Fertility Goddesses, Groundhog Bellies & the Coca Cola Company

Fertility Goddesses, Groundhog Bellies & the Coca Cola Company

The origins of modern holidays

Gabriella Kalapos

INSOMNIAC PRESS

Library and Archives Canada Cataloguing in Publication

Kalapos, Gabriella, 1969-
    Fertility goddesses, groundhog bellies and the Coca-Cola Company / Gabriella Kalapos.

Includes index.
ISBN 1-897178-14-X

    1. Holidays. 2. Holidays--History. 3. Rites and ceremonies. I. Title.

GT3930.K34 2006   394.26   C2005-907628-3

The publisher gratefully acknowledges the support of the Canada Council, the Ontario Arts Council and the Department of Canadian Heritage through the Book Publishing Industry Development Program.

Printed and bound in Canada

Insomniac Press
192 Spadina Avenue, Suite 403
Toronto, Ontario, Canada, M5T 2C2
www.insomniacpress.com

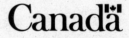

THE CANADA COUNCIL | LE CONSEIL DES ARTS
FOR THE ARTS | DU CANADA
SINCE 1957 | DEPUIS 1957

ONTARIO ARTS COUNCIL
CONSEIL DES ARTS DE L'ONTARIO

Canada

For Marcus
To what was, is, and is yet to be

For Amber and Dylan
Thanks for being so accepting of "Mommy time"

Acknowledgements

This book became a reality because of the work of numerous people who shared their ideas and knowledge. There are many authors who have done so brilliantly, and while all the works mentioned in the bibliography provided guidance in the development of this book, I would like to highlight a few in particular:

Tom Robbins for piquing my curiosity on holidays; Merlin Stone and Riane Eisler for enlightening me to a part of history that I should have been taught in University (especially since I studied Ancient Near East History), but wasn't; Riane Eisler again for her book *Sacred Pleasure*, which was instrumental in the development of the May Day chapter; Joseph Campbell for being such a proficient writer, not submitting to dry academia, and for inviting non-historians into the world of mythology; Elaine Pagels for providing an alternative view on the development of Christianity that is far more complex and interesting than I ever imagined; Leonard Shlain for his book *The Alphabet Versus the Goddess*, which convinced me that maybe there is a way to make history entertaining; Sue Ellen Thompson for her book *Holiday Symbols*, which was an excellent source for the interesting origin of obscure holiday traditions; and Barbara Walker for *The Woman's Encyclopedia of Myths and Secrets*, I am in awe of the research required in undertaking that book.

I would also like to thank Mike O'Connor at Insomniac Press for taking a chance on me; Dan Varrette at Insomniac Press for his amazing editing; and Nancy Forgrave for being the matchmaker extraordinaire. Thank you to Gordon and Michele North, Janice and Tom Ginder, David Renzetti, Lauren McKinley-Renzetti, Naomi Robinson, Philip Jessup, Cindy Robertson, and Irene and Leslie Kalapos for sharing your insight on the meaning of the holidays and/or dedicating numerous hours to providing comments back on the manuscript.

I am indebted to Marcus Ginder for going out of his way to provide me with the time required to complete this book and to my family and friends for putting up with my incessant questions and for providing me with the encouragement I needed to see this book to completion. Thanks are also due to Arni Mikelsons for developing the origins of holidays web site. For more information on the book or to send me a comment, visit www.originsofholidays.com.

Gabriella Kalapos
Toronto, 2006

TABLE OF CONTENTS

PREFACE

This book was written thanks to a mixture of curiosity, frustration, and anger. Curiosity is the easiest emotion to describe, but curiosity on its own would not have given me the will to start, never mind finish, a book. Yes, it is a great emotion to get you thinking and it may even be energetic enough to get you asking a few questions here and there. But by itself, curiosity is rather lazy and without anything else to give it a good boot in the butt, it will quickly end up back on the couch, watching *The Simpsons*. That is where frustration and anger come in. I would have to agree that frustration and anger will never be the life of the party that curiosity is, but there is no denying they are better equipped to handle the long haul.

My initial fascination for holidays started when I was reading *Jitterbug Perfume* by Tom Robbins. He touched on the origins of Easter, Valentine's Day, Lent, and Carnival and mentioned things I've never heard before. Heartfelt is my appreciation of his helping me realize my lack of understanding regarding the purpose and meaning of the holidays I celebrated. Yes, I would agree that it is not necessary to know the history of a holiday in order to participate in it. After all, it is nice enough just to have a day off work or school, an excuse to break up the sheer ordinariness of a day, or the opportunity to have a little fun with family and friends. But it got me wondering why it would never occur to me to wonder what I was celebrating. How many other things are there that I do every day simply because it is a "tradition"?

Thinking about this reminded me of an anecdote my mom told me about a little girl who was watching her mother cook a Christmas pot roast. After seasoning the meat, the girl's mother cut off an inch from each end of the roast and placed it in a pan and into the oven. The little girl asked her mother why she cut the ends off before putting it in the oven and the mother replied, "Oh, that is just tradition, it is how my mother used to do it."

The daughter, understandably not satisfied with such a lame answer, went to her grandmother, brought her into the kitchen, and asked her why she cut an inch off each end of the pot roast before placing it in the oven. The grandmother replied, "Well, that is just the way I was taught to do it from watching my mother."

The daughter, getting a little frustrated at this point, decided not to settle with another lame rationale; thankfully her great-grandmother was still alive and sitting in her wheelchair in the living room. The little girl snorts out an exasperated sigh, goes into the living room, and wheels her great-grandmother into the kitchen. With four generations in one room, the daughter gives it one more try. "Great-Nanna, why did you always cut an inch off each end of the pot roast before putting it in the oven?"

Great Nanna looks at her great-granddaughter and says, "Oh, I did that because my one and only oven pan was never big enough to fit a whole pot roast."

I don't use this anecdote to try to belittle traditions, but rather to question why after a certain age many of us stop asking the simple and often very justifiable *why*? Little kids do not have a problem with it. Parents often think that children keep asking the same questions over and over again as an attempt to drive them insane, but often this is because parents keep giving unsatisfactory answers. True, sometimes they do it just to drive their parents insane, but they probably just consider that an added bonus. So why do we stop asking "why"? Maybe we stopped because we kept getting unsatisfactory answers, or maybe because our parents chewed us out by yelling "enough already!" Maybe we realized that society and people do not look up to those who don't appear to have all the answers. So in our attempt to look competent and intelligent we did not want to let on that we were clueless as to why we do many of the things we do.

Either way, something happened to all those "whys" as we left childhood and headed into adulthood. Where did they all go? Are they gone forever? Can we ever get them back? I don't believe they have left us. I just think that in our drive to have it all, earn a living, survive the drudgery of basic day-to-day necessities, and so on, we have swallowed them down into our gut where they sit waiting for something that will allow them to get out. No one said curiosity is a neat and clean emotion; rather, it often has the ability to bring disruption and much messiness into our lives. For this reason we often go to considerable lengths to make sure we slow down—some of us have even stopped—the curiosity digestive system.

So that deals with the curiosity, but what about frustration and anger? What do they have to do with the story of holidays? This is where religion comes in. The origin of the word *holiday* comes from *holy day* and there is no denying that the holidays of most cultures are hooked up with their religions. Holidays and religions evolved as a human response to the mysteries of nature and life.

During the course of human existence, people faced with the uncertainty of life have found it important, perhaps even essential, to gather together and pay homage to the cycles of the year and the cycles of life. We knew with some certainty when the birds and herds migrated; when the fruits ripened; when the grains, nuts, and roots should be harvested; when the rivers flooded; when the rains were likely to come; when it would get cold. We held out for the promise of food and life in the spring, the joy and freedom of summer, the necessity of a good harvest, the fear of winter and death. These special and momentous times of the year were not merely noted, but celebrated. It was the legacy our ancient ancestors passed on to their descendants in an attempt to ensure their survival.

Our ancestors, who were directly dependent and connected to the land for their survival, understood better than anyone that nature defied human control and was unpredictable. But humans dislike the thought that they have no control over what happens to them, so as time went on, people started to anthropomorphize nature and create deities that took on the characteristics of the aspect of nature they controlled or represented. People began to believe paying homage to these deities would influence nature, thereby giving them an active role in determining their fate and survival. I guess they figured it was worth a try.

Interestingly enough, the deities and religions many of these rites were originally intended to honour have come and gone, and yet, despite much human intervention and abuse, the traditions and customs have withstood the test of time. We often think of holidays as belonging to one religion or culture, but the celebration of holidays is a phenomenon shared by all people. Each religion and culture has its own rituals to mark the times of the year it considers significant and while the names and dates of the holidays may vary, their meaning and symbolism share remarkable resemblances. Despite all the similarities, few religions are built on acknowledging the consistency between the stories, histories, myths, customs, beliefs, and celebrations of all humans. Personally, I have experienced much frustration with the way we spend 95% of our energy and time on the 5% that are unique and 5% of our energy and time on the 95% we have in common. To add further frustration, the overwhelming time and energy we put into discussions of our cultural differences is not invested with curiosity or with a feeling of "oh, isn't that neat (or interesting)" but rather spent pointing out how one is superior to the other.

This tendency became obvious to me at an early age, especially when it came to religion. Most people at some point in their lives experience frustration with religious instruction. (Sorry, but I think I might have used up more than my allocated amount). It took me going to Sunday school to realize there were adults who were not only exasperated by my "why" questions but downright hostile. My experience growing up under Catholic instruction taught me that my purpose was not to understand but simply to believe. While it might have made life easier for others if I accepted their world view hook, line, and sinker, my goal was to find a way to make sense of the world and my place in it, and asking questions was the only way I knew how.

I remember one incident that for some reason has had a far bigger impact on me than mere common sense would think appropriate. One beautiful spring day after another long hard winter in Montreal, the sun was shining, people were taking off their winter jackets, strolling down the street smiling at the world and all its inhabitants. I was one of the multitudes who felt like winter's yoke had finally been taken off and I could once again prance around freely. A friendly looking man approached me with a religious handout. I politely declined the pamphlet and was merrily heading on my way when he asked, "Don't you believe in God?"

I replied, "On a day as beautiful as this, I believe in Everything—the sun in the sky, the buds on the tree, the warmth on my face. If that is what you mean by God, then I guess I do." He looked at me with shock and told me that was not God, that was nature. Personally, I did not see all that much difference between Mother Nature and God. I always felt closer to some divine presence in nature than I ever had in a church or temple of any denomination. I tried to show him the error of his ways by enlightening him to the divinity of Mother Nature and he spent his time trying to show me the error of my ways by enlightening me to the divinity of his God. I do not know if this was as much an epiphany for him as it was for me, and I'm guessing it was not, but it certainly did something for me: it got me really angry, not with him, because he seemed like quite a nice and kind man, but at the arrogance of religion for thinking it could possibly have a monopoly on spirituality. How dare any religion think there was and is only one way to be spiritual and their way being *it*?

There is little difference between anger and frustration. In my experience, whether I felt anger or frustration over a certain circumstance depended more on me than it did on the situation. If I was feeling energetic, it was anger. If I was in a lethargic mood, then frustration was my calling. We are more acquainted with the negative characteristics of anger and frustration and less likely to see their positive attributes. But they do have positive attributes: they get us off our haunches to challenge things. It took time, but that is what they did for me and I am very grateful for the motivation and persistence they have graced me with.

One of the first things to occur to me while researching this book was that the study of holidays was a far bigger topic than any one book or one person could ever do justice to. I was often tempted to include holidays from numerous religions and cultures. There are so many fascinating traditions and similarities between all religions and cultures that it seemed a waste to miss out on them. Having said that, I had to admit to myself that there was little chance that I had the patience and energy to take on such an extensive task. I admit that I am slightly embarrassed by my limited selection of Western/Christianized holidays, but, going with the old proven formula of picking the low-lying fruit first, I decided to stick with the holidays I grew up with. If it is true that you need to understand yourself before you can understand others (and I think it is true), then it must also be true that we need to understand our own culture before we can understand other cultures.

The little girl in the pot roast anecdote was fortunate in that she had access to the origin of the tradition. If her great-grandmother had not been around or coherent, the origin of the tradition would have been lost to her forever. That is our problem with the histories of many holidays and their associated traditions: they go so far back in time that we do not have any living ancestors around to answer our seemingly simple "whys." Few people know why many of the holidays exist in the first place, much less what purposes many of their associated traditions and rituals serve. Why are fireworks set off at New Year's? What does Groundhog Day have to do with the Virgin Mary? Why does the Easter bunny defy physiology and lay eggs? Why do boys and girls dance around a maypole on May Day? Year after year, many of us continue to emptily perform holiday rituals because we have little or no understanding of what they mean or what purpose they serve.

Many may think holidays serve little purpose other than to encourage our already rampant materialism. There is no doubt that holidays are and probably always have been a commercial activity. Any time you have a large gathering of people, there are going to be individuals smart enough to realize a great opportunity to make a buck or two. That was just as true 2000 years ago as it is today. The difference is that 2000 years ago, while they may have had less scientific knowledge, they seemed to have more understanding of everyday life. While it may be the case that the outside shell of the holidays is encased in commercialism, the real purpose of the shell is to provide shelter and safety for the animal living inside it. Nowadays, we have forgotten all about the little snail inside the shell and only pay attention to its ornamental exterior. Maybe the time has come for us to allow ourselves the luxury to sit back and get better acquainted with this little snail inside the shell because it has quite a few interesting stories to share with us.

This book attempts to tell that cute slimy critter's story by answering many of the "whys" regarding the legends, customs, and symbols of the holiday legacy left to us by our ancestors. The story starts long, long ago in a land very far off, with people who lived under very different circumstances than we do today, but, who, when you really come down to it, weren't all that different from you or me. It doesn't start a mere few generations ago, or even a few centuries. In fact, it is even older than the advent of Judaism and Christianity and predates even the Greeks. Instead, many of our holiday traditions and customs have been in existence for at least the last 5,000 to 10,000 years and for possibly far longer.

Having to go so far back in time means the elusive sources of our holiday traditions have long been dead and buried and are therefore unavailable to answer our "whys." On the other hand, the complexity and universality of our present-day customs have left us with enough relics and fossils buried in the dirt to at least help us get an idea of what the mysterious holiday puzzle is supposed to look like. If we are patient and open enough to allow ourselves to get a bit dirty and dig through the dirt, the history of our holidays is still available to us. While this version of the story of holidays may be more complex than the so called explanations we were provided in grade school, religious school, high school, and even university and adulthood, I think you will find it makes infinitely more sense and provides us with a much deeper understanding of the world, human nature, and ourselves.

NEW YEAR'S DAY
January 1st

New Year's is a loot bag full of emotions and each time we reach in, we never know what will get pulled out. Try as we might, we cannot stop ourselves from partaking of at least a part of the emotional loot. It is almost as if at this time, when the old year gives way to the new, we are emotionally manic. We go from periods of euphoria and exultation, to feeling subdued and intro-spective, to wanting to hold on to the person next to us and cry. And sometimes we just want to be left alone.

For people who try not to get all caught up in the hoopla and would rather think of New Year's as just another day, it isn't and we know it. We may not allow ourselves the freedom to indulge all the emotions in our loot bag, but no matter how willing or unwilling we are, something heightens our emotions during this time period. More than any other day of the year, it marks the passing of time—a transition from the old to the new, a journey from the known to the unknown.

The New Year's festival is one of the oldest and most univer-sally celebrated holidays the world over. No matter what culture, or even what historical era, humans found it important to mark this passage. What is even more wonderful, despite all our per-ceived differences between time periods and cultures, there is amazing similarity in the way all humans have marked the ending of the old year and the beginning of the new one.

Noted mid-twentieth-century anthropologist and mythologist Mircea Eliade found a number of recurring and consistent themes influencing the way humans mark this transitional time. He found New Year's to be used by almost all cultures as a ritual of regeneration and/or re-enactment of the creation of the world. The basic New Year traditions include:

1. The elimination of the past and a chance for a new future starting from a clean slate.
2. The use of a sacrifice or scapegoat that dies in order to start the new year without any of the bad elements of the previous year being carried into the new one.
3. The return of the dead to the world.
4. Mimed combat between good and evil.

You might be thinking that none of these factors influences the New Year's parties you go to, but read on. The story of New Year's reminds us that despite all our sophistication and technology, we still mark this yearly transition the way countless generations have before us. New Year's Eve, which may at present simply appear to be a chance to go out and party, wear fancy clothes, and have a good time, is much more than that. New Year's presents us with the opportunity to gain insight into ourselves, our memories of the past year, and our hopes, dreams, and fears for the future year.

When Is New Year's?

It shows an amazing similarity between people of the world when the biggest difference in the way we celebrate New Year's is not how we celebrate it, but when we celebrate it. Deciding when the New Year begins has not been easy. You may wonder, what could be the problem? New Year's is January 1st, the first day of the calendar. Celebrating New Year's on January 1st, however, is a relatively modern occurrence.

The date chosen for when the old year ends and the new year begins depends on what influences a culture. Since crops and harvests were important to people's survival, it makes sense that the central part of an agricultural cycle would mark their transition from one year into the other.

In ancient Egypt, the New Year depended on when the Nile River flooded. Among the ancient Celts it was November 1st, the time of year they brought their herds home for the winter. The Jewish New Year of Rosh Hashanah is celebrated at the end of their summer, close to the autumn equinox, the time of year when the parched and barren land of summer would hopefully receive at last some much needed rain. In India, the Hindus celebrate the first day of each season, so they have four New Years on their calendar. The Chinese and Vietnamese celebrate their New Year in the spring as determined by their lunar calendar, and it falls sometime between January 21st and February 19th. In the ancient Near East, the spring equinox heralded the New Year. The spring equinox marked the beginning of most of Europe's New Year festivities until very recently. March 25th was the most common date for the start of the new year, with festivities lasting for a week, thereby ending on April 1st.

It makes sense New Year's would start in the spring. After all, it is the season of rebirth, of planting new crops, and of mating. January 1st, on the other hand, has no agricultural or astronomical significance; instead, it is completely arbitrary.

The Romans came up with the idea of January 1st for the start of the new year in 153 B.C.E.[1], when they revised their ten-month year into a twelve-month year. They added January and February to the year and changed the date of New Year's from March to January. In this revised Roman calendar, January 1st denoted the start of the political year when recently elected politicians had their first day in office. The ordinary folks, however, who likely paid little attention to politicians, also paid little attention to this attempted New Year's date change and continued to celebrate their New Year in March.

The Romans had bigger problems with their calendar than simply convincing the masses that New Year's was now the 1st of January. The difference between the solar year and their lunar calendar, plus the constant tampering by Roman emperors, resulted in the calendar becoming totally out of whack with the seasons. The calendar days marking the start of the planting season actually fell when farmers were harvesting their crops. In the mid-first century B.C.E., Julius Caesar, between staking out new turf for Rome and spending some quality time with Cleopatra, decided to take it upon himself to come up with a long-term and scientific reform to the messed up Roman calendar. With a little help from an Alexandrian astronomer named Sosigenes, the Julian Calendar was instituted in 46 B.C.E. A total of ninety days were added to the year in order to bring the calendar back into accord with the seasons. As a result, what would normally have been April 1st was now January 1st.[2] And we thought Y2K was confusing!

No one had really paid attention to the date of the New Year being changed from March to January the first time around in 153 B.C.E., and they did not pay too much attention in 45 B.C.E. either. People considered January 1st merely the start of the civil year. While there were festivities and feasts to honour that date and the newly appointed politicians (the Romans were not ones to say no to a festivity), the real New Year celebrations still started in March.

The symbolism of the New Year being near the spring equinox was too important for people to let go of. It made so much sense: it was the end of winter and famine, the start of the spring, of planting the new crops, of trees and flowers blooming, and a time of fertility and mating.

The spring equinox is one of two times in the year (the other being the autumn equinox) when the day and the night are of equal length all over the world. To many ancient cultures, the equinoxes not only had astronomical significance (since most people had better things to do with their time than measure the length of the day versus the night) but mythological significance as well. The spring equinox was also often the conception date of the various sun gods, who were almost always born on December 25th.

Based on a human gestational time period of nine months, if the birth of that sun deity took place on December 25th, then the conception date would have been nine months earlier, making it right around the vernal equinox. These sun deities were usually born of a goddess and a god, or sometimes by a mortal woman and a god. Let's face it, deity birth stories are definitely not limited by the usual rules of human conception, pregnancy, and birth. Mythological stories have goddesses creating life on their own without sperm anywhere in their vicinity (Hera and Ares), and gods incubating their offspring in their loins and giving birth to grown adults who slice their way out through the god's head (Zeus and Athena). Why they would be subject to the normal human gestational time period in this case isn't really consistent, but so the story goes.

It seems all cultures have crazy birth stories. In the Old Testament, when the senile and post-menopausal Sarah finally gives birth to a son, she names him Isaac, meaning laughter, because having a child at her age was certainly a joke.[3] Based on Christian doctrine, Mary became pregnant with Jesus not by having sex, but because God willed it so. The Roman Catholic Church and its priests spent a few centuries preoccupied with the intactness, or lack thereof, of Mary's hymen. The Church's doctrine was that if Jesus was born of a normal conception, then he would have been tainted with the sin of Eve and born of original sin. This was not the way the Church wanted their saviour, Jesus Christ, to start out. Incidentally, Mary's conception date, if we went by human standards, would also have been March 25th. To this day, March 25th is celebrated in many Christian countries as Lady Day, commemorating the appearance of the angel Gabriel to Mary announcing to her that she would be the mother of Christ.

As crazy as these birth stories are to us born of the DNA generation, there is no denying they had an important connection to special holidays and festivities and they were not given up quickly or easily. The Romans and the cultures they conquered were not very interested in ignoring all the significance and mythology of their March 25th New Year and moving over to the arbitrary date of January 1st.

The next chance for January 1st to get some glory came in 1582 when the Roman Catholic Pope Gregory XIII adopted the Gregorian calendar and instituted its use in Roman Catholic countries. France was quick to accept the new calendar with its New Year, but Europe's more Protestant countries were less willing to make the switch to their rival's religious calendar. Scotland accepted January 1st as the start of the New Year in 1600, but Britain and its colonies in North America and elsewhere continued to celebrate the New Year in March until 1752, when the so-called New Style calendar was finally accepted.

It was no easy journey for January 1st and it took over 1700 years for it to finally receive the honour of being the day that marks the transition from the old year to the new year. While our modern day New Year's may not have the astronomical and mythological significance of past New Years', it still marks our own changeover from the old to the new—from what was to what can and will be. There is enough symbolism and significance in that to warrant its special treatment.

What Does New Year's Really Mean?

Before we go any further, I have a confession to make. Up until writing this chapter I was one of those people who tried to consider New Year's as just another day. Deep down I knew it was more; I just did not understand why. I would go out to the parties, kiss at midnight, drink copious amounts of alcohol to have some fun or to numb myself, but it all felt very superficial and fake. I was trying too hard to have a good time and it seems the more we try to have a good time, the less likely we are to achieve it. I always expected something significant to happen on this date and was always disappointed when New Year's Day came around and felt like just another day. I had the right actions, but I was missing the point. I kept expecting something significant to happen on the outside, not realizing that the change is supposed to happen on the inside.

It is irrelevant what date the New Year actually falls on. What is important is that there is some date when one cycle ends and the next begins. If we just continued to track our days without breaking them into years, we would have fewer opportunities to review our lives and our deeds as individuals and societies. New Year's, as much as we may not want it to, forces us not only to look ahead but also to look back. Our birthdays also provide us with opportunities to look back and ahead, but birthdays only mark the New Year for individuals, not for everybody. New Year's is society's cleansing ceremony. It is not just a recreation of the world and the year but a point when we try and recreate ourselves.

To most cultures, New Year's is a day of reconciliation. It provides an occasion for closing rifts and healing disputes. A chance to look back upon the last year and figure out what good things happened, what bad things happened, our hopes for a better year ahead of us, and our fear of a worse.

New Year's Scapegoat

The New Year ceremony has been a cleansing period for many cultures. Many hunter-gatherer tribes used rituals to cleanse their tribe. The cleansing process usually took place through a ritual sacrifice or scapegoat who would be responsible for carrying the bad deeds of the last year away with them.

In *The Alphabet Versus the Goddess*, Leonard Shlain describes a reconstruction that may give us some insight into the New Year scapegoat/sacrifice:

> Usually once a year, hunters stalked and captured a live specimen of the tribe's particularly animal totem, for some unknown reason a recurring choice among a diverse range of cultures was the bear. They would then stake it in the centre of a magic circle. Each member of the tribe approached the straining, snarling animal. Out of earshot of everyone else, but just beyond the reach of the leash's radius, the tribesperson whispered into the totem's ear all the taboos that he or she had broken during the previous year. After the last confession, the entire tribe danced in a circle around the animal. Wild music and intoxicating substances transported them into a frenzy. The shaman then abruptly signalled the musicians to stop and amid mad shrieks the entire tribe turned and fell upon the sacrificial animal en masse. Death was usually swift but messy. Because everyone participated and everyone came away bespattered with blood, no one individual bore sole responsibility for the totem's death. During the feast that followed, each tribe member ate the flesh and drank the blood of the sacrifice. The ritual absolved all who participated [except, of course, the totem animal] allowing them to begin a new year with a clean conscience.[4]

Even with this being quite a riveting story, I don't think that is how I would like to spend my New Year's Eve. I do, however, recognize the purpose it served for cultures and believe it very much highlights the principles and purpose of what our modern-day New Year's can be. It is an opportunity to make amends for the past and do away with the bad so we can make room for the good. We also have our very own modern-day scapegoat. On the midnight of December 31st, Father Time, a long-bearded, wrinkled, bent over old man walks off into oblivion. There is something inherently sad about watching the image of this old man walking towards his end. Maybe it is because when he walks off we realize part of our time has also walked off into oblivion and there is always a part of us asking, did I waste that time?

The "Auld Lang Syne" Song

The custom of playing "Auld Lang Syne" on New Year's Eve is all that remains of a much broader custom that originated in the British Isles in the late eighteenth century when all New Year's parties and festivities ended with the guests standing in a circle singing this traditional song. In all probability, the custom first took hold in Scotland, since Robert Burns, the country's favourite folk poet, wrote the lyrics in 1788.

Even the rowdiest modern-day New Year's Eve party often ends with a relatively quiet, if drunken, tribute to the old tradition. In Scottish dialect, *auld lang syne* is translated to mean "times long past." Each year, I was surprised by how at a time when fireworks are going off, when everyone is hugging and kissing, and when there is a general air of happiness and expectation, we have this tradition of playing a really sad song that in a few seconds flat can reduce me to feeling melancholy, if not downright tearful. And I did not even know the words! For those of you who also don't know the words, but are curious....

> Should auld acquaintance be forgot,
> And never brought to mind?
> Should auld acquaintance be forgot,
> And days of auld lang syne?
> For auld lang syne, my dear,

For auld land syne,
We'll take a cup of kindness yet,
For auld lang syne.
Should auld acquaintance be forgot,
And never brought to mind?
Should auld acquaintance be forgot,
And days of auld lang syne?
And here's a hand, my trusty friend,
And gie's a hand o'thine;
We'll tak' a cup of kindness yet
For auld lang syne

It is almost as if at the same time we are celebrating, we are also mourning. Then it hit me—we *are* mourning. There is no way we can welcome in the new year without saying goodbye to the old one. Even if the old year was a crappy one, and especially if it was a good one, we are not all that keen on letting it go. We are at that threshold where we have to step into the unknown future of the coming year. Will it be better? Will it be worse? What will happen? What won't happen? Our ambivalence towards letting go is not exclusively a New Year handicap. Our biggest challenge to setting off on any new adventure or challenge is in letting go of what we can't take with us. There is an enormous level of insecurity and anxiety surrounding change. The realization that starting something new requires our letting go of the past is not easy for us.

The Dead and the New Year

The transitional time when the old year and the new year pass each other by has been regarded as a critical time when unseen powers are at large and the dead return to their old haunts. These dead require either welcoming or expulsion. This belief is very apparent in the Celtic New Year of Samhain, or Halloween, as we now know it, but it is also still practiced in our modern-day festivities. The belief was that the ending of the old year and the beginning of the new year marked the time when the veil separating the spirit world from the earthly world was thinnest. Our modern-day New Year's festivities are still heralded by loud noise, the ringing of bells, beating drums, cracking whips, rattling bamboos canes, setting off fireworks, all of which were used as attempts to scare away malicious and mischievous spirits who apparently did not enjoy such rambunctious behaviour. The attempt to banish not only the forces of darkness but also the old year and its evil led to the custom of opening all the doors and windows of the house at midnight to let the spirit of the old year escape unimpeded lest it stick around and carry over into the new year.

Mock Battles Between the Forces of Good and Evil

One of the most common ways people in the United States spend the first day of the year is to watch the numerous football games on television. There are four football games that take place on New Year's Day—the Rose Bowl in Pasadena, California; the Cotton Bowl in Dallas, Texas; the Sugar Bowl in New Orleans, Louisiana; and the Orange Bowl in Miami, Florida. What on earth could have prompted the networks to schedule four different games on one day?

In many homes in the United States, having friends over to watch football has replaced the more social visits paid on this day in past centuries. Is this a sign of our deteriorating social situation and our lack of connection with each other? Maybe it is our modern-day continuation of the way New Year's has been celebrated for thousands of years. Ever since the first known New Year's celebration took place in Babylonia sometime around 2000 B.C.E., mock battles between the forces of good and evil have signified the passage from the old year to the new year.[5] Who would have thought our superficial modern-day football obsession on New Year's Day might actually be an ancient relic of our mythological heroes' annual battle with the forces of evil and darkness?

A Good Beginning Makes a Good Ending

Many of our New Year's traditions are based on the idea "a good beginning makes a good ending." This principle stems from the idea that whatever happens on the first day of the year affects one's fortunes throughout the year and people want plenty of everything to set the pattern for the coming year. The feasting and drinking so popular on New Year's Eve serves as a kind of charm guaranteeing abundance. In order to set us on the right path for the new year, a whole host of do's and don'ts have emerged.

For Wealth and Prosperity

The ancient Romans exchanged gifts on New Years Day. The gifts were usually coins bearing the portrait of the two-faced god Janus, whose one face looked forward and the other face looked backward. Although gift giving at New Year's is rare in North America, it remains quite popular in France, Italy, and some other European countries. These gifts were the precursors to our modern-day Christmas presents. They were based on the belief that acting wealthy by spending money on gifts would attract good financial luck in the coming year. The trick (isn't there always one?) was you could not go into debt in order to appear wealthy as that would negate the effect of the presents.

The belief was—and still is in many cultures, especially for the Chinese New Year—that it was bad karma for a household to begin the new year in debt, no easy feat for those of us who go a little wild on Christmas presents, but it might explain why our financial problems seem to follow us into the new year. It would be great if New Year's was not only a symbolic cleansing of the past but also a day when past debts were miraculously wiped out. Since this is not likely to happen, it is left up to us to partic- ipate in the excess and still walk into the new year debt-free. Sure we may have to start saving in July, but maybe planning ahead is not such a bad option. Who knows what can happen when we start planning ahead?

A continuation of this theme of ensuring wealth and prosper- ity says that the new year must not be ushered in with bare cup- boards lest this pattern continue throughout the year. Pantries must be topped up and plenty of money placed in every family member's wallet to guarantee a prosperous year.

New Year Omens

The principle of the New Year is how the year begins; this fore- tells how the upcoming twelve months will unfold. For this rea- son, we are always trying to make sure we are around our loved ones, or those important to us, close to the time the clock strikes twelve. Planting a big juicy kiss on a significant other, or even on the person beside us at the time (this is part of the reason we place emphasis on our positioning for that midnight stroke), will ensure our affections and ties will continue, and maybe even improve, throughout the next twelve months. To not smooch our significant other, or someone who represents someone we would not mind as a significant other, would be to set the stage for a year of loneliness and lovelessness. Who wants that?

First footing, a tradition originating in Scotland and England, is said to set the stage for the family's fortune in the coming year: the first guest to set foot inside the door is believed to influence the family's fortunes for the year. If it is a woman, a red- or light-haired man, or an undertaker, it was considered a bad omen. A dark-haired man, on the other hand, brought good luck. In some villages, dark-haired men hired themselves out as professional first footers to go from house to house immediately after the new year arrives. In addition, no one should leave the premises before the first footer arrives—the first traffic across the threshold must be heading in rather than heading out. Otherwise, it foretells a year of loss instead of gain. To make things even more challenging, nothing, not even garbage, is to leave the house on the first day of the year. Doing laundry is also a no-no on New Year's Day because it was considered an omen that a member of the family will be washed away.

All of these do's and don'ts certainly make it difficult to go about New Year's as just any other day. Maybe the do's and don'ts are not really the point. Maybe they are just a means to ensure we do not treat the first day of the year as any other, but rather as a day to think about our actions and what we would like to get out of the coming year.

New Year's Resolutions

When all the singing, drinking, merriment, and fireworks are over, many of us try to become more serious about life. We take stock and plan a course of action to better our lives. On New Year's, we remember last year's achievements and failures and look forward to a new year and a new beginning. With the regeneration of the year comes the potential for the regeneration of the individual, time for a fresh start, turn over a new leaf, and a whole host of other clichés. All the thinking and analyzing brings us to the resolution thing. Oh come on, you knew it was coming, didn't you?

It is hard to resist the urge to make a resolution on New Year's Eve. On average we each make 1.8 resolutions per year, the most common being to lose weight, exercise more, quit smoking, and drink less. I think it's great that New Year's is an active-minded holiday that gets us thinking of what we want to achieve, giving us that little boot in the butt to remind us we are in control of our lives. We are not mere victims of fate or circumstance; instead, we can make choices and in turn change our lives. What does it say about us, however, if we continually fail to succeed in our resolutions? John Norcross, head of Scranton University's Department of Psychology, has spent six years studying our annual exercise of New Year's resolutions. His findings are not reassuring: 25% of those surveyed break their promises within a week and only about 40% are sticking to their goal by June.[6] My guess is that the people answering the surveys were lying to him or themselves. I would bet good money the percentage of broken resolutions is much greater. Few New Year's resolutions ever achieve prolonged success, but year after year we stick with the tradition. A positive way of looking at it would be that at least we don't lose hope as easily as we lose our will power. Then again, it might also tell us a bit about our level of sanity. As the saying goes, "A true indication of insanity is doing the same thing over and over again and expecting a different result."

But why? Why are New Year's resolutions such notorious failures? I choose to blame the Romans. They are the ones who jinxed the January 1st date. They made it the date when their politicians took their first day in office—a date when politicians were supposed to start making good on all the promises they made in order to get elected. Well, we all know what happens next. It set a bad precedent for the whole date of January 1st and keeping promises. It was doomed from then on.

Unfortunately, the Romans can't take all the blame. I suppose we too would have to take some of it since we make the promises. Perhaps our biggest weakness when we make New Year's resolutions is that we choose things we think we should do, not the things we really want to do. It almost becomes a guilt thing. "I could stand to lose a few pounds, so I should, but what I really want to do is learn to dance the tango." We know which is more likely to become the failed New Year's resolution.

Another problem we have is that most of our New Year's resolutions are too general and vague. "I will lose weight, save more money, exercise more…" What is the difference between a dream and a goal? A goal is a dream with a plan and a deadline. For example, if we want to lose weight, maybe we should think about what we need to do in order to lose weight: eat less, eat better foods, cut out junk food and sugars, have some type of physical activity everyday, set a goal to lose ten pounds in the next year, something by which we can measure our progress, or lack thereof. If, for example, you want to save money, you could set a goal for how much you want to save in the next year, divide it by 52, and then you know how much you have to save each week in order to reach your goal. Few, if any of us, can make our dreams come true without a plan. Try it, who knows what could happen? It's not like you have to fear failing in your New Year's resolution because that is what is expected. Rather, all you would have to fear is making others look bad when you succeed.

The Evolution of New Year's
One of the most interesting aspects of New Year's is that, more than any other holiday, the way we celebrate it changes with who we are. Our stage of life determines how we spend New Year's Eve, and how we spend New Year's Eve also tells us something about what is important to us.

When we are in our late teens, New Year's is all about going wild and pushing the code of conduct as far as we possibly can— anything short of death is permissible, even encouraged. As we move into our mid-twenties, it's about spending New Year's with friends. If we are with a significant other, we may decide that how we really want to spend our time welcoming in the New Year is by sipping champagne in the bath with our loved one. As children come into our lives, New Year's becomes more of a family affair again. Then when our children leave us with an empty nest and are off creating their own New Year's mayhem, parents may again decide to attempt some of their own New Year's mayhem.

One of the mistakes we may make is that we don't really stop and think about how we want to spend New Year's. Instead, we usually spend the night doing what we think we should be doing. New Year's has a lot to teach us about ourselves. We all need time to reflect and New Year's is an ideal time of year for self-reflection. Yes, sometimes it is easier not to look back on unfulfilled hopes and dreams, but even if we don't consciously deal with them, those same unfulfilled hopes and dreams seep into our subconscious and will get us in the end. If we don't take the time to figure out what we want for ourselves we may just do what others think we should and end up disappointed and depressed. New Year's is your very own personal therapy festival—work with it instead of against it.

GROUNDHOG DAY
February 2nd

Every year on the second day of February, a groundhog is given the task of determining whether spring has arrived or if there will be six more weeks of winter. It's not a bad gig for the cute little rodent; it gets the distinction of being the only mammal to have a day named in its honour. Starting from when we were school children, we were taught the folklore of Groundhog Day. If it was sunny and the groundhog saw its shadow, it signalled that winter would go on for six more weeks. A cloudy day and no shadow meant spring was just around the corner.

Although we might not suspect it, the history of Groundhog Day is far more complex and interesting than what it has become: a staged event in which a poor groundhog is physically forced from its burrow into the glare of television cameras so news stations and meteorologists can have a cute sound bite and a brief close-up of the groundhog's bewildered face.

I don't think that too many of us believe the groundhog has true divining powers. Why would we trust a rodent still groggy from a few months of sleep when the weather person who has access to billions of dollars of sophisticated equipment still can't get it right? Try as they might to find a correlation between February 2nd and a cloudy day / early spring, or a sunny day /

extended winter, the numbers are not encouraging. Weather researchers have found the groundhog has been correct only 28% of the time.[1] Let's not be too hard on the little critter; it is usually not the groundhog's idea to wake up and check out the weather on February 2nd. Most groundhogs do not come out of hibernation until March, or April in northern regions. More often than not, people awaken and prod the poor bewildered groundhog rather rudely so it can provide us with some guidance on what has become our day for seeking reassurance that spring will indeed come again.

Where did we get the crazy idea February 2nd could possibly foretell the arrival of spring? February may be the shortest month of the year but after dealing with cold weather for almost three months, it feels like the longest. February is the point of the winter when we begin to doubt spring will ever come again. There may be moments when we feel the warmth of the sun again and think maybe spring really is just around the corner, but that is just a tease because winter does not end in the beginning of February. February is the high point of winter's hurrah.

Groundhog Day falls right in the middle between the winter solstice and the spring equinox. The equinoxes mark the points each year when the day and night are the same length. The solstices distinguish the days with the longest period of day and the longest period of night. So no matter what groundhogs do on February 2nd, by our reckoning of the seasons, spring will not start until the spring equinox on March 21st. This is one of the points of Groundhog Day: it marks the day when we are at the midpoint between the winter solstice and the spring equinox— the day we are halfway through the winter.

But why was spring thought to begin with the spring equinox, summer with the summer solstice, autumn with the autumn equinox, and winter with the winter solstice? How did that come about and is that the only way to do it? Much as with many other things in life, just because we do it one way, it does not mean everyone else does likewise. The Egyptians had three seasons— flood, winter (planting), and summer (harvesting)—that had nothing to do with the solstices or the equinoxes. Instead, their seasons were based on their lifeblood, the Nile River.

So why do we use the equinoxes and the solstices to mark the seasons? The equinoxes and the solstices marked the seasons of the Sumerians and Babylonians. This was later adopted by the Greeks, then by the Romans, and spread to all the places where the Romans managed to get a foothold, which was pretty much all of what is now Europe. Since the Babylonian seasons have become our modern-day seasons, we might sometimes wonder why we occasionally come across a different way of reckoning the seasons, as in Shakespeare's *A Midsummer Night's Dream* where midsummer night is June 23rd, the night before Midsummer Day. By our reckoning of the seasons, that day should be the beginning of summer, not midsummer. Did Shakespeare get his sources wrong or is something else going on we are not aware of?

In both Celtic and Chinese astronomy, the seasons are measured to start in the middle and not at the beginning of the equinoxes and solstices. These days are known as cross-quarter days. Although the existence of these cross-quarter days is largely unknown, the holidays that have grown up around them are still celebrated in our own culture, with spring starting on Groundhog Day, summer starting on May Day, fall starting on Lammas Day, and winter starting on Halloween. The days of February 1st, May 1st, August 1st, and November 1st were important seasonally for many cultures in Northern Europe and the traditions and customs surrounding these holidays were incorporated into the Roman and Christian traditions as they colonized these areas.

Groundhog Day Unleashed

German immigrants known as the Pennsylvania Dutch are thought to have first brought the Groundhog Day tradition to North America in the eighteenth century. While they were in Europe, it was the badger who acted as their winter/spring barometer. Upon arriving in North America, the job was reassigned to the groundhog. The groundhog and badger were not the only animals used to predict spring. Other Europeans used the bear or the hedgehog, but the honour always belonged to a creature that hibernated.

Hibernating animals have what many people might consider the good fortune of being able to sleep through the winter. They bed down in the fall and for all intents and purposes don't arise again until the spring. Hibernation is a survival strategy that can be very successful in environments where food is scarce during the long cold winter season. Groundhogs first begin to disappear for their hibernation in September, and by October, they are all underground.

Amazing physiological changes take place during hibernation. During their winter sleep, groundhogs are able to drop their body temperature to 3°C (just above freezing) and their heartbeat drops from its normal rate of 80 beats per minute to only 4 or 5. Its breathing and oxygen consumption are also greatly reduced. Hibernation is still a bit of a mystery for scientists. They don't really know how an animal knows it is time for hibernation, nor do they know how these animals survive the slowdown in their metabolism during their hibernation. Scientists have found a special substance in the blood of hibernating animals, however, called HIT (Hibernation Inducement Trigger). If blood is taken from a hibernating animal and injected into an active animal in the spring, that active animal will go into hibernation. Pretty cool, isn't it? They must have had some messed up animals after that experiment. Scientists continue to study the mysteries of hibernation for clues from everything to organ preservation and kidney disorders (many hibernating animals, such as the black bear, do not urinate or defecate during the whole winter; instead, their body reabsorbs their waste). Ultimately, we hope to unlock the secrets to human hibernation with the goal of enabling long-distance space travel.[2]

Whatever the mysteries of hibernation, the emergence of hibernating animals from their burrows has symbolized the arrival of spring. For this is the time of year when, despite the bleakness and lack of life on the surface of the earth, the re-emerging animal world reminded people that seeds and other vegetative life still existed underground and was getting set to stage its entrance back onto the surface.

Groundhog Day was originally celebrated by the Celts in honour of Brigid, the Celtic goddess who in later times became revered as the Christian Saint Brigit. Originally, her festival was held on February 1st and was known by different names, including Imbolc, Oimelc, or Brigid's Night, but whatever name was used, the point was always the same: her festival reminds people that, just like them, the rest of nature also eagerly awaits the coming of spring.

Imbolc translates to mean "in the belly," the "belly" being that of Mother Nature. This rite sought to remember that even when you look all around you and everything seems bleak and dead, there is always life and hope to be found. The womb of Mother Nature was not dead; instead, it was getting ready to bring forth new life. *Oimelc*, which translates to mean "ewe's milk," was the name for lambing season. Early February is the time of year when farm animals (cows, goats, and sheep) are giving birth, creating a fresh supply of milk. While not as important an event these days with supermarkets, this extra food in days past may have meant the difference between life and death.

In Ireland, Imbolc was known as Brigid's Night and was celebrated, like all Irish holidays, on the eve of the holiday through to the following night. Brigid was known as the goddess of healing and birth and was honoured with bonfires symbolizing the heat and warmth of the sun.

Christianity was unwilling to find a place for the goddess Brigid in their newly developing religion and, despite numerous attempts, found it difficult to banish her influence and devoted following. Consequently, Pope Gregory I decided to do away with the whole goddess image and give her the status of saint instead. This Saint Brigit was allegedly Ireland's first convert to Christianity and the founder of Ireland's first convent in the fifth century.

When Sabinianus took over from Gregory in 604, he found this thinly veiled goddess worship hard to take and decided to appropriate this pagan holiday for the church. He renamed it Candlemas but kept fire as its symbolism. On this day, which used to signal the end of winter and the return of spring, churches all over Europe blessed the coming year's supply of candles. On many a dark, cold, and gloomy night in February in the shadowy recesses of medieval churches, each member of the congregation carried a lighted candle in a procession around the church to be blessed by the priest. It must have been a beautiful sight but I can't help but picture a group of firefighters standing by outside churches waiting for a clumsy fool to trip and drop their candle onto the floor of the tinder boxes known as churches in those days. It must have been one of the busiest nights of the year for medieval fire departments.

After the blessings, the candles were brought home to rekindle the doused home fires and just like the yule logs of Christmas, this rekindled fire was thought to keep away storms, demons, and other evils. The custom lasted in England until it was banned during the Reformation for promoting the veneration of magical objects.

In order to further Christianize the holiday, the Roman Catholic Church also made the second day in February the feast of the Purification of the Virgin. To reinforce the connection between Saint Brigit and the Virgin Mary, the Church added the new Saint Brigit to the Christmas nativity scene and called her the midwife to the Virgin Mary. The fact that the Virgin Mary and Saint Brigit lived in different centuries and different geographical areas did not seem a problem for the Church.

So, this feast of the Purification of the Virgin, what is that all about? It goes back to a Jewish tradition where women were considered unclean after the birth of a child and not permitted to enter temples of worship for forty days following the birth of a son and for eighty days following the birth of a daughter (because girl children were considered twice as unclean as boy children). Imagine! At the end of the forty or eighty days, the mother brought an offering to the temple or synagogue and was ritually purified. Now she was able to go to religious services again.

When the Catholic Church changed the date of Jesus Christ's birthday from January 6th to December 25th, the date February 2nd gained in significance, falling forty days after December 25th. There are quite a few references to the number forty in many mythological and biblical stories. It rained for forty days and forty nights; and the Israelites stayed in the desert for forty years.

On a different note, why was this purification needed in the first place? The fact that a woman was not able to go to the temple for at least forty days following the birth of a child does not seem like a big deal to me. After just having a child, she has a lot of demands and is not likely to have much time to spend in church, but it is insulting to think of the process of childbirth as "impure." Messy, yes, I will wholeheartedly agree on that, but "impure"? That puts a moral judgement on something that is a purely natural function. And considering a female child twice as impure as a male child—well, what type of scientific instruments did they use to determine that? It must have been the age-old religious/scientific instruments of bias, ignorance, and superstition.

What is it about the period following childbirth that would be cause to consider a woman impure? This taboo really derives from a fear of blood. Women bleed for up to six weeks, or about forty days, following childbirth. This type of bleeding goes by the term *lochia* and is a result of the uterus contracting to expel the remnants of the pregnancy after the baby and the placenta have been delivered.

The same taboo extended to a woman following childbirth was also in place when she was menstruating. It was not only a Jewish tradition: this blood taboo was common among many nations during this time. Traditional human thinking equated blood loss with injury and continuous blood loss with death. A woman's ability to bleed without much pain or loss of life and to do so regularly was viewed suspiciously by men. It was not only that women were considered impure during these time periods but their impurity was also viewed to pose a threat to others.

The Greek historian and scientist Pliny the Elder writes in his book *Natural History*:

Contact with the monthly flux of women turns new wine sour, makes crops wither, kills grafts, dries seeds in gardens, causes the fruit of trees to fall off, dims the bright surface of mirrors, dulls the edge of steel and the gleam of ivory, kills bees, rusts iron and bronze, and causes a horrible smell to fill the air.[3]

I get a kick out of all the fear menstrual blood inspired. It is a real pity I did not know that in high school. Instead of fearing the thought of others knowing I had my period, I could have had my revenge on all those brats who hounded or teased me. I can just picture myself chasing after them, yelling, "Ha, ha, run away you little bully! I'm bleeding and I'm going to turn your blood to vinegar, and watch you run home to mommy, who's also bleeding, and you won't be able to escape the curse of the menstruating woman!"

All these fears of contamination via a menstrual woman led to the custom of forbidding menstruating women from interacting with any non-menstruating person. This led to there being certain isolated areas of the house or the community where menstruating women would spend their blood days without risking contamination of their "clean" society.

This emphasis on restricting women kept her out of the daily business of life. Being taboo during her period meant she was not allowed in a common place, lest she defile others. This was just one more excuse to keep her out of places of economic, religious, and political power. Christian forefathers inherited quite a bit of the Jewish, Greek, and Roman menstrual superstitions. Saint Jerome wrote, "Nothing is so unclean as a woman in her periods, what she touches she causes to be unclean."[4] In the seventh century C.E., the Bishop of Canterbury forbade menstruating women to take communion or enter a church. From the eighth to the eleventh century, many church laws denied menstruating women access to church buildings. As late as 1684, it was still ordered that women in their "fluxes" must remain outside the church door.[5] If only I could have used that excuse in my teen years, when I was always looking for ways to get out of going to church. Even in our present day and age, Orthodox Jews might refuse to shake hands with a woman because she might be menstruating,[6] and the Catholic Church still considers itself on firm theological ground using the notion that a menstruating priestess would pollute the altar as the argument against the ordination of women.[7]

Believe it or not, these old traditions and customs influence our modern-day ideas on menstruation. I can't help but find it strange that such a continual influence on a woman's life is so rarely talked about. Menstruation is an experience almost all women have and these age-old taboos are responsible for real damage to women's view of themselves and their bodies. From all the advertising about pads with wings and non-leak/perfume scented tampons, it is obvious women are still embarrassed by the prospect of others knowing they are on their period. I can't help but wonder how we would view menstruation if men menstruated and gave birth. Would it still be nicknamed "the curse" or would it be highly esteemed?

Menstruation has not always been regarded with the fear, horror, and disgust our history would lead us to believe. It was noted by the earliest peoples that the bleeding was cyclical in nature and when a woman was pregnant, it ceased. So the link between menstrual blood and the singularly female ability to create life was recognized. Considering that the survival of the human race depends on this awesome and miraculous abilities women have to bleed for days without dying, produce new life from their wombs, and food from their breasts, it is likely that at one time menstruation must have been highly esteemed.

A connection between menstruation and pregnancy was established in ancient times. Early thoughts on menstruation were that the blood congealed to form a human being. In ancient Mesopotamia, the goddess Ishtar is said to have made humans from clay she infused with her "blood of life." The name Adam comes from the Sumerian word *adamah*, meaning "bloody clay," though scholars translate it more delicately as "red earth."[8] The Maoris stated explicitly that human souls were made of menstrual blood, which, when retained in the womb, assumed human form and grew into a man. Aristotle believed human life was made of a coagulum of menstrual blood.[9] This notion of the function of menstrual blood was taught in European medical schools up to the eighteenth century.[10] In fact, our modern-day understanding of the female menstrual cycle only took shape in the nineteenth century.

Who would have thought a chapter on Groundhog Day would end up discussing menstruation? In some strange ways, they are parallel: both represent the stirrings of life that are not always seen on the surface. On a monthly cycle, women have the potential for life, and on a yearly cycle, nature has the potential for life. While not as showy as the height of summer, the darkness of winter, or the life of spring, Groundhog Day represents the stage of nature where life is hidden from view and you have to trust it is at work even when you can't see it. It represents that stage of life everyone dreads: when everything seems bleak and we are not rewarded with any results from the efforts we make. Yet in order to keep going, we have to trust that feeling in our gut that things will work out, and hold out for the period of the spring equinox when we are finally able to see the results of the efforts we have made.

In early February, after many months of cold, we want and need reminding of nature's ability to bring forth life once again. For me, Groundhog Day always brings to mind a Bette Midler song called "The Rose." No matter how many times I hear this song, it always has the ability to give me goosebumps regardless of the temperature. It poetically reminds me that even when all seems lost, somewhere hidden from sight exists a seed that, if given time, will make its way to the surface so that hope, life, and love will flourish once again.

VALENTINE'S DAY
February 14ᵗʰ

There is a bit of a void in celebrations following the post-mortem of Christmas and New Year's. It is a good thing too, with all the extra pounds and debt that come with that holiday season. But just when things start to get too boring, along comes Valentine's Day.

In the middle of February, I always find myself longing for the sun and warmth. I eagerly await an end to the drudgery that winter inevitably becomes no matter how hard I try to be a winter person. A love festival would be most welcome but Valentine's Day also makes me feel like a nervous eight-year-old afraid of being the only one in my class not to get a Valentine's Day card. I remember writing out masses of cards to schoolmates trying to ensure I would receive at least a few in return. A friend once told me she used to write Valentine's Day cards to herself to save herself possible public humiliation in the event nobody sent her a card. It didn't really work because she still suffered intolerable anxiety thinking those would be the only cards she received. Unfortunately, it does not end at grade school—in fact, it only gets more complicated.

Valentine's Day is about giving and receiving love. Whenever we love, we risk the possibility of rejection, and with the possibility of rejection comes anxiety. We transfer that anxiety onto finding the right gift. "Hmmm...jewellery? Too committed. I'll scare him off. Chocolate? Great, she'll blame me for the few pounds added to her thighs. Flowers? Oh, they just die, is this a sign of our love? Lingerie? She'll think I think of sex every time I think of her. Even if that's true, I don't want her to know it." When we eventually settle on a gift, we realize we are required to pay three times the price it was last month.

Now, we might be more inclined to tolerate all this anxiety for the potential benefit of some love if Valentine's Day did not seem so commercially contrived. It is easy to become jaded about this day and it is easy to become jaded about love on Valentine's Day. So where did Valentine's Day come from anyway? Did the greeting card industry, chocolate companies, and florist industry create it? Or is there something original, pure, and maybe even carnal about it?

Who Is This Saint Valentine Guy Anyway?

The first question that comes up about Valentine's Day is who is this Saint Valentine guy and what does this day have to do with him? There are three possible characters vying for the original Saint Valentine position.

In one legend, he was a Christian priest during the third century in Rome who defied the orders of Emperor Claudius II. The Emperor was having trouble filling the vacanct positions of soldiers to fight his wars for him so, in his both twisted and logical mind, he decreed it illegal for young men to get married. He thought a married man would be more likely to stay home with his wife and family and a single man would be more inclined to join his army, go to new countries, meet different people, kill them, and claim him some more territory. Valentine (or Valentinius, as the name would have been known during those times) defied Claudius II and let it be known to young lovers he was available to perform clandestine weddings. When the Emperor discovered his actions, Valentine was beheaded.

The second legend also has him as a Christian priest during the third century in Rome, but this time as a physician who cured the sick with special medicines and ointments. He reputedly accepted a loaf of bread or whatever else the poor could spare in place of payment. He was also said to help Christians escape persecution by getting them out of the city and into the mountains. One day, a Roman jailer brought his daughter to see if Valentinius could help her regain her eyesight. Valentinius rubbed an ointment on her eyes and told the jailer to bring her back once a week to continue with the treatment. Not long after that meeting, helping Christians escape persecution landed him in front of Emperor Claudius II who, because he was impressed with his medical skills and kindness, told Valentinius if he converted to paganism he would be spared. When Valentinius instead tried to convert the Emperor to Christianity, he was promptly sent to jail to await his beheading.

While waiting in jail, Julia, the jailer's daughter whose blindness he had been treating before he landed in the slammer, visited him quite often. Valentinius and Julia ended up falling in love (Christian priests were allowed to have sexual relations and marry in those days). Julia's father, who was sympathetic to Valentinius but unable to help him, went to go see him moments before he was executed. Valentinius asked him for a piece of paper and some ink and wrote Julia a love letter signing it, "from your Valentine." Inside the letter was a yellow crocus blossom said to have cured Julia of her blindness.

Now these beheading judgements might seem harsh by our modern-day judicial standards but keep in mind what things were like at the time. The Romans controlled most of North Africa, the Middle East, a good part of Asia, and pretty much all of Europe. They were a force to be reckoned with. While the cruelty of the Roman regime was undisputed, they were not keen on practicing religious intolerance. They accepted that the cultures they conquered had their own religious beliefs and did not persecute people for continuing to practice their rituals; in fact, they encouraged them to. They did, however, require acknowledgement of the divineness of the Roman gods and goddesses, and, most important, the divineness of the Roman emperor himself.

Most of the cultures the Romans conquered had few problems satisfying this demand. There were numerous gods and goddesses and their names changed from region to region and culture to culture. This request did pose difficulties for the Jews and

Christians, who believed in only one God and that to worship or even acknowledge another was blasphemous. Constant uprisings took place within the Jewish Roman state known as Judea, where Roman army had a heavy military presence. The Roman army worked closely with the Jewish priestly class and allowed them complete religious freedom if they kept their populace under control.

The decentralized Christians, on the other hand, were a constant thorn in the side of the Romans. Christians were called atheists because they refused to acknowledge the divineness of the Roman emperor. When the Christians began challenging his authority, the Roman army was ordered to start persecuting.

At first, they did it half-heartedly, just trying to set an example so other Christians would keep a low profile. To the surprise of the Romans, the policy backfired. Instead of persecution driving the Christians underground, it brought them out of the woodwork. Christians were throwing themselves at the feet of the Roman army, begging to be crucified so they could emulate and join their saviour, Jesus Christ. The Romans did not know what to make of it all and sent away many Christians, until, that is, they realized they could use these Christians as entertainment to be ripped apart by lions and/or tortured in a public spectacle instead of the higher-cost gladiators used previously. It was then that the Roman persecution of Christians intensified.[1]

According to both legends, Valentinius was executed on February 14th in the year 270 C.E. There isn't any historical evidence that either Valentinius really existed; in fact, most historians believe these are just mythical stories created by the Catholic Church. Whether these stories are fantasy or reality is beside the point. The stories are sweet, romantic, and include the things a good story needs: love and death. The Catholic Church knew a good story when they heard one and Valentine was chosen to become the patron saint of lovers.

There is a third Valentinius who is not recognized by the Catholic Church as having any association with Valentine's Day, but he was a real historical person and not just a character in a sweet story. He was a second-century Christian mystic and poet.

During the first 300 years of Christianity many different

Christian sects developed. The largest and most influential sect was the Orthodox Christians, who eventually became the Roman Catholic Church after Christianity became the official state religion in the late 300s. The second biggest sect was the Gnostic Christians. The difference between the Gnostics and the Orthodox consisted not so much in their beliefs but rather how their beliefs were practiced. The Gnostics took the belief of the return of Jesus Christ after his crucifixion as one of the many resurrected God mythologies believed at the time. The Orthodox viewed the resurrection of Christ as a literal story and believed Jesus arose not only in spirit but also in body as a living, walking person. The Gnostics viewed religion and spirituality as a personal journey undertaken by an individual. The Orthodox believed religion and spirituality could not exist outside the church. The Gnostics included women in their practices on an equal basis with men. Women were excluded from any position of authority in the Orthodox Church.

The Gnostics challenged the authority of the Orthodox Church, and when the Orthodox Church gained control of the Roman state—and, more important, of the Roman army—they branded the Gnostics as heretics and instituted death as the punishment for heresy. Almost all of the Gnostic writings were destroyed and burnt (not to mention the Gnostics themselves). Up until the last fifty years, all we knew of the Gnostics was what the Orthodox Christians wrote about them, and none of it was very flattering. It was only fifty years ago, when some Gnostic writings were found hidden away in caves, that we were given the opportunity to get a better understanding of their beliefs and how they were practiced.[2]

This real-life third Valentinius was one of the best-known Gnostics. Even amongst his enemies in the Orthodox Church he was known as a wise and well-respected man. His Valentinian sect of Christianity gave women the right to practice their faith as they saw fit, encouraging them to act as spiritual leaders and perform rites such as baptism. One of the names the Orthodoxy called Valentinius besides "heretic" was "woman lover."[3] Ironically, according to the *American Book of Days*, some historians believe the name Valentine comes from a confused translation of the Norman French word *galantin* meaning "lover of women."

Where Did Valentine's Day Come From?

Valentine's Day did not start with the Christians. Instead, the Christians invented a day to honour Saint Valentine in order to replace an ancient Roman festival called Lupercalia, which took place on February 15th. Lupercalia was originally a fertility rite to honour the god Pan (known as Faunus to the Romans). The purpose of Lupercalia was to purify new life for the spring. In a fit of patriotic reform, Emperor Augustus decided it was meant to honour Lupercus (*lupus* means "wolf"), the she-wolf who suckled Romulus and Remus, the founders of Rome.

The celebrations began with the sacrifice of a goat (symbol of fertility) and a dog (symbol of protection) at the Lupercal cave near the Palatine Hill in Rome. Two virile male youths from upper-class families were anointed with the blood from the animals and then cleansed with milk and wool in a ritual of purification. Then the Roman Luperci priests made a whip from the sacrificed animal's hide. These whips were called Februa, which is where we get the name for our month of February, from the Latin *februare*, meaning "to purify."

The two young men then headed through the festival area of the city, whipping women with their goat strips and followed by a band of revellers. The whole festivity was accompanied by much drinking while huge crowds of people on the sidelines watched as women ran in front of the young men hoping to get whipped. The whipping was believed to help ease childbirth and promote fertility, no small feat considering the enormous risk women took in giving birth during those days.

The childbirth deathrate was so high that the average life expectancy of women was ten years less than that of men.[4] It was also important to a woman that she not be barren since women suffered a significant loss in status in Roman society if they were. Failure to provide offspring was a justifiable reason for divorce or annulment of a marriage in Roman society, so it is a bit easier to understand why women were eager to receive such a whipping.

The next entertainment after the whipping and the parade took place on the evening of Lupercalia and was known as the

Lupercalia lottery. The names of eligible young women were written on slips of paper and placed in a pot or urn. The available young men were then given the chance to pull a slip out and be paired with the woman whose name he picked. The pair exchanged gifts and the Roman men wore the names of the girls who were their Lupercalian partners pinned to their sleeves. Hence the origin of the saying "wearing your heart on your sleeve."

There is a lot of speculation about what these couplings entailed. Some speculate the couple would be paired up for either the duration of the festival or the duration of the year and be allowed license to sexually experiment with each other as both felt fit. As appealing and deliciously kinky as this lottery sounds, it is probably very unlikely young Roman women were allowed such sexual license. Too high an economic value was placed on a girl's virginity in Roman society. People believed that when a girl comes into her teen years her sexual appetite increases and her sexuality becomes almost uncontrollable. Fathers therefore decided to marry their daughters off early to ensure they went to their marriage as virgins. The average marriage age for females was fifteen and for males it was thirty. It is likely the Lupercalia lottery paired up males and females for something as simple as a social mixer with numerous chaperones checking on rules for how close and where one could touch the other. Still, considering the limited access males and females had with each other in those days, I am sure it was a highlight of the festival for many young men and women.

The origin of the Lupercalia festival is where the idea of such sexual license probably came about. In Rome, the period of mid-January to mid-February was called Gamelion, the month of the sacred marriage, or *heiros gamos* as it was known in Latin. For the majority of prehistoric human existence, the entity we now know of as God was worshipped as the Mother Goddess. From about 20,000 years ago until about 500 B.C.E., but especially before 3000 B.C.E., the worship of a supreme Mother Goddess was the main, if not the only, divine figure. For these goddess-worshipping cultures, descent was matrilineal, meaning inheritance was passed from mother to child, with the main benefactor being the daughter. This made the most sense to these people because you always knew who the mother was but not necessarily who the father was. It was only when descent started to become patrilineal (based on the identity of the father) that it became necessary to control women's sexuality. A sexual double standard did not exist in matrilineal societies the way it exists in patrilineal societies. In a patrilineal society before the advent of DNA testing, if a woman's sexuality was not controlled it was possible that at some point the husband's family would be passing all their wealth to some child not "really" of their lineage.

When matrilineal descent was the norm, the sacred marriage festival represented the yearly ritual when the Mother Goddess would take a lover, who was usually her son. This festival occurred at different times of the year for different cultures but was a common thread running throughout pagan cultures of Mesopotamia, Egypt, the Middle East, and most of Europe. The coupling of the Mother Goddess with her consort represented a fertility rite and the festival was celebrated by the couplings of human men and women who had sexual licence to fertilize themselves and the earth by mimicking the sacred marriage festival of the goddess and her consort.[5] The Lupercalian lottery was probably a tame and boring continuation of that rite.

The celebration of Lupercalia transformed and spread as the Roman Empire grew, especially in its lottery element. As Christianity became the official religion of the Roman Empire, Christians set out to convert the pagans. Try as they might to convert the pagans from their own gods and goddesses, the Christians had a tough time of it. Even when the pagans accepted Christianity, they accepted Christ as just another god in the family of gods and goddesses. The idea of there being only one God and no goddess was a hard sell to the average pagan. At first, the Christians tried to outlaw pagan celebrations but met with little success. So Christianity took special care to replace the festivals of the pagans with more "Christian" celebrations. The local populations would continue to celebrate on the same days and with similar activities, they would just be celebrating different things.

Lupercalia, with its rather suggestive lottery and ancient origins, had no place in the new Christian order. The trick the

Christians faced was how to redirect something as purely sexual as Lupercalia into something holy. So in 496 C.E., a stern Pope Gelasius I outlawed the mid-February Lupercian festival and instead set up the martyred Bishop Valentine as the patron saint of the new festival. The sacrifice and the whippings were for the most part done away with, although it is still a popular custom in Europe for little boys to chase little girls on Valentine's Day to "switch" them with pussy willow branches. The lottery, however, was far too popular to eliminate simply on pain of persecution.

Pope Gelasius was smart enough, even if a bit naive, to try and replace the lottery with a new Christian version. The pot that once held the names of available young women was replaced with the names of Christian saints. Both men and women extracted slips of paper and in the ensuing year they were expected to emulate the life of the saint whose name they had drawn. The saint lottery did not last long. As I am sure you can guess, trading companionship and flirtation with a young woman for the name of a dead saint did not really turn the cranks of many young males.

With Christianity having difficulty erasing the original meanings and memories of the ancient celebration of fertility and mating from Valentine's Day, numerous attempts were made to eliminate the holiday completely. Valentine's Day was banned by the Catholic Church more than once and in more than one country. It proved too popular, however, and the day always returned.

Valentine's Day Symbols

There are numerous Valentine's Day symbols, and where they came from, what they mean, and how they are laced together is as interesting a story as the origin of the festival itself.

Valentine's Day Cards

Young men replaced the Lupercalian lottery with the custom of offering gifts and handwritten greetings of affection to women they wished to court. As Christianity spread, so did the Valentine's Day card. Since parchment was scarce and the majority of people were illiterate, it was not until the fifteenth century that the first greeting cards were produced. Charles of Valois, the

Duke of Orléans, gave his wife the oldest known valentine after he had been taken prisoner by the English in 1415. The card is now in the Museum of London.

Many Valentine's Day cards had secret panels in them to hide messages to the girls to whom they where sent. Victorian fathers were very strict and would not allow their daughters to receive any sort of correspondence unless they had first read it and decided whether or not it was suitable. Messages were often hidden under lace or ribbons. This probably accounts for the reason valentines are by tradition anonymous. As the eighteenth century ushered in the less personal practice of mailing, it became easier to give Valentine's Day cards anonymously. This was taken as the main reason for the sudden appearance of racy verse in what was traditionally thought of as prudish Victorian times. The burgeoning number of obscene valentines caused several countries to ban the practice of exchanging cards. In England, new cards called the "penny dreadful" took the place of Valentine's Day cards. These cards were insulting, often crude and obscene, and even sometimes downright cruel. They were usually sent anonymously, for obvious reasons. In Chicago, late in the 1800s, the post office rejected some 25,000 cards on the grounds that they considered them unfit to be carried through the U.S. mail. I would like to see some of *those* cards in the museum.

Birds

Another possible origin of the Lupercalia festival, and maybe even of the date of the sacred marriage ceremony itself, was the belief that birds begin to mate in the middle of February. Many birds do begin to mate around this time of year and some birds, such as the missel thrush, the dove, the partridge, and the blackbird, have actually been seen mating on February 14th. Now, there aren't many things more romantic than birds choosing their mates. The males go to an enormous amount of effort to court the females. They do things such as offer them lots of food (grasshoppers and other tasty insects); build elaborate nests (the guy with the biggest nest wins); perform elaborate and sometimes downright weird dances; and wage mock (and sometimes real) battles.

On top of all the effort the male birds put into attracting a female, they also make extremely loyal and faithful partners. An estimated 90% of bird species are monogamous and a good percentage of those monogamous pairs are pairs for life. Only about 3% of mammals can be considered monogamous. If you consider only primates, then this number jumps to 12%, but that is only if you include borderline cases such as humans.[6]

Few animals co-parent as birds do. The female may lay the eggs but the male and female birds work in partnership to incubate the eggs and take turns tending the nest of young ones and going out to hunt and bring back food for their little ones and their partner.[7] Of all the birds, doves are the most popular Valentine's Day symbol; they also mate for life, share the duties of caring for their babies, and are often to be seen loving and cooing each other.

The Rose
In the Far East, the rose was called the flower of the goddess. Roses were sacred to Aphrodite, the Greek goddess of love, and are considered one of the strongest aphrodisiacs in aromatherapy. Cupid is responsible for the mythological origin of the rose. Cupid was carrying a vase of sweet nectar to the gods on Mount Olympus when he spilt it on the ground. On that spot roses grew. Romans also believed anything discussed under a rose was *sub rosa* and kept a secret. We still use this Latin expression today when something is confidential.

Cupid
The Roman idea of Cupid came from his Greek counterpart, Eros, who was the son of Aphrodite (known to Romans as Venus). It is the Greeks whom we have to thank for the words *erotica* and *aphrodisiac*. Cupid went through a transformation to become the little, chubby, baby-like creature we now know him as. Jupiter (Zeus to the Greeks) had apparently married Venus off to the ugliest man he could find just to stop the feuding taking place amongst the male gods vying for her favour. This marriage arrangement did not please Venus, so while she felt compelled to marry the blacksmith god, Vulcan (Greek: Hephaestus), she refused to be faithful to him. She had many dalliances and in one of these, with Mars (Greek: Ares), Cupid was the result. He was originally depicted as

a young man carrying a bow and quiver who sharpened his arrows on a grindstone coated with infant's blood, using them not for romantic purposes but for entertainment.

This fits well with the way romantic love used to work: marriage and love usually did not go together but adultery and love did. Marriages were conducted for political and practical reasons and love very rarely played a role in determining matches. Cupid's use of his mother Venus' arrows probably served as a mythological explanation for why love was very often accompanied by inconvenience and had such power to wreak havoc.

It is interesting to see how Cupid's appearance changed over time. In ancient times, he was the symbol of infatuation, a young, handsome, Adonis-like mythological man. Now he is a chubby playful cherub. The image change was helped by the fact the Catholic Church wanted to eliminate the social upheaval of infatuation, lust, and love from the holiday, while merchants were also looking for a way to make the holiday more appealing and what they viewed as more suitable for women and children.

The Heart Symbol
The Romans believed the heart contained the soul. Egyptians believed the heart was the centre of intelligence and reasoning. The arrow that pierces the heart is a symbol of death and the vulnerability of the heart. In addition, the heart and the arrow represent the merging of the male and female principles. The actual organ that pumps all the blood throughout our body does not look anything like the conventional heart-shaped symbol. Where the symbolic shape came from is all speculation, but some ideas include: the heart being a representational shape of the human buttocks, a female torso with prominent breasts and an arrow pointing down to the mount of Venus, or even the shape of the lips when they pucker up to give a kiss.

Chocolate
Chocolate and Valentine's Day have become connected only very recently. Chocolate came from the Aztecs in what is now Mexico, where it was considered a royal aphrodisiac. The Aztec emperor Montezuma II apparently drank liquid chocolate all day to

enhance his libido. But the chocolate of the Mayans and Aztecs was a far cry from the stuff we eat today. They took cocoa beans and crushed them with spices to make a bitter drink. When the Spanish first brought chocolate back to Europe in this form, it was considered extremely vile until it went through an important evolution—the chili pepper was replaced with sugar.

Scientists seem to know as much about how chocolate affects the body as they know about why people fall in love. They know chemicals are involved but they don't know what triggers them. Chocolate is made up of 300 compounds, many of which (such as caffeine, theobromine, and phenylethylamine) are known to have mood-altering effects: caffeine brings along its usual energy-boosting properties; theobromine stimulates the heart and nervous system; phenylethylamine is an amphetamine-like substance said to simulate the same reaction in the body as falling in love. Some scientists also say chocolate contains substances that have the same effect on the brain as endorphins, naturally occurring chemicals similar to opium. The opiates dull pain and promote a feeling of well-being.

Mind you, these same scientists will also tell you these compounds found in chocolate do not exist in amounts sufficient to produce a reaction in the body. But the fact is, in practical studies, people do experience these chemical and mood-lifting experiences when they eat chocolate. Maybe it is because, even in their minute amounts, these chemicals are enough to trigger the body into recognizing the chemical changes taking place and to continue the production of these or similar types of chemicals the body can produce on its own, like serotonin, a mood-lifting hormone naturally produced in the brain when a person is happy. This reaction is similar to the way homeopathy is believed to work. Even a minute amount of a substance introduced into the body can trigger the body to create that chemical or start a chain reaction causing the body to create similar types of hormones or chemicals. Then again, maybe it is simply the placebo effect. However it works, chocolate seems to make people happy and happiness is always an aphrodisiac.

Whatever the origin of Valentine's Day, there is no denying the present-day commercialization and superficiality of this holiday. We have become convinced Valentine's Day is our yearly quota of romance. We may not believe this in our emotions and thoughts but unfortunately we tend to show it in our actions. The florist, greeting card, and chocolate companies are smart enough to prey on our guilt. It is up to us to reclaim the holiday's original intention of reminding people of the joy of life, love, and sex. Even our primitive ancestors understood the need to celebrate these basic human needs at least a couple of times a year!

St. Patrick's Day

March 17th

March 17th is dedicated to celebrating the life of some guy named Patrick who became one of Christianity's best-known and best-loved saints. Patrick has so many legends attributed to him that his life seems more fairy tale than real life. The fact is, when it comes to his life we can't separate history from fable, but our inability to do so doesn't matter anyway; his life is a good story—fact or fiction.

All we know about Saint Patrick and his life comes from two writings—his Confession, a spiritual autobiography, and a short letter he wrote to a slave trader named Coroticus, slamming him for the abuse perpetrated against Patrick's followers. His writings, supposedly written by him in the fifth century, were not heard of until 400 years later, making some people think Saint Patrick was only a fictional character created by Christian priests to prove Ireland was Christianized earlier than it really was.[1]

Either way, Ireland has adopted Patrick as its patron saint and the Irish give him the credit (or the blame) for converting Ireland to Christianity. One of the legends attributed to Saint Patrick was that he managed to introduce Christianity to Ireland and convert the entire population to his religion in a mere thirty years. It is highly unlikely the Irish were converted as early as the fifth century, since in the twelfth century a Christian bishop (who also rose to sainthood after his death) complained the Irish were still given to "barbarous rites as Christianity has failed to take root among them."[2] To take even more legend away from poor old Saint Patrick, there is some evidence he was not the first to introduce Christianity to Ireland. Numerous followers of either Saint Paul or Saint Peter trying to escape Roman persecution landed in Britain and made their way over to Ireland as early as the first century C.E. I would agree it is highly unlikely one person could convert an entire culture to a new religion in a mere thirty years when they already had one that served them well. However, just like painters who live in destitute poverty, unable to sell their paintings for a pittance only to become famous and have their paintings sell for millions a century or two after their deaths, Patrick's legacy went unrecognized during his lifetime. But he did leave a legacy: today, 93% of the Republic of Ireland's population is Catholic.[3]

Strangely enough, Patrick was not born Irish but Scottish. He was given the name of Maewyn Succat by wealthy parents near the end of the forth century. In his sixteenth year, slave traders ransacked his family's estate and carried off poor Maewyn. He was shipped off to Ireland and sold into slavery where for six years he tended sheep for his owner. In the sixth year of his captivity, he heard a voice he believed to be God's telling him, "Thy ship is waiting for thee." Maewyn heeded the voice, ran away from his position as a slave, and walked over two hundred miles to reach the coast, where he eventually managed to find himself passage on a boat. He was taken on for what he believed was to be a crewmember only to be made a slave once again. He eventually managed to desert his shipmates and spent a few years wandering through Southern Gaul (France) and Italy.

After having enough of wandering, he hooked up with the Catholic Church and began religious training that lasted fifteen years. Upon his ordination, Pope Celestine I gave him the name Patrick. Soon after becoming Patrick, he heard another message from God telling him the Irish people wanted him to come back to them and bring them God. Despite numerous attempts by family and friends to dissuade him from taking a posting regarded as the equivalent of a modern-day diplomatic posting in Siberia, Patrick insisted God was sending him a message and he intended to heed His voice. It was probably in the summer of 432 C.E. that Patrick landed just south of Dublin. Despite the constant threat to his life from village warlords and landowners, Patrick travelled widely, baptizing and preaching and building churches, schools, and monasteries to educate his followers. There are over sixty churches and cathedrals named after Saint Patrick in Ireland alone. He made his way across the country as a missionary and somehow managed to survive to a ripe old age. He is thought to have died on the March 17, 460 C.E.

Unlike many of the missionaries exiled to Ireland, Patrick was familiar with the Irish language and culture and went there willingly. Unlike many of his contemporaries, he did not consider the Celts to be primitive barbarians unworthy of salvation. He respected their beliefs and tried to incorporate the message of the Christian God into their existing religious stories, festivals, and rites.

These so-called barbarians whom Patrick went to Ireland to convert were actually Celts and Scandinavians, the ancient pagans whose rites and rituals were performed by the priestly class of Druids. They were not just savages that practiced human sacrifice and worshipped fire and a heap of stones as they were often portrayed. The Celtic Druids were required to study for a lengthy twenty years to master their knowledge. Their scholastic endeavours in natural philosophy, astronomy, mathematics, geometry, and medicine reached an incredible level of sophistication far exceeding what was known in mainland Europe during the same period.

Theirs was a nature-based religion filled with mythology and symbolism. We owe holidays such as Halloween, Groundhog Day, May Day, Christmas and their associated traditions to this ancient culture. But instead of acknowledging their contribution to our society, our perception of them as axe-wielding savages who practiced human sacrifice (an image perpetuated by the likes of Julius Caesar and many of their other enemies) clouds our ability to truly appreciate what modern-day Western culture has absorbed from them.

The Celtic concept of religion was based on a very personal

appreciation of life in all its stages from birth to death, and good to bad. Nature's goodness in providing life, food, and shelter, as well as nature's harshness (via death and starvation) were considered one and the same. The Celts understood their dependence on nature for their care and considered it their duty to take care of her so she would not turn against them.

This is not to idealize the culture as some sort of a utopia, not in the least. Just like in mainland Europe, warfare, slavery, and brutality were also part of the culture. But the Celtic appreciation of nature is something we lost in the Western world when we started our grand separation from nature over three thousand years ago and came to the conclusion that we needed to subdue and control it. Religions became based on the idea we were bigger and better than nature and it was there for our use and abuse. Our perception of the world became separated into light and dark, good and evil, nature and civilization.

It is understandable that people would want to protect themselves from the negative side of nature since hurricanes, drought, tornados, and getting lost in the woods can be downright scary. With our attempt to reduce our vulnerability to the ways of nature, we have done away with much of her strength as well. Our fear of nature's negative side has weakened our appreciation of her positive side; we have lumped all of nature into one parcel that needs to be tamed and put under our control lest it wreak havoc on our lives. The Celtic understanding of the world as both good and bad rather than our perception of either good or bad is something that may benefit us in our lives.

Proving once again that no one is more Irish than one who has left Ireland, St. Patrick's Day is a far more commercial and rowdy event in North America than in Ireland, where it is downright tame and even solemn in comparison. For example, up until the 1970s, Irish law mandated pubs be closed on March 17th. Parades are another example: St. Patrick's Day parades are largely an American invention. The first St. Patrick's Day parade took place in the United States when Irish soldiers serving in the English military marched through Boston on March 17, 1762. During the potato famine of 1845–49, masses of Irish immigrants migrated to the United States and faced heavy prejudice from the American

Protestant majority. The majority of Irish immigrants had trouble finding even menial jobs. St. Patrick's Day became one of the few opportunities available to them to express pride in their national heritage.

Unfortunately, the rising political tensions between British Protestants and Irish Catholics resulted in many early St. Patrick's Day parades ending in fights and violence. Although statistically the Irish are only moderately heavy drinkers by European standards (Belgium and Germany both consume more beer), the stereotype of the drunken Irish was popular in America.

The Irish soon began to realize their great numbers endowed them with a political power that had yet to be exploited. They started to organize and their voting block, known as the "green machine," became an important swing vote for political hopefuls. Suddenly, annual St. Patrick's Day parades became a show of strength for Irish Americans as well as a must-show event for political candidates. Ironically, as the Irish became more influential in New York City politics, the parade became less about politics and more about fun. Today there are more people of Irish descent in the U.S. than there are in Ireland, and St. Patrick's Day has become the biggest annual parade held in New York City and is also celebrated with over thirty parades all over North America.

But why does a supposedly nationalistic holiday appeal to so many people of non-Irish descent? How can we explain why "Everybody's Irish on St. Patrick's Day"? Well, it is because St. Patrick's Day is not only an Irish holiday; it is a rite of spring.

Like so many other people of ancient beliefs who retained their connection to the passing of the seasons and realized their dependence on nature and the influence of gods and goddesses, the Celtic Druids honoured their deities of plant life. The plants that best represented these deities were the plants that stayed green year round. These were considered a symbol of hope and eternal life. Even to this day, it is customary in Ireland to plant something new in the garden the week following March 17th.

In Ireland, green has always been considered the symbolic colour of healing and hope. With the coming of Saint Patrick and other missionaries, many of the old pagan rites were linked to days of importance in the Christian calendar. The traditions remained pretty much the same but the message was changed over the centuries. The pagan vernal equinox/springtime celebration was gradually replaced by St. Patrick's Day and Easter. It is a day when Christians and non-Christians, Irish and non-Irish, cast off that dark shroud of winter and welcome the warmth of the sun and the rebirth of nature. Our modern-day society does not really have a festival or any other significant marker for the spring equinox, so St. Patrick's Day has become our opportunity to mark this change of season.

One of the famous legends attributed to Saint Patrick is that he used the shamrock to illustrate the Christian doctrine of the Holy Trinity (three persons in one God). He demonstrated to the unconverted Irish pagans that the shamrock has three separate leaves but is a single plant with a single stem. This legend likely arose to justify the high esteem in which the Irish people traditionally held the shamrock. The shamrock, which looks like a clover, was called *seamroy* by the Gaelic Celts and was a sacred plant in ancient Ireland because it symbolized to the Druids the coming of spring and the rebirth of the natural world at the spring equinox. In addition, it is likely the Irish worshipped the shamrock as a sign of their own triple deities, where the Mother Goddess was represented in her three different stages: virgin, maiden, and crone. It is likely that Saint Patrick would not have had difficulty explaining the concept of the Holy Trinity as a result.

The significance of the number three was not original to Saint Patrick or Christianity; it was considered significant in many ancient religions. Scholars speculate that the number three has always been important and may have come from the wonder our ancient ancestors had for the birth mystery once they got it figured out. They observed that two humans or two animals created a third entity after mating. It might also be derived from the significance or symbolism of the past, present, future; or even the idea of the underworld, earth, sky.

While the shamrock still grows freely all over Ireland, where the mild climate resulting from the North Atlantic Drift keeps the country green all year long, the symbolism of the shamrock has changed quite a bit over the centuries. Although it started out as a symbol of the arrival of spring, and then of St. Patrick's Day, it became symbolic of the way the Irish felt about their country. As the English began to seize Irish land and make laws against the use of the Irish language and the practice of Catholicism, many Irish began to wear the shamrock as a symbol of pride in their heritage and of their displeasure with English rule. By the seventeenth century, the shamrock had become an emblem of Irish rebellion and, more than ever, a symbol of national pride.

Of all the legends attributed to good old Saint Patrick, the most famous was that he banished all snakes from Ireland. He is often depicted holding a shamrock in the act of ostracizing the snakes. It has long been recounted that during his mission in Ireland, Saint Patrick once stood on a hilltop—now called Croagh Patrick—and with only a wooden staff and his faith, banished all the snakes from Ireland. Perhaps this story is really a metaphor for the elimination of pagan ideology from Ireland, the last stronghold for pagan nature-based religions in all of Europe.

One story recounts how he had banished all the snakes except for one that refused to go. Saint Patrick made a box and invited the serpent to enter it. The serpent objected on the grounds the box was not big enough to hold him but Saint Patrick insisted it was big enough to be comfortable. After a long discussion, the serpent finally agreed to enter the box to prove it was too small. As soon as the serpent was safely inside, Patrick shut the lid and threw it into the sea. There is another legend claiming Saint Patrick magically made the Irish soil so repugnant a serpent would die if it touched it. The eighth century English scholar Bede went even further; he claimed that when a snake got even the slightest whiff of Irish air it would die. Just goes to show you how stories become more and more embellished over time. Yes, it is true there are no snakes in Ireland but it was not Saint Patrick that got rid of them, it was an ice age.

Starting 1.8 million years ago in an icy period called the Pleistocene epoch, a series of great ice caps covered all of Northern Europe and North America practically down to the Missouri. During this time of the glaciers, Ireland was buried under a deep sheet of ice. No snake would be able to survive this and any snakes that existed in Ireland at this time met a cold icy death. Only after the great freeze finally ended in Ireland some fifteen thousand years ago would a snake have been able to survive in Ireland and by then twelve miles of icy North Channel Ocean barred the way to Ireland for any snakes thinking of making the trip. There are no snakes in Ireland today for the simple reason of there being no way for the critters to get there.[4]

Perhaps what is more important than what Saint Patrick did or did not do is what he represents. Thomas Cahill, the author of *How the Irish Saved Civilization*, believes a better advocate cannot be found for anyone disadvantaged or living on the fringes of society. Despite whether Saint Patrick was real or just made up, he represents a person who turned a disadvantaged position into something that put him on top. Here is a person who lived his life by following his heart.

Saint Patrick really is one of the few people who fought for recognition for the downtrodden no one else wanted anything to do with. The Catholic Church did not have a lot of priests breaking down doors to go to Ireland and convert the Celts. Patrick volunteered for this position and, based on his confessional, continually defended his choice to an unsympathetic papacy in England and Rome.

Whether his arrival in Ireland and Ireland's conversion to Catholicism was a good thing or a bad thing is open to debate and there is no real answer anyway. Ireland is largely Catholic today, and while Saint Patrick is honoured among them for bringing them Christianity, the Irish have paid a high price for their religious conversion. Not many people know that Britain's Oliver Cromwell murdered or starved to death 5/6[ths] of Ireland's population in his holy quest to purge the country of Catholicism in the 1600s. Nor do many realize Ireland was a potato exporter to England during the potato famine in which nearly a million Irish starved to death and another million fled to America. There is little doubt the Irish can easily be considered the underdogs of Western Europe.

Women, as another of society's underdogs, also find a very rare advocate in Patrick. Unlike his Christian contemporary Saint Augustine, who wrote about women as the bringers of evil into the world and as the personification of the temptations of the flesh and original sin, Patrick was actually the first male

Christian since Jesus to speak well of women. There are clear instances of him saying warm and appreciative things about women—an absolute rarity in Christian writings.

In his Confessions, Patrick criticizes himself quite a bit as being uneducated. The six years Patrick was enslaved in Ireland put him permanently behind his peers in terms of classical education, and one might suspect the papacy never let him forget it. But it seems Patrick's enslavement as an adolescent was a critical development in his unique attitude towards the Irish and to people in general. According to Thomas Cahill, Saint Patrick's experience in captivity left him with a virulent hatred for the institution of slavery and he would later become one of the first human beings to record his negative feelings towards the idea of slavery. "The Catholic papacy did not condemn slavery as immoral until the end of the fifth century," Cahill writes, "but here is Patrick in the mid-fifth century seeing it for what it is. I think that shows enormous insight and courage and a tremendous fellow feeling to the suffering of others and to understand what other people's suffering is like."

I admire people who put themselves out on a limb and fight for what they think the world should be rather than accept the world as it is. Sometimes their ideas may be considered unrealistic and even naive if they are viewed only as a single person in a single lifetime. But then again, just think of where the world would be if we did not challenge a status quo we consider unfair, if not downright wrong.

Each of us at some point in our lives will find ourselves the underdog, and hopefully there will be someone who will help us in our cause. There will also hopefully be many times when we are in the position where we can take up the cause of an underdog and make a difference in their life. The problem is there are so many worthwhile challenges to the status quo; to take it on can easily become overwhelming. Sadly, many of us just give up and think one person can't possibly make a difference. To be realistic and not let our lives be overrun by good causes, and even to be effective in undertaking a cause, we have to pick our fights, otherwise we will become disillusioned and burnt out and will inevitably come to this unfortunate conclusion.

Spring's unwillingness to let winter continue on its way even though it feels like it will never end, reminds us we can also make a difference as Saint Patrick did, even though everyone seems against us and the odds seem insurmountable. No matter what happens, the change of the seasons reminds us that change is inevitable. And if this is the case, we might as well make an effort to try and make that change for what we see as the better. People who take on the fight of the underdog can't help but make a change and they often create a legend or two in the process. The world needs more legends.

EASTER

The Sunday Following the First Full
Moon after the Spring Equinox

Easter has always signalled the beginning of spring for me. It is a time when I can not only finally see the light at the end of the tunnel that is winter, but I can feel it too. The warmth of the sun has come back from the dead of winter to grace us. Hallelujah, this is the part of Easter I rejoice at. On the other hand, there is also a part of me that can't help but feel uncomfortable with the whole religious significance of the holiday. Nothing throws a damper on a party faster than the crucifixion of someone who seemed like a really cool guy. I don't understand why I or anyone else would want to celebrate that. Okay, I like the idea of a wake just as much as the next Irish. Actually, when I go, I sincerely hope there is a party on my grave, but there must be a different sort of vibe to the wake of a person who has been assassinated or murdered. It can't be the quiet acceptance of death we feel when a person who has lived a long full life dies peacefully in their sleep. No, when someone's time is violently cut short we cannot help but ask *why*?

Asking "why" only increased my discomfort with the Easter story. There was this underlying current of blame for Jesus' death being placed on the Romans and since they no longer existed as a culture, the blame went on the Jews. Now I was not only lamenting the wrongful death of what seemed like a cool guy but I was also lamenting the wrongful conviction of countless generations of Jews for something their religious elite might or might not have done over two thousand years ago—especially when, according to Christian theology, it was God himself who decreed Jesus' death, in which case the Jewish priests were merely obeying the will of God. Execution? Crucifixion? Persecution? Yuck. It all forced me to realize how unfair and depressing life can be sometimes.

Then to add confusion to depression, I was told that even though this guy named Jesus did die, he was miraculously brought back to life. I still remember the look of disbelief and relief on the faces of the kids in my Sunday school when we were told this story. You have to feel pity for the person who is supposed to explain this to a bunch of questioning kids. "Miss Foster, what about my dog? Can he come back too?" "Does that mean I can come back to life if I get run over by a car?" And then came the doozy: "Miss Foster, if he can come back from the dead, why hasn't my mother come back to me? Did she not love me enough?"

As you can imagine, after that question we were quickly sent out for recess and it was never addressed again. It was probably that question and the look on the girl's face when she asked it that caused my ongoing feeling of depression during the Easter season. I didn't get it. At a time of the year that seemed all about life and its return to the surface of the earth, why were we all talking about death? I hope this chapter will help you and me find an answer to this question.

Where Did the Name *Easter* Come From?

The origin of the name *Easter* in most languages other than English and German comes from the old Hebrew word for *Passover*. In Spanish, it is *Pascua*; in Greek, *Pascha*; in French, *Pâques*. The English and German name for Easter, however, is taken from the Teutonic dawn-goddess known variously as Ostare, Ostara, Ostern, Eostre, Eostra, Eostur, Eastra, and numerous other variations. Her name is derived from the ancient word *eastre*, which means "season of the growing sun," which also sounds very close to the word *estrus*, the term for when a female mammal goes into heat and is ready to mate. On an even stranger note, it turns out that the name for Easter in all languages pre-dates Jesus by a few millennia. Hmm…what is that all about?

The Easter-Passover Connection

The Christian celebration of Easter is linked to the Jewish celebration of Passover. It is generally believed that Jesus was crucified on the eve of Passover and died on Passover itself. Passover is one of the most important feasts of the Jewish calendar and it is celebrated on the first full moon after the vernal equinox. In 325 C.E., Emperor Constantine set the Easter festival on the first Sunday after the full moon following the vernal equinox. If the full moon should fall on a Sunday, Easter was then celebrated on the following Sunday. They devised this system in order to put some distance between the Jewish Passover festival and the Christian Easter festival by ensuring they would never fall on the same day.

In the Old Testament, the Jews settled in Egypt at the invitation of Joseph (the guy with the colourful cloak). Shortly afterwards, the pharaoh (from the vague dating in the Old Testament, it is not possible to know which pharaoh) launched an ambitious building program. The Jews were forced into service and before they knew it, they were slaves. This continued for a few centuries until Moses politely asked another pharaoh (believed by scholars to be Ramses II) to let his people go free. The pharaoh thought this request ludicrous and told Moses that if his God really looked out for his people they would not have had to endure centuries of slavery. He also suggested to Moses and his people that they should rethink their allegiance to this God of theirs. If you really think about it, he did have a point but not one that won him the favour of Yahweh (as the Jewish God is named). Yahweh sent the pharaoh nine plagues, including an array of frogs, lice, locusts, fire, and hailstorms. With each plague, the pharaoh remained unmoved and still refused Moses' request to let him lead his people out of slavery.

So Yahweh, seeing he would have to play hardball, devised a tenth plague—he came down for an earthly visit and went throughout Egypt killing first-born sons. The Jews, however, were conveniently warned ahead of time to sacrifice a lamb and sprinkle the blood on the doorsteps so God would know to "pass over" their homes and spare their sons. According to the story, in the morning when all the non-Jewish households woke up to find their first-born sons dead, all hell broke loose. The pharaoh finally relented and allowed the Jews to leave but shortly thereafter changed his mind and sent the army to recapture them. This is when the story of the Red Sea parting comes in.

Passover is an eight-day celebration of the Jews' deliverance from slavery in Egypt and their rebirth as a free culture. It turns out, however, that the festivity goes back even further. The earlier inhabitants of the region the Jews eventually settled in after their forty years in the desert were an agricultural people called the Canaanites who held seasonal rites to honour their local gods and goddesses. Their spring festival involved the sacrifice of lambs. The ancient Canaanite spring festival may have later been reinterpreted to mean the "skipping over" of Jewish homes by God on his Egyptian killing spree.

People seem to forget that Jesus was actually a Jew, as were many early converted Christians, so it is no surprise that many of the traditions of the Passover festival were carried over into the new Jesus-worshipping religion. The Hebrew custom of the sacrificed lamb blended with the Christian custom and its meaning changed. To Christians, Jesus became the sacrifice and the lamb became the symbol of Jesus.

What is this obsession with sacrifice on Easter? We are told Jesus laid down his life in order to save the lives of his followers and ended up paying the price for past, present, and future sins of humanity. No small feat indeed. But let's be more practical and wonder how the death of one person, even if divinely inspired, can achieve such a lofty goal. What does one person's death have to do with the salvation of the multitudes? This leads us to the backdrop of the political and religious intrigues and power plays during the time of Jesus. While this subject is worthy of a book in itself, it is such a good story that I can't resist the opportunity to get into it a bit here.

After their narrow escape from Egypt and their forty years of exile in the desert, the Israelites decided to settle into the land of "milk and honey" only to be faced with the fact that this land was not empty and free for the taking. It was populated by various other cultures, with the Canaanites being the most numerous. Not willing to let this keep them from their "Promised Land," they embarked on what they considered a God-inspired takeover. Their leader, Joshua, led them into numerous Canaanite villages and instructed them to kill everyone but virgin girls.

With such heavy-handed tactics, it did not take them long to gain a substantial foothold in their new land, but then the tables were turned. The Israelites underwent their own experience of being repeatedly conquered by other nations. In 922 B.C.E., the Egyptians came back to haunt them; in 722 B.C.E., the Assyrians gained control; in 586 B.C.E., the Babylonians took over; in 332 B.C.E., under Alexander the Great, the Greeks came into town and set up shop; in 198 B.C.E., the Syrians took over; and then in 63 B.C.E., the Romans claimed Judea as their territory.

Despite their brutality and success in gaining territory, the Romans were smart enough to realize that there is a difference between getting land and keeping land. With too much territory and too few soldiers, the Romans made alliances. In Judea, they made their alliance with the Sanhedrin, the Jewish religious elite. The deal was this: the Jewish priests could have religious independence and control if, and only if, they were able to keep their population from organizing insurrections against Rome. If they were unsuccessful in honouring their side of the bargain, then a Roman administration would be set in place and the present priestly administration and the Jewish people would be taken as the sacrifice.

Along comes this guy called Jesus. We might think he is something special nowadays, but to the people of his time, he started out as just another one of the multitudes of travelling preachers roaming Judean neighbourhoods talking about freedom, peace, and everlasting life. Not having taken any media-savvy courses, he did not really have the two-minute sound bite down pat either. More often than not, it was hard to understand what he was really going on about since he constantly spoke in parables and riddles. This must have been the modern-day equivalent of

Shakespeare to a teenager who is left wondering why people think the guy was so brilliant when he could not even come out and say what he wanted to say. While Jesus may have thought he was talking about spiritual freedom and peace, the practical people of Judea understood this to mean freedom from the Romans and their heavy hand and heavy taxes. He never came out and said, "Fight off the Romans," but then he never said to accept them either and that was good enough for many who were just dying to find a reason to rise up against Rome.

This was the first concern the Jewish priestly elite had. If Jesus was successful in bringing people together then he might be the Messiah they were waiting for who would finally release them from under an oppressor's thumb. On the other hand, he might just be a regular guy who would start a rebellion against Rome, lose the rebellion, and leave them and the whole population of Judea to face Rome's wrath. You can't really blame them for being overly cautious. These were serious risks. If there were to be an insurrection, it would have to be a successful one because a failed one would mean their lives, the lives of their family, and the lives of many of their people. A few decades after Jesus' death, this is exactly what did happen when the Jews staged a failed rebellion and Rome came down hard. In 66 C.E., when the Jews revolted against their oppressors, the Romans levelled the state of Judea, killed a good one-third of the population, put another one hundred thousand Jews into slavery, and dispersed what remained of the Judean population from one end of the Roman territory to the other.

This reality, which came a mere few decades after Jesus' death, is what concerned the Jewish priestly elite during Jesus' life. They wanted to find out what this Jesus guy was really like and whether he had any hope in hell of defeating Rome. It turned out that Jesus was a slippery sort of guy who was quite hard to track down. Until, that is, his best bud, his spiritual brother, ratted him out. Ah, the worst deception, the one you hold closest to you betrays you. Our worst fear becomes a reality, *ooch*; we all can imagine how that hurts.

They held Jesus in custody because they could not really be sure who or what he represented, especially since he spoke in parables. Consequently, the Sanhedrin powers that be decided to play it safe and hand Jesus over to the Romans. You have to admit it was very strategic for them to hedge their bets. I guess they figured that if he was the Messiah, he would get the people to revolt against Rome and maybe even win. But just in case he wasn't and he lost, then the Jewish priests couldn't really be blamed because they handed him over to the Romans. We all know how this story ends. After some deliberation, the Roman prefect Pontius Pilate decided to do away with him. But, hey, even that can't keep this guy down. Three days after his death and funeral, Jesus is found out roaming the hills.

Wow, maybe this was no ordinary guy after all. He must have been a god since no one else in the last two thousand years has been able to pull off that trick. Many began to think that maybe he really was the Messiah they had been waiting for—and let's face it, death has the ability to bring people together. It really is a great story. But wait a second, this is not supposed to be just a story, we are told this is something that really happened—this is history.

Okay, I have to admit it seemed very far fetched to me as a child and I still have problems buying it. So to deal with my scepticism, I decided that the coming back to life bit is part of a story, but the real life person named Jesus was probably just a regular guy who had some amazing things to say and was able to move people in a way that was miraculous. That comforted me. I had finally found a way to make sense of it all in my own mind. But just when it all seemed to add up, along comes more information to complicate matters. I just love it when that happens.

What do we make of the fact that the story of a prodigal son born to a virgin in a mangy manor with the ability to perform miracles such as turning water into wine, curing the incurable, and bringing people back from the dead, only to be cruelly betrayed, needlessly killed, and then brought back from the dead in order to bring salvation to all of humanity is at least three thousand years older than Jesus?

In Egypt he was called Osiris, brother and husband to the goddess Isis. Osiris is betrayed, killed, and dismembered by his brother Seth. The whole earth is barren until Isis finds him and brings together the dismembered pieces of his body. When she finally succeeds in putting his body parts back together, she finds out she is missing a vital organ. She cannot find his penis anywhere. Being a resourceful goddess, she fashions one from wood and attaches it to him. He comes back to life, they make love, and she becomes pregnant with a son.

After performing his conjugal duty, Osiris dies once again and is reborn as their son Horus, who is born in a mangy cave on Old Christmas Day (January 6th) and brings back salvation to the earth and all its inhabitants.

In Babylonia he was called Dumuzi, or Damu, "only begotten Son." He fertilized the earth with his blood at the time of his death and was called Healer, Saviour, and Heavenly Shepherd. Each year on the Day of Atonement he was sacrificed in the form of a lamb.

In Syria he was known as Adonis, son of the Virgin Myrrha— a temple woman—and born in Bethlehem in a scared cave and killed at Easter time.

In Anatolia he was called Attis, born of the Virgin Nana, who miraculously conceived him by eating an almond. He grew up to be a sacrificial victim and saviour, slain to bring salvation to humankind, and his worshippers ate of his body in the form of bread. His death and rebirth (after three days in the underworld) were celebrated on March 25th, exactly nine months before the festival of his birth on the 25th of December.

In Greece he was Dionysus, son of the supreme father god Zeus. Dionysus' birth was prophesied by a star, he was able to turn water into wine, was surrounded by twelve disciples, was unjustly accused of heresy, was hung on a tree, died, and miraculously came back to life after three days in the underworld. And this is just the top of the "god's dying/resurrected son sacrifice barrel."

Comparing all these stories got me wondering, did Jesus ever really exist or is he just a mythological story we have turned into history? The idea at first seemed preposterous. Could it possibly have been all made up? Isn't there just too much evidence that a person named Jesus really did exist?

As it turns out, almost all the so-called evidence that Jesus did in fact exist is in the New Testament. Okay, if you buy into the line that God himself divinely dictated the writing of the New Testament and a few helpful scribes helped him put it down on parchment, then this might be enough for you. But the history of the writing of the New Testament shows all the intrigues and betrayals rampant in the hands of humans, not some benevolent god. We now know the New Testament to be made up of four gospels, but when they were doing the biblical cut and paste job, there were hundreds of different gospels being passed around.[1] What we are left with is just what was considered to be the word of God at the time, but we have to ask by whom and for what ends?

The meticulous paper-trail bureaucrats known as the Romans have absolutely no mention of Jesus' life, trial and execution. The sole Roman reference to someone named Jesus occurs four hundred years after his death and makes mention of some guy named Jesus being talked about in Judea. Even the Jewish priests never wrote anything about Jesus during his lifetime.[2] So did he exist or is he just the next evolution of the ongoing dying/resurrected sun god or Son of God story? After much deliberation, I have to say I came to the conclusion it does not really matter.

What I believe to be far more important is what this story—be it fact, fable, myth, or history—means and what purpose it serves for humans, which would explain our ongoing attachment to this theme. This brings us back to the sacrifice thing. According to many ancient cultures, there is this ongoing story of a sacrifice being offered to the goddess, gods, or other divine beings that they believed wanted an offering in order to ensure the divine's continued care of nature and humans. It started out that a king would provide this service, then it became a mock king chosen at random who represented the king, and then it became an animal—either way, something had to go.

Now I have to be honest and say that I don't really get it. How could people possibly think the Creator of the World could really be swayed one way or another depending on who or what was offered up? It seems so ridiculously superstitious. I would never think of taking my dog out back to try and ensure that choice job, the hoped-for baby, or even the lucrative book contract. Uh Oh, but wait a second, I do remember offering up deals in an attempt to try and ensure a hoped for outcome: "Please, God, if you allow me to pass this exam I did not study for, I promise to never be unprepared again"; "Please, God, if you cure me of this nasty flu, I promise never to smoke again." When you come down to it, it is really the same principle, the belief that in order to get, we have to give. Something needs to be sacrificed. Thankfully, I wasn't contemplating sacrificing family members or pets, but then again, the concerns and trades I have attempted were utterly petty and insignificant. None of these were life-and-death matters. What if they were? Our ancestors were much more aware of the thin line between life and death. Would I take my dog out back if I thought it would ensure the life of my family and community? In our modern Western world, we do not see our animals butchered for food, but to those who regularly killed animals in order to eat, it probably wasn't a big deal.

During the time of the year when spring is fighting with winter for supremacy, we know that one will have to lose in order for the other to win. We have it with some assuredness that by this time of the year, while winter may have made it seem like everything was dead and buried, the plants and animals on which humans depend will be reborn. Even though on the surface this season was all about life, maybe our ancient ancestors understood that the line between life and death is not as wide as we in our modern-day Western society think it is. Oh sure, we have all seen the Disney movies and understand that it is all part of this great big Circle of Life but we are sheltered from our everyday vulnerability to this Circle of Life much more than our ancestors were. Crop failures, drought, floods, famines, pestilences, persecutions, inquisitions, and death in childbirth are things that happen to other people, in other places, in other times. We see death as something that happens when your time is up and you have lived a nice full life.

We know that people betray, that evil exists, that bad things can and do happen to good people, and many of us have had loved ones taken from us before their time. At some point we have to face up to the fact that someone we love will not make it to the next spring; they will be gone forever. This is when we feel cheated, betrayed, and overwhelmed by the unfairness of it all. This is not easy for us to accept and this is when, like no other time, we are looking for some reason, explanation, and consolation that this is not really the end. Having this story where bad things happen, where people are betrayed, unjustly accused, persecuted, and taken from us before their time, and yet they still manage to rise again and go on to an afterlife provides us with a tool to make sense of the fact that life is not always fair. Maybe this is what this "persecuted-hero-who-rises-again" story gives us, some consolation that bad things happen to good people, and not just the average Tom, Dick, or Jane but to the Son of God. This story tells us that this is not just bad luck or random chance but part of a greater plan. The hope remains that death is not the end—that there really is something more. This story provides an enormous amount of comfort when someone we love has been taken from us before his or her rightful time.

Easter Side Festivals

On a lighter note, Easter is also about life and there are numerous side festivals and traditions that highlight this.

Lent

With the double entendre of life and death at Easter, the early Christians could not figure out if Easter should be celebrated as a happy or a solemn occasion. They finally came to the compromise that Easter was to be a period of celebration and honouring of Jesus' sacrifice preceded by a solemn period of spiritual preparation called Lent that included fasting, penance, and prayer. Various Christian groups originally established Lent as an interval ranging from a few days to several weeks. In the eighth century, it was eventually fixed at forty days. The number forty appears time and time again in numerous cultures' mythologies. This number recalls the interval that Jesus and Moses and Elias spent in the desert; for forty days, Demeter wailed for Persephone; forty days after Christmas, Mary goes through her post-birth purification period and presents Jesus to the temple. Lent did not originate with the Christians; instead, the observance of the forty days of Lent was derived from the worship of the Babylonian goddess Ishtar.

This Lenten period may have originated as an easier way to

deal with the late winter rations that would inevitably take place for our ancestors. Forty days before the spring equinox corresponds to the halfway point of winter. Depending on the success of the fall harvest, the amount of food left to carry people through to the spring would either be just enough or, in many years, not enough. Halfway through the winter, our ancestors would have to take stock of their supplies and decide how much would be available to the family and the community to carry them through to spring. Fresh, dried, and smoked meat would likely be one of the first rationings to take place. The Lenten fast may have made it easier to deal with food limitations, where, instead of rationing being forced upon our ancestors because of lack of supplies and the likelihood of starvation, it was viewed as an offering or a sacrifice that would ensure the return of the sun, warmth, and life.

Carnival

Many cities and countries around the world celebrate some form of Carnival. The two most well known Carnivals are the ones that take place in Rio de Janeiro, Brazil and New Orleans, United States. Few people realize, however, that Carnival and Easter are connected. Carnival (which is a name believed to be derived from the Latin *carnis + levare*, meaning "put away meat") is the last fling before Lent. Again, this ritual comes from the Babylonian New Year festivities, which were held around the spring equinox. New Year/Carnival time represented a period of chaos—a reversal of the way society defines how things should be. Rules and societal norms were eliminated or reversed, which served numerous purposes. In one way, it allowed people to act out their wishes and fantasies in a form that would not receive as much societal disapproval as it would normally. They got it out of their system; they could finally cut loose. At the end of the year, they would be able to leave their naughtiness behind and start the new year with a fresh slate—sort of like a Catholic doing a whole bunch of naughty things before going to confession to absolve themself. Ironically, allowing people to throw caution to the wind and flaunt societal norms also reinforces the acceptance of these same societal norms outside of Carnival.

Easter Symbolism
Easter is rich in symbolism with the Easter egg, Easter bunny, bonfires, fireworks, candles, and hot cross buns. Each of these symbols begs the question, where did these come from and what do they have to do with Easter?

The Easter Egg
The egg is probably the most popular Easter symbol, with the Easter bunny running a close second. Now we all know that bunnies don't lay eggs, so how did these two become connected? The symbolism of the egg belongs to all the world's cultures and forms part of the creation stories of many different mythologies. The ancient Egyptians, Persians, Phoenicians, Hindus, and many North American Native cultures, to name just a few, believed that the earth was created from an enormous egg. The egg was a sacred symbol among the Babylonians. Babylonian legend tells of an egg that fell from heaven to the Euphrates River and hatched to release the goddess Ishtar. The egg represents fertility, birth, and survival.

It is easy for us to understand why eggs represent fertility for birds, but why people? This is because the uterus and the ovaries of the female are egg-shaped. The egg represents the source of life for birds, mammals, and humans as well.

In addition, birds have just started to lay their eggs at the time of the spring equinox and eggs would have been one of the first foods for people coming out of a cold winter. They are probably a symbol of survival and the resurrection because they served to bring many people back from the brink of starvation and death after the winter.

The Easter Bunny
It is understandable why rabbits have been linked with sexuality and fertility. The saying "breeding like a rabbit" is not meant for those who limit their procreation. Most female mammals go into heat (estrus) once or, at the most, twice a year. When estrus and mating take place depends on the gestation period of that animal, but the birth is set to coincide with the time of year when resources are most plentiful and therefore most favourable to

rearing young. The animals that are an exception to the above rule are mice, squirrels, and rabbits. For these animals, estrus is a continual process—they keep going and going just like that Energizer Bunny. Rabbits are associated with spring and procreation because of their fertility and were companions to many of the fertility goddesses such as Eostre for whom Easter is named.

New Year Festivities

Before the Romans tried to standardize the use of one calendar, most cultures' calendars were based on their agricultural year. The spring equinox was the start of the agricultural year in many places and therefore the New Year for many cultures. Many New Year's symbols and festivities accompanied the arrival of the spring equinox and are still practiced in our modern-day Easter. Joyful spring festivals were held and people would gather around blazing bonfires and chant, sing, dance, and leap through the flames. These gatherings were banned by the Catholic Church when it came into power. Bonfire festivities were continually broken up until Saint Patrick set up huge bonfires outside of churches in Ireland to try and replace the old pagan traditions people were still unwilling to give up. The practice quickly made its way back into Europe, where the practice of annually blessing a new bonfire was still so popular, and it eventually became part of the Roman Catholic Church's Easter ceremony. The Easter fire is now the opening rite of the Easter vigil service.

Our present-day Easter candles and Easter sunrise services represent the same message as the old spring fire rites. It means that after the darkness of winter, comes hope in the life of spring. Through fire comes growth. Through death comes life.

Fireworks

Easter fireworks are used to celebrate Easter in Italy, Spain, Portugal, and many Latin American countries. The fireworks are a continuation of earlier New Year's festivities. Many cultures believe that New Year's heralds a time when the veil between the earthly world and the spirit world is thinnest. The fireworks are intended to frighten away evil spirits or ghosts that may have crossed from the spirit world into the earthly world.

New Clothes on Easter

The custom of wearing new clothes on Easter, or a new Easter bonnet when bonnets were popular, is an old New Year's custom. It was believed that starting off the New Year by being freshly groomed and sporting new clothes increased your likelihood of having a prosperous year. The custom of baptizing people at Easter continued the tradition of wearing new clothes at Easter. People were baptized in new white frocks. New clothes symbolize the baptism and a new and better Christian for those who were already baptized.

Hot Cross Buns

The custom of eating hot cross buns on Easter grew out of an earlier pagan tradition of offering wheat cakes to Eostre. At the feast of Eostre, an ox was sacrificed and the ox's horns became a symbol of the feast. The horns were carved into the ritual bread. The word *buns* is derived from the Saxon word *boun*, which means "ox." In many cultures, there was a symbolic link between the ox and the goddess. The ox is thought to represent her son/lover/consort and was a common sacrifice offering. While we are much more acquainted with the macho symbolism of the ox, it represented female fertility in many of the goddess-worshipping cultures because, as Georgia O'Keefe noticed, if you look at the skulls and horns of the ox, it looks just like the uterus, fallopian tubes, and ovaries of a human.

In an attempt to influence the pagans to abandon their old customs and deities, the Christian Church replaced the wheat cakes with hot cross buns. They used the symbolism of the cross because it was familiar to many pagans. The symmetrical cross is believed by some to represent the four quarters of the earth (north, south, east, and west) or the four elements (earth, air, water, and fire), some also think the cross represents the moon— the heavenly body associated with the goddess—and the four quarters of the moon (the waxing, waning, full, and invisible moon). Diana, the Roman goddess of the hunt and the moon, used the cross on her sacred cakes. Crosses were also incised or tattooed on the navel or near the breasts of the goddess and her priestesses.[3]

As this chapter comes to its own rightful end, I feel the urge to confess. Of all the chapters in this book, this is the one I have found the hardest to get my head around. I think it is because the death of Jesus has so many religious and political overtones that I was tempted to deal with it superficially. Honestly, I tried but just couldn't. It is not my intention to overly criticize religion— no matter which religion. We should all be allowed and encouraged to have beliefs that provide us with comfort, especially at the times we need it the most. The greatest (and cruellest) irony is the fact that so much sadness has been caused, too much blood has been spilled, and way too many lives have been lost simply because we have been convinced that there is only one true story and everyone must adhere to it. Easter's history reminds us that while the stories might have their own slight variations, they are much more alike than they are different, as are we. Only by remembering and honouring that can the death of one bring salvation to the many.

April Fool's Day
April 1st

April Fool's Day is an unusual holiday. It is not linked to any religious denomination and, unlike most other holidays, April Fool's Day has escaped the blight of commercialization. Nobody is expected to buy gifts for anyone or take their significant other out to eat in a fancy restaurant. Government and bank employees don't even get the day off work. April Fool's is not a serious or stuffy holiday; rather, it is celebrated just for the fun of it. It's a day dedicated to testing the imagination and gullibility of the human race.

Why do we have a day on our calendar specifically dedicated to tricking people? What purpose does this day serve and how did it originate? Well, this is another April Fool's prank, no one really knows for sure how or why this day originated. There are lots of theories, however, and some are more believable than others.

Some believe April Fool's Day is a vestige of an early spring Celtic custom. Some of the fertility practices of the Celtic Druidic priests were attempts to deceive evil spirits intending to interfere with fertility at the time when planting, sprouting, and mating was occurring. Some thought that by pulling pranks, the ill doers and spirits would become confused and the Druid fertility rituals would be more successful.

A connection exists between April Fool's Day and the Hindu festival of Holi. Although there is no historical evidence showing a connection between the two, it is interesting that Holi marks the New Year and the advent of spring and one of the principal customs is playing practical jokes on people and sending them on fool's errands.

The most common modern explanation for our April Fool's Day custom is that it came about when the Old Style (Julian) calendar made way for the New Style (Gregorian) calendar. When the Romans instituted the Julian calendar in 46 B.C.E., it was a marked improvement over their previous calendar that had become totally out of whack with the seasons. Those in charge of keeping track of the days of the Julian calendar, however, made a small mistake in calculating leap years and by the 1500s the calendar was out by ten days. In 1582, Pope Gregory XIII adopted the Gregorian calendar (which fixed this small error) and instituted its use in all Roman Catholic countries.[1]

While the date of the New Year changed often over the course of European history, the most common date for the start of the New Year amongst the peasantry was March 25th and ending after a week of festivities on April 1st. The Gregorian calendar tried to institute the date of January 1st as the New Year instead of the date of the spring equinox.

The origin of April Fool's Day customs is said to have come about because of the people who were unwilling to make the switch from New Year's being in the spring to January 1st. They were made fun of and teased, given mock gifts, and sent on fool's errands. Okay, that makes sense. But I think it is more likely that the custom of pranking now celebrated on April Fool's Day did not start when the calendar change took place but was instead a part of the New Year festivities that had taken place at this time of year for centuries, if not millennia.

New Year's was viewed as a time of reversal of the normal order; chaos before rebirth, a time of buffoonery and license. April Fool's Day carries on an old New Year tradition that people should have a chance to make fun of their rulers. For the first day of the new year, slaves switch roles with their masters and children switched roles with adults. In times when rules of behaviour were strict and breaking them was often punished by death, festivals like these gave people a chance to relax, burn off some steam, and enjoy themselves.

This old New Year's custom allowed people the freedom to act out their fantasies and, in doing so, release at least some the frustrations they more than likely felt with their lot in life. Allowing people with a lower lot in life some power and control to express their point of view in a creative and often flamboyant way probably reinforced the status quo. Without this one meagre day, it is very likely all that frustration and resentment would boil up to the surface and result in a possible attempt at social upheaval.

Whatever April Fool's Day's ancient origins, the celebration of this day of freedom for all pranksters spread quickly throughout France and Europe. It came into common practice as early as 1582 in France and as late as the early 1700s in England. The British and French settlers migrating to the New World were responsible for the spread of pranks to North America.

In France, the fish takes the place of the fool. Chocolate candies shaped like fish are sold everywhere and people often try to pin a paper fish on someone else's back without being caught. The people known as April Fools in English-speaking countries are called Poisson d'Avril (April Fish) in France. Since fish begin to run again in the spring, it is likely the April Fish is a symbol of rebirth and fertility. Or it may be because fish are easier to catch in the spring as they are just coming out of their winter dormancy and are hungry and less likely to be as cautious in taking the hook as those who make it to August.

In England, pranks need to be played before noon. Superstition has it that the pranking period expires at noon on the 1st of April and any jokes attempted after that time will call bad luck down on the head of the prankster. Additionally, those who fail to respond to being pranked with good humour are said to attract bad luck to themselves.

In Scotland, April Fool's day lasts for 48 hours. The second day is called Taily Day and is dedicated to pranks involving the buttocks. It seems logical that our butts would become game on this prankish day. There is no end to the amusement our derrières will provide to others. Those Kick Me signs and fart jokes will always get a rise out of the young and old alike. The Scots call their intended April Fool an April Cuckoo.

Although the cuckoo was welcomed as a symbol of spring by our ancestors and the cuckoo call in April was a sign for rejoicing at the death of winter, the word *cuckoo* came to mean "foolish" or "insane" in many European countries. This might have been because of the bird's unusual nesting habits. It doesn't make a nest and instead lays one egg in another bird's nest, removing one of the eggs already there. Upon hatching, the cuckoo chick then proceeds to tip out the remaining resident eggs, leaving the mother bird to bring up the cuckoo in the nest as if it were her own. This is perhaps one of the best tricks in nature, which leads me to wonder whether the fool is the one who gets tricked or the one who does the tricking.

There is no better character than the fool to represent the spirit of April Fool's Day. Not just on April Fool's Day but on everyday of the year the fool is willing and able to take on the challenge of making a comment on society, or even to have a little fun with those who are normally untouchable within the social hierarchy. The fool as a character stands in contrast to the king as the lowest and the highest in hierarchical powers. The fool, jester, or clown occupied the humblest place in the court and symbolized the forces of chaos and licence, while the king represented those of law and order. Since the jester was not expected to be smart enough to follow social graces, his assumed stupidity and innocence allowed him the freedom to speak his mind. In most courts, the fool was given considerable licence and could mock and caricature the secret scandals and failing of people—most often their masters. In Shakespeare, for example, it is often the fool who speaks the most profound truths. The performances of the fool in court were often political and social satires used by smart royalty as a way to get some insight on what the general population thought about the antics, policies, and practices of the royal family. Since the fool posed no threat to the authority of the king and the court, he could get away (at least most of the time) with presenting this insight to the court. On April Fool's Day, however, we all get the chance to play the fool, and the social hierarchy protects no one—everyone is a target.

The role of the fool in the tarot reading deck also has a lot to say about why this character was chosen to represent the spirit of April Fool's Day. "The Fool" card is the first card of the Major Arcana (the bigwigs of the tarot card deck) and is symbolized by an androgenous youth skipping along and looking completely blissful even though he is about to step off the edge of a cliff. As a card, "The Fool" represents freedom of the mind, heart, and body from worldly concerns and the boundaries of the social world. He represents the mysterious impulse within all of us to leap into the unknown.

The conservative, cautious, practical side of us watches with horror as this wild youthful spirit who, trusting in heaven and the universe, is prepared to take that leap without a moment's hesitation. The card is sometimes interpreted to mean to be careful of what lies ahead, to play it conservatively—the look before you leap approach. It can also be read in a different way. "The Fool" showing up in a reading may mean we need to draw more upon our own foolish characteristics we have lost touch with.

The fool is afraid of nothing, he is hindered by nothing; in fact, he believes he is charmed. The fool is still in that wonderful state of childlike security making them oblivious to the dangers around them; they are unafraid to frolic and play, and are convinced that the dangers the world will not touch them. They are courageous and do not know the meaning of limitation. This fool starts out in all of us to various degrees and then our parents and society, in an attempt to more easily control us and help us survive, try to minimize our foolish aspects.

If compassion and maturity did not temper our foolish aspects, it is likely we would rush head-on into life without thinking and foresight and really walk off that cliff, falling into the unknown below, oblivious to not only what is around us but also to how we affect others around us. If this lack of foresight does not lead to death, then it will usually lead to disillusion, loss, and hopelessness.

It is these negative characteristics of the fool that we are most acquainted with, but just like all things in life, it is all about balance and the fool in many of us is unbalanced. In order to create a sense of security and routine, we have suppressed our inner fool. Sure, this has allowed us to temper some of the negative aspects and outcomes that result from being too much the fool but it also means we have lost many of the positive characteristics as well. And the fool has lots of positive characteristics that if allowed to come out to play when appropriate, can lead us to a more fun and rewarding life.

Our fool reminds us we have to take chances in life, stop worrying so much, and sometimes just have fun. Our fool also shows us that an act of foolishness might be necessary in order to get results and reminds us that choosing not to take chances makes us less likely to achieve our dreams and sense of freedom. The fool is the ultimate expression and representation of freedom. Even if the fool is aware he has something to lose, losing it does not bother him in the least. We all have romantic notions of freedom and while most of us would loath to be in a position where we have nothing left to lose, we still long for just a taste of that freedom.

In order to get a taste of freedom and joie de vivre we need to become a wise-fool. A wise-fool is someone who can relax and let their playful, confident, and secure inner child emerge. Our inner child is the part of us that knows that spontaneity, surprises, innocence, and a sense of play and trust in the world are all valuable tools to guide us through life. When we allow that part of ourselves to come out, especially under negative or stressful conditions, we have achieved a taste of that longed-for freedom. The challenge in life is to figure out when it is the time to let our fool out and when it is the time for our fool's temper tantrum to be ignored or given a time-out. Just working on this balance will make us happier, more interesting and fun, and, believe it or not, more successful. Our increased success will be achieved by allowing us to be more of a free spirit who doesn't worry about the things we can't change and instead works on the things we can. It is this striving for balance that is highlighted so well in the famous prayer:

God, grant me the serenity to accept the things I cannot change,
The courage to change the things I can,
And the wisdom to know the difference.

Not listening to our inner fool causes us to overestimate the things we can't change. Listening to our inner fool too much or at the wrong time, causes us to overestimate the things we can change, leading us to disillusionment and exhaustion. It is the wisdom and maturity we try to achieve throughout life that enables us to find the right balance. There are a few of us who let our fool control us too much and then there are a larger number of us who control our fool too much. We need to find a balance that allows the negative aspects of our fool to be curtailed so we don't hurt ourselves and others but not enough that we don't give the fool in us a chance to come out.

The symbolism of the fool in the tarot card game gives us even more insight into our quest to achieve this balance and, more important, what the fruits of our labour to find this balance will get us. When we think of tarot cards today, we most likely think of the cards used by fortune tellers. But before being used for divining, the tarot was used in Europe during the Middle Ages as a normal card deck. The fool is one of the main characters in the tarot card game. Of all the trumps, only three are worth points in the game, "The Fool," "The Magician," and "The World." Whereas "The World" beats every card in the deck, "The Fool" beats none. So why play it if it can't win? The power in playing "The Fool" lies in its ability to momentarily exempt you from the rules of the card game. When you play "The Fool," it is like taunting all the players by saying, "You can't touch me, you can't touch me!"

In addition, "The Fool" card is a lucky card because it is worth a whole lot of points and you get to keep it even after it is played—no one can take it away from you. This is also true of our own fool-like characteristics. No one can take away our sense of humour, optimism, adventurousness, or enthusiasm. They can make us hide it and suppress it, no doubt, but it is still in us and we can call it out in the right supportive environment. When we honour our foolish traits, we are also able to exempt ourselves from the rules and codes of conduct of the world, at least for a certain time period.

Mark Twain, who was certainly in touch with his fool in his writings and hopefully in his life too, has dibs on the most famous April Fool's Day quote when he said, "The first of April is the day we remember what we are the other 364 days of the year." It is only by giving our fool some freedom to come out and play, not only on April Fool's Day but for the rest of the year, that we will be able to teach our inner fool the wisdom and the maturity it needs to become the wise-fool who will empower us to change our lives and ourselves.

MAY DAY
May 1st

When we think of May Day, cute maypole dances, and sweet May Day baskets come to mind. The deepest meaning we might be inclined to attach to this day is the arrival of warmer weather. In many socialist countries, the May Day celebrations have been replaced with the message of patriotism and celebration of the common hard-working folk, or a time for Communist governments to show off their biggest and best phallic military war toys. This, however, is not how May Day started. May Day used to be all about fertility and the return of life to the earth. As perverse as it may appear to us uptight Western folk, May Day used to be all about sex and the celebration of sexual love and pleasure.

The festival of May Day was observed, and still is to a smaller extent, by many nations each according to their own customs and traditions. Called Beltane by the Celts, Walpurgis by the Teutons, and Floralia by the Romans, the message was the same. May Day was essentially a festival concerned with celebrating the arrival of summer, fertility and sexual love—a period of the year dedicated to paying due respect to the wonderful, lazy, hazy days of languid summer. With all the crops planted, all the animals out at fresh pastures, and harvesting still a month or two away, May was a month dedicated to celebrating love, attraction, courtship, and mating—the things that made life worth living.

May Day festivities would begin on sundown on the 30th of April with bonfires alit all through the villages and surrounding woods and hills. Bonfires were a big part of Beltane and Walpurgis. May 1st represented the separation of the year from winter to summer. Just as Samhain (Halloween) was the time of year when animals were brought in from pastures for the winter, May 1st marked the day when animals were sent out from their winter confines into fresh new fields of green. Before being let out to pasture, however, they were walked between a mass of bonfires believed to protect them from illness, parasites, and disease. Getting animals to walk past huge bonfires is not an easy task and people would all work together to convince the animals this was not as bad an idea as it might have seemed to them.

After this work was done, the fun began. As people celebrated around the bonfires, couples would begin to slip away into the woods to perform their very own fertility rites. They would not return until May Day morning, and with them they would carry garlands of flowers, branches of hawthorn, and a specific group would be responsible for bringing in the maypole. What these couples did in the woods...well, that was part of the fun stuff. May Day gave licence to "go into the green together." This was not limited to married couples; it also involved unmarried folks and even folks who were married but would rather go off into the green with a different partner. On this one day, people were entitled to indulge themselves. Blessed by the gods and goddesses on this sacred night, such unions were seen as wholly proper and were referred to as "greenwood marriages." As Christian morality surrounding marriage and sexuality become more influential in Celtic society, a renegade friar would preside over mock marriages before couples would leave to go "into the green." Children born to women nine months following May Day were called "Merry Begets" and were usually not acknowledged as coming from the father; instead, people believed God fathered these children.

People believed they were celebrating in the same way the goddess and her chosen god were celebrating. When our ancestors realized women only gave birth following sexual intercourse, they concluded that the rebirth of vegetable and animal life every spring and summer was also generated via some kind of sexual union.[1] In the sacred marriage, the goddess and her chosen consort would mate and thereby bring back fertility and life to the plants and animals of the earth. The celebrations in the woods on the eve of May amongst the mere mortals were believed to encourage and enhance the fertilizing powers of the goddess and the god, and therefore the earth. In addition, by engaging in an activity that allowed for the experience of sexual fulfilment, people paid honour to the heavenly powers they believed gave humans the gift of sexual pleasure.

There was no double standard here like in so many other cultures. What went for men also went for women. All marriage ties were revoked for the month of May and future marriages were put off until June. May was not about marriage; it was about love and sexuality. We might not see the disconnect between marriage and sexual love, but for most of our recorded history, marriage was not about love and sexuality, it was about political and economic alliances. Up until only the last century or two, arranged marriages were the norm, and in many countries it is still common practice. Young men, but especially women, in royal and aristocratic families were just political pawns. They were sent all over the place in an attempt to forge familial, political, and economic alliances. Love and sexual compatibility were only a bonus if couples were lucky enough to get it. More often than not, love and sexual attraction did not result in marriage; they were in direct conflict with marital ties.

We might place all our present-day moralistic sexual baggage onto this day and consider it a day of excess and orgies, but as Riane Eisler writes in her book *Sacred Pleasure*, "that is because we have been taught to think of sex as sinful, dirty, titillating, or deviant. The possibility that sex could be spiritual, much less sacred, may be shocking." We might think our secular Western society is immune from religious perceptions of sexuality, but it isn't. We make the mistake of thinking of sexuality as a matter of physical fact, when it is only sex that is a physical fact. Sexuality, on the other hand, is a cultural construction. Sexuality is a highly, if not the most highly, socialized aspect of our life and each culture designates various practices as appropriate or inappropriate, moral or immoral, normal or abnormal.

Until the last century, the Church dominated both the political and emotional aspects of society. It was not simply that the Church provided spirituality or salvation; without the approval of the Church, there was no political life, no education, no career, no social standing, and in some cases, no life. Our modern-day views of sexuality and morality—what is proper and improper, and right or wrong—is still heavily influenced by religious norms. For this reason, we find it hard to imagine a time and a culture where sex and human sexuality was not debased and relegated to the "dirty and not talked about" side of life and instead was a celebrated activity that added meaning to people's lives and brought them as close to the divine as they were likely to get...short of death that is.

Our modern-day separation between spirituality and sexuality is not a natural phenomenon but rather a cultural one. There is a lot of compelling evidence that for many thousands of years (far longer than the thirty to fifty centuries we call recorded history) sex was sacred. What is even harder for us to imagine is a time when female genitalia were revered as the magical portal of life and pleasure. Yes, I realize it is hard for us to imagine a world where female genitals could be sacred! For women and men to view their bodies and each other's bodies as sacred is countered by everything we have been taught about sexuality and to many people, the idea may even seem sacrilegious.

Most pagan religions saw sexuality as a part of the natural order, a part of the same generative force that ultimately resulted in fertility. Sexual behaviour did not make people less like the gods and goddesses; on the contrary, it reinforced their resemblance to the upper order of beings. In the wake of the acceptance of one God with no female counterpart, the sexual dimension of the divine was eliminated. In Christianity, the sexual and the divine have nothing to do with each other. Sexual activity brings people into a realm of experience that was unlike God. To become more like God, one had to therefore leave or surrender the sexual.

In the Judaic culture, sexuality was to be celebrated only within the confines of a marriage and even then, the main point was to "multiply and be fruitful" not to celebrate the wonder, pleasure, and magic of sexuality. As Christianity became the dominant religion in the ever-expanding Roman world, sexuality became even more restrictive, reaching its climax of limitation because of a guy named Augustine.

Augustine lived during the fourth century C.E., just as the Christian movement was being transformed from a persecuted sect to the religion of the emperor himself and all the attendant political, economic, and power blessings that went along with that transformation. Augustine agreed with the Jews and Christians that Adam's sin brought death upon humankind but he went even further. Augustine believed that the sexual urge was so involuntary and troubling that only Satan could be behind it. According to Augustine, as punishment for Adam's act of disobedience, God had contaminated Adam's seed. During sexual ejaculation, Adam passed the infection to his partner and Eve in turn polluted the fetus. Each newborn babe emerging into the world was inescapably contaminated and therefore born a sinner. He believed Jesus Christ was the only exception to this because he was conceived via God immaculately.

As far as Augustine was concerned, the only way to break this cycle of original sin was to be celibate and only then could man become one with God. I don't know if Augustine realized that if the human race actually achieved this oneness with God, it would mean the end of our species. Perhaps Augustine (and I would guess many others) did not have high hopes for the ability of humans to achieve this. Or maybe it was because humankind's earthly existence did not concern Augustine; he believed that it was only once humans achieved this celibate oneness that the New Kingdom of God would arrive.[2]

Either way, from the fifth century onwards, Augustine's pessimistic view of sexuality and human nature became the dominant influence on Western Christianity. Now you may wonder, as I do, how one guy can have such an overriding influence on shaping a religion and a culture but it happens—sometimes for good but, more often than not, also for bad.

Augustine's legacy of advocating celibacy as a means of getting closer to God resulted in women being viewed as a temptation leading man away from godliness. The Church started preaching about the body as separate and lower than the soul. The idea that in sex, man is at his most physical and so furthest from God increased Christian disgust for sex and the body. The natural result of this fear of loss of control via sexuality was that the Church and society started to see women as sexually dangerous. According to early Christian teachings, every woman was the embodiment of Eve the temptress and was responsible for man's fall from innocence. Women, sex, and sin became fused together in the Christian mind. In order to save man from sin, women must hide themselves away, veil their faces from men's lustful eyes, hide their beauty, and make themselves ugly and sexless. If a man succumbed to his lust for her it was her fault for flaunting her sexuality or for not hiding it well enough.

It was because women gave birth and were more influenced by their bodies that they were considered to be more animal-like and less civilized than men. The need to separate and place humans above nature did not start with Judaism or Christianity; it goes way back to the Greeks, who popularized the idea of the separation of the body from the soul, nature from civilization, and masculine from feminine. In all cases, the ones attributed to the male—soul, civilization, and masculine—were viewed as superior to the ones viewed as female—body, nature, and feminine. They believed the male elements needed to dominate and subdue the influence of the female elements.

Christian sexual self-help books taught that if you must have sex, have it within marriage and then at least you won't go to hell. But people were reminded that sex was for procreation, not fun, and enjoying sex was like signing yourself up for a one-way ticket to hell. Christian dogma taught that enjoying sex or having sex only for pleasure must be avoided because it was a base animal instinct and took us further away from our soul and God. Strangely enough, if there is anything that does separate us from our other mammalian relatives it is the human interest in sex simply for pleasure's sake.

While there are lots of similarities between the reproductive and sexual drives of humans and other mammals, especially the primates, there are still some important differences that play a huge role in making humans what we are. The human female is sexually distinct from other female animals. Hormones largely direct a female primate's sexual receptivity. For human females, however, estrus (or heat) plays no, or very little, role in their lives. Instead, they largely choose to have sex on the basis of social and psychological factors.

Although the female orgasm is not unique to human females, as many field researchers have reported similar orgasmic responses in other female primates, the human female's ability for multiple orgasms and the frequency and intensity of those orgasms is unparalleled in the mammalian world. Humans have certainly complicated matters by obsessing with the different types of orgasms women were thought to experience, starting with Freud's obsession with the vaginal orgasm versus the clitoral orgasm. Freud believed women who were mentally and sexually immature experienced clitoral orgasms and only women who had reached a certain level of maturity were able to have the superior vaginal orgasm. It is now realized that the clitoris plays a role in almost all female orgasms but, unfortunately, Freud's belief persisted for decades during which time many women who were lucky enough to be getting some, thought, "They were doing it all wrong."

In failing to fully recognize the importance of the clitoris and its purpose in female sexuality, scientific and religious authorities also failed to fully recognize that in the human female there is an anatomical separation of the central locus for sexual pleasure (the clitoris) from the vaginal opening through which coitus (or the act required for reproduction) takes place. Their ignorance or denial of this special function of the clitoris helped maintain the sham even to this day that sex purely for pleasure is a base or animal nature, whereas, contrary to popular opinion, it is precisely our capacity for sex purely for pleasure, rather than reproduction, that distinguishes our species from most other animals.

To our prehistoric ancestors for whom sex was integral to the cosmic order—to the body of men and women who believed it was not, as the medieval Church proclaimed, "a source of carnal evil" but rather an attribute of the goddess and god—erotic rites would have had a very different meaning. Partaking in the pleasures of sex at the rites of Beltane, then, would not have been sinful or immoral but rather a way of coming closer to their spirituality or divineness.

Though complaints about Beltane's "immoral" sexual practices started in the early twelfth century, its rites continued throughout the centuries until the increasing Puritan persecution of those who continued to partake in the festivities instead of "staying home and reading the bible." The Puritan and Protestant protests against May rites came to a head in 1555 when the British Parliament banned May Day observances.

When Charles II regained the British throne in the mid-1600s, May Day rites were once again permitted. Beltane's sexual component, however, became much less a part of the holiday as Christianity and its obsessesion with sex and morality became more influential in Celtic and Saxon lands. It was at this time that dancing around the maypole became the central ritual of the holiday, not the bonfires and "going into the green." Modern celebrations of May Day rarely involve any mention of the sexual aspects of the original festivals but instead concern themselves with flowers and the celebration of warmer weather.

Since the Puritans frowned on May Day customs, they brought that attitude with them to the New World where they also sought to have the holiday outlawed. So May Day has never been celebrated in the United States with as much enthusiasm as it was in Great Britain. Attempts to Christianize Beltane focused on Mary, the mother of Jesus. In many places in the United States where May rites are celebrated, the central focus of the holiday is the crowning on the May Queen who then leads a procession to a local church where the Queen of the May places a crown of flowers on the statue of the Virgin Mary.

While Beltane was the main holiday that influenced our present-day traditions and customs associated with May Day, festivals of similar sorts were celebrated all over Europe with local variations to the theme. Each of these celebrations had elements of sex and the renewal of life even if, as in the case of Rome, the message of sexuality had become a bit seedier. The Roman May rites were called Floralia and were held in honour of Flora, the goddess of flowers and gardens. The Floralia was instituted in 238 B.C.E. and was at first a movable feast that depended on when the flowers bloomed and the conditions of the crops, but in 173 B.C.E., the Roman senate made it an annual festival extending for six days from April 28th to May 3rd.

From the very beginning, the Floralia was characterized by wild behaviour. Prostitutes claimed it as their feast day and courtesans are said to have performed mimes and dances in the nude and medallions showing various sexual positions were distributed to revellers. Roman prostitutes believed Flora was originally a courtesan who left a small fortune to the people of Rome to celebrate her memory and was later elevated to divine status. It is perfectly understandable that Roman prostitutes would want to try to bring some honour and credibility to their profession. For the rest of the fifty-one weeks of the year they were not accorded much respect and their profession certainly did not improve their social standing.

As exciting as the Floralia festival sounds, it was not a holiday for everyone as Beltane was. There most certainly was a double standard to this festivity. Women who were not prostitutes were not involved in the festivities and the sexuality that was celebrated was not the same sexuality being celebrated at Beltane. Beltane was more about the spirituality and pleasure associated with sexuality and Floralia was more of a celebration of sexual excess. In addition, Floralia was more concerned with men's sexual pleasure than with women's sexual pleasure. Let's face it, even if you are a giving lover, when you pay someone for sex, you are most concerned about your own pleasure.

Prostitutes might have been the first profession to lay claim to a specific day to honour their profession and to give them some credit for work that was largely taken for granted the rest of the year, but they most certainly were not the last. During the Middle Ages, various trade guilds celebrated feast days for the patron saint of their craft. The shoemaker's guild honoured Saint Crispin and the tailor's guild appropriately celebrated Adam and Eve. The two most popular feast days for medieval craft guilds were the feast of St. John the Baptist on the summer solstice and May Day. As late as the eighteenth century, various trade societies and craft unions would participate in local parades by entering floats depicting Adam and Eve being clothed by the tailors and Saint Crispin blessing the shoemaker.

May 1st, trade unions, and the rights of the everyday working folk became linked even more in 1889 when a congress of world socialist parties held in Paris, France voted to support the United States labour movement's demand for an eight-hour day. It chose May 1, 1890 as a day of demonstration in favour of the new standard workday. Eventually, May 1st became known as Labour Day and was turned into a holiday honouring working folk. Countries with socialist or Communist forms of government still celebrate May 1st with parades, speeches, and their very own phallic displays of military strength. Moscow's Red Square is one of the better-known examples, although it has been toned down somewhat due to military budget cuts and super-hyperinflation since the dissolution of the Communist Soviet Union. The United States and Canada celebrate Labour Day in early September rather than May 1st. Why? Well, that's another story, so check out the Labour Day chapter.

May Day Symbolism
The Maypole and Its Dance

The maypole and the accompanying dance has so much symbolism surrounding it that it is difficult to figure out where to start. But let's start with the most obvious: to those of us born in the post-Freudian era, we can't help but see the maypole as a phallic symbol. As we see it, the pole represents male sexuality but we might not be aware that the maypole actually represents a blending of male and female sexual energy and power. The pole itself…well, we can quite easily guess what that represents, but encircling the top of the maypole is a wreath of flowers and sometimes even a female figure, representing the female sexual organ intertwined with the male phallus. The maypole represents more than just the fertility associated with the joining of the sexual organs of the male and the female—it also represents the blending and unification of the masculine and the feminine, the yin and the yang.

Most maypoles were trees cut down and stripped of their

branches and set up in the village square each May 1st, but as the competition became more intense to be the village with the thickest and the tallest maypole, they became permanent fixtures. The dance around the maypole is performed by an equal number of young males and females who dance around the pole and the wreath. The boys face one direction and the girls face the other. They then begin to dance past each other, in and out from the centre to the circumference, intertwining the ribbons until they get ever and ever closer to each other. The maypole dance is an important aspect of encouraging the return of fertility to the earth but it is also a dance celebrating the power and pleasure of human coupling and sexuality and the blending of the masculine and the feminine.

This seems simple enough but the symbolism doesn't stop here. Cutting down a tree and stripping it of its branches to create the maypole also represented the worship humans believed trees were due. Why would people honour and worship trees? Trees naturally lend themselves to rich mythological symbolism: they represent rebirth, immortality, and the passageway between the worlds.

Trees have been a part of the human story for eons, probably ever since we climbed down out of them and started walking upright on the grassy plains. Even to our present day, we have the infamous Garden of Eden's Tree of Knowledge and the mythological Tree of Life that creeps up in almost every culture's mythology. Even through the hardest droughts, trees continuously grow. Some trees can survive fires and most have a lifespan of hundreds of years, with a few even lasting thousands of years. This far surpasses the average human lifespan, making people think trees were immortal. Many trees look like they die in the fall and are reborn again in the spring, leading to the symbolism of rebirth. In addition, trees span three different worlds. Their roots reach deep into the underworld, their trunk stands strong on the earth, and their branches reach high up into the sky and the heavens.

For most cultures, but especially to the Celts, trees were important religious sites and many temples and places of worship were located amongst groves of trees because it is here that one could be closer to the gods and goddesses who dwelled in the other worlds. For this reason, deforestation was a big part of the Christian persecution of the Celtic religion and beliefs.

Flowers

As the Romans conquered northern Europe, Floralia's emphasis on flowers merged with the local customs and flowers became a larger part of Beltane and Walpurgis festivities. Flowers have always played a role in summer rites and it makes sense they would. Flowers are a symbol of life and reproduction; after all, they are a proud and very colourful display of a plant's sexual organs. Plants have none of the shyness or moralism we humans do regarding our sexual organs. Imagine if there was a time of year when humans showed off their sexual parts in the same unselfconscious way plants do. Children remind me of flowers; they have the same unselfconsciousness as flowers do regarding their bodies. It is only as they grow up and become more socialized to our present-day norms that they become shy and self-conscious about their so called "private parts." While this is necessary in our modern-day society (as such a display can cause some social faux pas), I can't help but find it a little sad too. It is almost as if they have lost some of their purity, innocence, and their connection with the rest of the animals inhabiting the world with them.

Flowers are still very much a part of our modern-day May Day festivities. Even in North America, where the celebration is downright tame in comparison to modern-day European festivities, never mind the festivities of days past. May baskets are probably the most popular aspect of North American May Day traditions. The custom of hanging May baskets became popular in the United States in the nineteenth century and is still enjoyed in many classrooms across the country today. Baskets are woven using strips of coloured paper, then decorated with lace, doilies, and ribbon. The basket is filled with flowers and then anonymously left for a special someone to let them know someone out there thinks they are special and wants to get to know them better. The problem, of course, is that May Day baskets are usually anonymous, so the receiver has to guess whom it is that gave it to them. Unfortunately, the giver might not be the person they would like to get to know better, but such are the risks of courtship.

May Day Dew and Well Dressing

Young women, and probably a few men too, prayed for a good fall of dew on May Day morning as they went into the fields to wash their faces in it believing it would improve their complexion and bring them eternal youthfulness. A similar belief and custom also surrounds the dew that falls during Easter and the spring equinox festivities. Perhaps it is because there is something special to the morning dew that falls on these auspicious days, or it might simply be that the wrong associations were made. After a night frolicking in the woods, people would probably use the early morning dew to freshen themselves up and we all know how a night of frolicking can improve a person's complexion (not to mention their demeanour).

May was the traditional season of "well dressing" and the tradition is still practiced in parts of the United Kingdom, especially Ireland. People go out on May Day morning and hang colourful cloths around wells and throw flowers and garlands into the water. Wells and caves were seen as holy places because they were believed to be the earthly representation of the goddess' portal of life and pleasure (i.e. her vagina). Many early Christian temples continued this tradition but many of the wells and caves that were worshipped as sacred sites dedicated to pagan goddesses were renamed after the Virgin Mary. Of course, the whole vagina reference was done away with.

The May Queen and King

The custom of choosing a May Day Queen was an attempt to find an earthly representation of the goddess. Since this was believed to be the time of the year when the sacred marriage between the goddess and her chosen god would occur, this led to the tradition in some places of also crowning a May King. The May Queen and King lead the village May Day celebrations. Nowadays, the May King has mostly disappeared but a May Queen is still chosen in many places. Usually, the girl thought to be the prettiest is chosen as the May Queen. I'd hate to think the old celebration of the power of sexual energy to bring pleasure to people and bring life back to the earth has become a modern-day beauty contest but weirder things have happened.

Can It Be?

It is hard for us to imagine that our ancestors believed human sexuality, rather than taking us further away from our soul, actually brought us closer to it. Could there really have been a holy day dedicated to paying honour to the divine by engaging in sexual pleasure? Well, yes, there was. The original intention of May Day was to set aside a day of the year to pay honour to the bringing together of the sacred and the sexual.

Now let's not get overly romantic and think the sexuality they honoured was limited to sex between two people who were in love and intended to spend the rest of their lives together. Just as we all know, there is more to love than sex; there is also more to sex than love. Voyageurs on the quest in search of what it is that makes sex meaningful are loaded down with so much conflicting social baggage that it is hard for them to move about. In one hand is the suitcase overflowing with the message that sex is only meaningful when accompanied by "true" love or marriage. In their other hand is the suitcase filled by our sex-obsessed culture telling us that all sex is meaningful, even if the act of sex is about as sacred and intimate as an aerobic workout.

In our post–sexual revolution days, there are still many of us, both men and women, who are totally out of touch with our sexuality and our basic human need for connection and intimacy, which let's face it, is most easily attained via sex. The person who is sexually experienced but is frightened and threatened by the passion and emotion associated with sex is a common phenomenon in our culture. We yearn for the elation that accompanies sexual pleasure and at the same time we dread it. Sexual pleasure is a balance between our desire for intimacy and connection and our fear of attaining it. To get in touch with our sexuality, we have to be open to more than just the penetration involved in the sexual act. We need to allow the sexual act to open us up to the penetration of love, intimacy, and the connection between our bodies and our souls.

The sexual has been relegated to either a physical act or a romantic act and the idea that our soul might be connected with our sexuality, or sex as a means of getting in touch with our own divineness, is considered sacrilegious. We need to stop separating our body, our mind, our heart, our soul, and our lives into different departments; they are all one and the same. When we are able to get these departments working with each other instead of competing against each other, we have a better chance of experiencing the divineness of our sexuality and seeing it for what it really is: magic. This is not simply because it has the amazing ability to create new life from a simple egg and sperm, or even because it is absolutely essential to our survival as a species. Our sexuality can also bring such pleasure to our bodies, our minds, our lives, and to the world. A force that has the ability to do all of that has to be magic.

MOTHER'S DAY
The Second Sunday in May

On the surface there does not seem to be much history to Mother's Day but let's not allow Mother's Day's book cover, back flap, or even the reviews fool us into thinking this is all there is to this day. We need to delve deeper to discover the real origin and history of Mother's Day. Sure the ten-second sound bite tells us it all started when a woman, intent on honouring her mother, lobbied to have a day dedicated to recognizing the role of all mothers. What does it say, however, when that same woman later regretted the result of her efforts and died bitter and all alone? She might have been disgusted by the rampant commercialization of Mother's Day but little did she realize she had good reason to be bitter, and commercialization was the least of the reasons. Mother's Day has undergone radical revisions, and the changes have not always been pleasant.

I could get away with saying that all festivals were celebrated in honour of the Mother. How, you ask? Well, there is a lot of evidence to lead us to the conclusion that before the advent of our modern-day religious belief in one male God lording upon us from up in heaven, there was a religious idea based on the worship of a Mother Goddess. This Mother Goddess reigned from at least 7000 B.C.E. until 500 C.E. Most of the evidence—the statues, murals, inscriptions, clay tablets, and papyri—was found spread from northern Europe, to the Soviet Ukraine, to the coasts of the Mediterranean, and into the heart of the Middle East. The Mother Goddess was known by many different names, but whatever her name, she was the maker, the creator, the giver, the nurturer, the taker, and the destroyer.[1]

Motherhood and Sex

Why were the earliest religious beliefs based on the idea of the worship of a Mother image? When you really stop to think about it, this idea makes perfect sense. In both the animal and human world, the first bond most of us experience is that of mother and offspring. This mother was responsible for our existence and, more important, she was the key to our survival.

What about the father, you ask? Good question, but the role of the father in procreation was not understood for the most part of human history. This might seem silly to us who know the connection between sex and conception but if you think about it, it really wasn't that easy to put together. Sex takes place one day and a birth nine months later. I can't remember the details of what I was doing nine months ago, much less whether I had sex that day or not. To complicate things even more, conception does not take place every time a woman has sex. There is only a 24 to 48 hour time period per month when a woman is fertile.

Even for those smart enough to suspect the truth, there were many cases to disprove it. Some women can copulate frequently but rarely, if ever, become pregnant. Other women can remain childless when living with one man but conceive when living with another. In addition, women past menopause or before menarche can take any number of lovers without conceiving, leading to the suggestion that menstruation was the crucial factor, not intercourse.[2] Our modern-day understanding of sex and conception probably took place after the establishment of a common practice of animal livestock farming. Observing animals with shorter gestation periods mate and relatively shortly thereafter give birth made it easier to realize the connection.

The dissociation between sex and conception still existed until recently among many of today's tribal cultures. Trobriand

Islanders attributed pregnancy to spirits, not sex. A woman's husband might help care for her children but he thought of them as "the children of my wife." The Islanders laughed at the White men who first tried to tell them about impregnation.[3] Australian Aborigines thought women became pregnant by eating special foods, or by embracing a sacred tree hung with umbilical cords from previous births.[4]

Most anthropologists agree that just like the few primitive societies still around today, all the world's people for some time during prehistory knew nothing of man's part in the process of reproduction. If this was the case, then the belief must have been that women alone held the divine power to give life.[5] No small feat indeed. If women were able to generate life on their own, this gave them a divine-like quality, making it perfectly natural for the first divine being to be thought of as female.

"Mother Right"

Even once the sex/conception connection was understood, our ability to always know who the mother is, but not necessarily the father, led to a matrilineal descent system known as Mother Right. Mother Right was a lineage and inheritance system that flowed through the female line. While all children took on the name of their mother, it was daughters who inherited the property, wealth, and position of their mothers. Sons, brothers, and husbands gained title and property through the women to whom they married or were related.

This matrilineal social system gave women a high status in society, not only because the female was viewed as the giver of life but also from an economic aspect. Females had the freedom to determine how they would like to use their inheritance and were not dependent on the approval of a male guardian in their economic and/or personal dealings as later became the case. Early writings from Egypt describe women as independent and in complete control of their personal and professional lives.[6] The earlier Sumerian writings also indicate that women had significant economic and personal independence.

We do have to keep in mind that a matrilineal descent system and worship of a female deity does not necessarily mean a matriarchy. A number of nineteenth- and early twentieth-century scholars came to the conclusion that if prehistory was not patriarchal, then it must have been matriarchal. In other words, if men did not dominate women, women must have dominated men. When the evidence did not seem to support female dominance, many scholars returned to the more conventionally accepted view that male dominance must have always been the human norm.

According to Riane Eisler in her book *The Chalice and the Blade*, the evidence supports neither a matriarchy, nor a patriarchy:

> To begin with, the archaeological data we now have indicates that in its general structure pre-patriarchal society was, by any contemporary standards, remarkably egalitarian. In the second place, although in these societies descent appears to have been traced through the mother, and women as priestesses and heads of clans seem to have played leading roles in all aspects of life, there is little indication that the position of men in this social system was in any sense comparable to the subordination and suppression of women characteristic of the male-dominant system that replaced it.

She expands further to state that while the goddess-worshipping societies seem to have been more egalitarian and communal and less violent than the societies that replaced them, "it is important to stress, however, that these were not ideal societies or utopias, but instead a real human society, complete with problems and imperfections."

The Coming of the Son

When the male's part in procreation was understood, a role for him appeared in the Creator of Life script. The god's role began with the bit part as son of the goddess. Later, he took on the more prominent role of lover/consort to his mother. While the god's role had been part of the goddess religion since early times, according to Professor E. O. James, author of numerous books on the history of prehistoric Europe, "the fact remains that the Goddess at first had precedence over the young God with whom she was associated as her son or husband or lover." This relationship of the goddess and her son is known in Egypt by 3000 B.C.E. It also occurs in the earliest literature in Sumer; emerges later in Babylon, Anatolia, and Canaan; survives in the classical Greek legend of Aphrodite and Adonis; and is even found in pre-Christian Rome as the rituals of Cybele and Attis, possibly influencing the symbolism and rituals of early Christianity.[7]

What happened to the goddess? Sometime around 3000 B.C.E. came the arrival of the Kurgans, or Indo-Europeans/ Aryans as they are more commonly known. These Aryans seem to have undertaken a series of aggressive invasions, resulting in the conquest, area by area, of the goddess people. In modern times, Nietzsche and then Hitler idealized these Indo-Europeans as the only pure European race. They were not actually from the European continent but were nomads from the Asiatic region. Marija Gimbutas, author of *Goddesses and Gods of Old Europe*, suggests they came from the steppe lands between the Dnieper and Volga rivers.

The Indo-Europeans led a predominantly nomadic life, worshipped warrior sky-gods, and rode horses, which they had domesticated as early as 5000 B.C.E. Being on horseback enabled them to cover large distances unimaginable on foot and also gave them a formidable military advantage. As the Indo-Europeans conquered more territories, they imposed their supreme father/thunder god on the goddess cultures, often by marrying their god to the goddess. This, however, was no equitable marriage; the god played the part of the conqueror people and the goddess played the role of the conquered people.

The Indo-Europeans also aggressively substituted a patrilineal descent system for the previous matrilineal descent system. In addition to giving women access to an economic or professional life, matrilineal descent structures gave women a large amount of sexual freedom. There was no need to control female sexuality when the father's identity made little difference. In order for a patrilineal descent system to be effective, however, it must control women's reproduction. If women still retained their previous freedom as independent beings able to control their finances and therefore the resources of their offspring, the male would be less likely to ensure that her child was really his child. By eliminating their direct access to resources, males ensured that females became dependent on them. In his book *The Masks of God*, Joseph Campbell, one of the most popular mythological historians, writes, "There can be no doubt that in the very earliest ages of human history the magical force and wonder of the female was no less a marvel than the universe itself and this gave to women a prodigious power, which has been one of the chief concerns of the masculine part of the population to break, control, and employ to its own ends."

The God Gives Birth

As the father/thunder god gained influence at the expense of the goddess, he began to take over many of her rights and responsibilities. One of the last roles he took over was the role of procreation. By evading the simple reality that pregnancy and birth was a female act, these thunder-god cultures were able to change the social view of the importance and credit for procreation. Along with these Indo-Europeans come myths where the male god creates humanity from his ejaculate, his blood, or by incubating the baby himself.

In Greek myth, by killing his father Cronus, Zeus is considered to have rebirthed his sister and brothers that were eaten by his father. Zeus also gave birth to Athena, Dionysus, Artemis, and Apollo. The Egyptian god Atum claimed to give birth to the primal couple from his penis by masturbating. In Judaism, the mother of the Jewish people, Sarah, was unable to conceive except through the divine intervention of Yahweh (as the Jewish God is known) thanks to her husband Abraham's loyalty to Him. In Christianity, it is God alone who is responsible for the impregnation of Jesus' mortal mother Mary.

The Fall of Motherhood

These ideas of the father reflect the view of the earthly role of the female in procreation. No longer was she thought of as the creator of life. Instead, that role was attributed to the male, starting with the ancient Greeks and the idea that sperm contained a tiny individual who developed in the womb. The role of the menstrual cycle and the female egg in conception was not understood until the last century.

Even when science replaced religion in helping to guide the beliefs of society, many scientists used it to justify this bias. For example, in the eighteenth century, the light microscope was the scientific toy of the century. As Mariette Nowak writes in her book *Eve's Rib*, "While the resolving power of their microscopes were limited, their imaginations were not. Throwing scientific discipline aside these men looked at the human sperm and claimed to see in its head the miniature replica of a human being—they called it the *homunculus*."

Perhaps the story that best describes the change in attitude and respect for the role of motherhood in ancient Greece is well illustrated in the third play in Aeschylus' *Oresteia* trilogy (458 B.C.E.). The *Oresteia* details the blood feuds and misfortunes that consumed the house of Atreus. This generational continuum of despair started when Tantalus wanted to show everyone how important he was, so he invited the gods to dinner. Unfortunately, he did not have Martha Stewart around to help him organize his little dinner party, so when the Gods arrived he had nothing prepared. Making use of what was around, he served up a dinner that contained his son Pelops. Strangely enough, this is where the word *tantalizing* comes from. Go figure.

Zeus and the other gods, horrified by this, laid a curse on Tantulus and all his offspring. Tantulus' two other sons, Atreus and Thyestes, were bitter rivals. Thyestes seduced Atreus's wife and as an act of revenge, Atreus murdered his brother's sons and cooked them in a vat. He then invited his brother to a banquet and served the unsuspecting father tender parts of his sons' flesh. And you thought your family was messed up!

In the next generation, Atreus's son Agamemnon sacrificed his daughter Iphigenia in order to enable his army to set sail for the Trojan War. Clytemnestra, his wife, avenged her daughter's murder by killing Agamemnon with his axe upon his triumphant return from the sack of Troy. This regicide is the subject of the trilogy's first play, *Agamemnon*. In the second play, *The Liberation Bearers*, their son, Orestes, murders his mother to avenge his father. The third play, *The Eumenides*, recounts how the Greek god Apollo interceded on Orestes' behalf and rescued him from the Furies. The role of the Furies was to protect the role of the mother and relentlessly pursue anyone guilty of the heinous crime of matricide.

In the opening scene of *The Eumenides*, Orestes seeks refuge from the Furies in Apollo's sanctuary in Delphi. The Furies demand Apollo hand over Orestes and Apollo tries to get the Furies to agree to a trial to be judged by the goddess Athena to determine Orestes' guilt. While the Furies are hesitant and do not see the need to defer to a third party, even if she is a woman, they are nonetheless convinced by the sweet-talking lawyer-wanna-be Apollo. Athena empanels a jury of twelve male Athenians over which she presides. The Furies obtain Orestes' confession of his mother's murder. They naively rest their case confident that the old laws governing the crime of matricide will enable the court to find him guilty.

Pleading for the defence, Apollo sets out to change the old laws by claiming that Orestes should not be punished because his duty to his father supersedes any loyalty he might have towards his mother. Apollo argues that mothers play a very minor role in pro-creation. According to Apollo, it is the man's sperm that contains the miniature individual and the woman's role is simply to act as a passive incubator via her womb. Apollo therefore tells Athena and the jury that a mother is not actually related to her son by blood. So if a son kills his mother, the act should be considered no more serious than killing a stranger. Whoever said a good lawyer can't get you off, even if you are guilty?

When the jury returns with a split verdict, six for and six against, Athena breaks the tie by siding with Orestes. She claims that respect for motherhood is misplaced because she herself emerged fully-grown from the brow of Zeus. She conveniently omits the fact she was initially sheltered in the womb of the goddess Metis, Zeus' first wife who he killed and ate in order to take over her power. Free to go home, a very happy Orestes leaves the stage with Apollo. Athena urges the Furies to join her as upholders of the new laws. In his book *The Alphabet Versus the Goddess*, Leonard Shlain writes, "This play explained to the Greek populace how they came to live by the new patrilineal rule of law, and in the course of doing so, denigrated women and belittled motherhood."

Most school curricula contain at least small references to the contributions made by ancient Greek culture to our modern-day world, with the most common contribution being the creation of democracy. What is not taught in most school classrooms is that democracy, as we think of it, was never part of ancient Greek society. The participants of their version of democracy consisted of Greek-born landowning men. The rest of the 85% of the population made up of women, foreigners, and slaves had absolutely no say in the workings of their country or society.

It is more likely that the biggest influence of ancient Greek culture was not democracy but rather the transition from matrilineal succession to patrilineal succession. As the Hebrews and Romans followed this Greek/Indo-European trend, matrilineal descent went the way of the dinosaurs and woolly mammoths. In some northern European areas, the matrilineal system survived to a much later date. For example, the rule of matrilineal succession existed in some areas of the British Isles up to the ninth century and matrilineal descent still exists in some native cultures of Africa.[8] Exchanging matrilineal inheritance for patrilineal inheritance changed the course of history. Women were forced to trade in their financial and social freedom for economic dependence and social control and women and their offspring were given a new status as property of the father and/or husband.

Control Via Economic Dependence

In general, Roman society had a higher regard for motherhood than Greek society. After all, their founding story was based on a she-wolf that suckles and raises Romulus and Remus, the founding brothers of Rome. Women in the Roman Empire were at least given a small measure of control over their lives. By the end of the republic, women were granted access to divorce and the courts revoked a father's ability to annul his daughter's marriage against her will. Women regained at least part of their right to inherit and to enter into contracts and manage their own financial affairs.[9]

Women in Greece and Judea (as the Jewish state was known) were unable to do any of the above things. To ensure that women were not involved in financial transactions, the Greeks and the

Hebrews made it a crime for anyone to enter into any type of contract with a female without the signature of her father or husband. The consequences for anyone who did so varied from a heavy fine to the total loss of one's business, and even death. By eliminating a woman's access to resources, she was thereby made completely dependent on her husband or father, who if they grew tired of her were legally able to sell her into slavery.

If a man divorced a woman, or in places like Rome where a woman was also entitled to divorce her husband, the children, because they were considered the property of the father, remained with the father. The woman was at most only allowed to leave with her dowry or half of her dowry depending on the circumstances surrounding the divorce. If a couple divorced because of an actual or even a perceived adultery on the side of the wife, she was either stoned to death, as was the case in Judea, or if she was lucky enough to be Roman, she was required to leave the marriage without her dowry. Children always remained under the ownership of the father. Sons could hold out for some independence and free will upon the death of their father; daughters, on the other hand, remained under the ownership of the father until his death whereupon she then became property of her uncle or husband.

Christianity continued the Father God tradition and used every tool at its disposal to justify the status quo of male dominance. Saint Paul, the founding father of the religion now known as Christianity, put much effort into ensuring women would not attain power or responsibility in Christianity despite numerous strong and influential early Christian female figures.

One of the main aims of the Roman Catholic Church was the acquisition of property. In order to achieve this goal it meant overturning the system of matrilineal inheritance. Simply by using the age-old strategy of forcible seizure and warfare, the Church managed to acquire over a third of all the landed property on the European continent by the early Middle Ages.[10] The other two third's proved a bit more difficult. Much of this so-called "unclaimed territory" was in northern Europe where patriarchal rule had less of a stronghold than it did in the heart of the Greek, Roman, Jewish, and Christian world. For example, until the tenth century, priests in some parts of pagan northern Europe married to gain property via their wives, claiming that without their wives they would succumb to "hunger and nakedness."[11] In addition, women were still listed as the landowners and men identified themselves by their mother's clan name up until 1200 C.E. Church laws revised the old system between 1031 and 1051 by instituting a series of decrees ordering priests to abandon their wives and sell their children into slavery.[12] The property and monies thus acquired by a priest would revert to the Church upon his death, since he no longer had any legal heirs and women could no longer inherit.

The legal/ecclesiastic war on female property ownership went on century after century, until women were so hamstrung by the laws of God and man that they had almost nothing left to call their own. By the end of the nineteenth century, English wives could not administer their own property even if they had any, nor make a will disposing of it without their husband's consent.[13] As late as 1930 in France, a woman was forbidden to do any business with a bank without her husband's permission, not even to make small deposits.[14]

This economic dependence helped ensure that a woman would not stray from her marriage and risk losing everything, including her life, by engaging in an adulterous relationship. This worked in the favour of the patrilineal descent system by helping to ensure that the children she bore where actually the children of her husband.

Eve – The Mother of All Living

Jewish and Christian leaders have referred to the Adam and Eve myth as a justification for women not to have power. I don't want to go into too much detail about the symbolism that is rife in this Old Testament creation story, there is just too much to cover and its interpretation alone is worthy of a book or two. While I am weary of not covering it in enough detail and belittling the symbols associated with this story, we can't talk about motherhood without bringing up Eve, whose name means "mother of all living."

In this story, birth is again turned around. Yahweh creates Adam first and when Adam was unable to find a suitable "helpmeet" amongst the animals, Yahweh decided to fashion woman from Adam's rib. Once again we see things turned around by making woman from man, rather than the usual way of conception where man comes from woman. Anyway, after finishing his newest creation, Eve, Yahweh instructs the new couple to make themselves at home in His Garden of Eden and live a carefree worry-free existence. He places only one condition on this relaxed lifestyle: He tells them they are not to eat of the fruit of the Tree of Knowledge "lest they die."

Along comes the antagonist serpent. After all, every story needs one. The snake creeps up in almost every one of the earlier goddess-worshipping cultures as an important and potent feminine power symbol. In this story, however, the serpent is the villain who tells Eve that partaking of the Tree of Knowledge's fruit will not cause her death. Instead, the serpent says, "In the day ye eat thereof, then your eyes shall be opened, and ye shall be as gods, knowing good from evil." Finding it hard to resist such a temptation, she "took of the fruit thereof, and did eat, and gave also unto her husband with her; and he did eat."

The "all-knowing" Yahweh pretends not to know what has transpired. When He confronts Adam with the transgression, Adam blames Eve. She confesses but blames the serpent. Yahweh first curses the serpent, pronouncing, "I will put enmity between you and the woman, and between your offspring and her offspring. He will bruise your head, and you will bruise his heel." Turning to Eve, Yahweh pronounces, "I will greatly multiply thy sorrow and thy conception; in sorrow thou shalt bring forth children; and thy desire shall be to thy husband, and he shall rule over thee." Lastly, Yahweh sentences Adam and all his descendants to labour for their food, and tells him that they will die, "for dust thou art and unto dust shall thou return."

In *The Alphabet Versus the Goddess*, Leonard Shlain writes, "Because of Eve's transgression, humans would know pain, hardship, suffering, and death. In a turnaround with far reaching consequences for Western womanhood, woman who had been primarily associated with life in all previous cultures, was now blamed for the death of every mortal." He goes further to question why these sentences seem excessive in light of the circumstances under which Adam and Eve disobeyed God. Eve's decision to transgress was made before she had eaten of the magic fruit, when she could not have known the difference between good and evil. A mere few passages later, Cain kills Abel. Cain knew good from evil (due to his mother's actions), yet Yahweh treats him with the unmistakable compassion of a parent discipling a wayward but beloved child. Yahweh banishes Cain, but when the youth protests, Yahweh reconsiders and marks Cain forehead to protect him from harm. "In these two morality tales less than one page apart, Yahweh judges murder by a man a less egregious crime than disobedience by a woman."[15]

Let's face it, whatever the symbolism or however you interpret the story, there is no denying Eve got a bum rap out of the whole deal. She alone, among the planet's myriad creatures, would bear children with great difficulty and high mortality. Which brings us to the real reason why giving birth is a much more painful, difficult, and dangerous experience for the human female in comparison to other female mammals. It has to do with the simple consequence of walking upright.

In the evolution of humans from their four-legged position to their two-legged position, the two-legged pelvic bone needed to be smaller than its four-legged counterpart. Not only did we move from four feet to two feet but we also evolved ever-bigger brains. The large size of the human baby's head and the smaller size of the human female's pelvic bone made for an exceedingly tight fit. Where primates have ample room for the baby to squeeze through the pelvic opening, the fit is so tight in humans that unless the baby turns its head at a specific angle it will be unable to fit through the pelvic opening. This is why delivering babies is so much tougher for women when compared to labour in apes. For example, labour for a gorilla is short, in the order of twenty minutes, and enviably easy. By contrast, human births take far longer and range from easy to extraordinarily difficult and deadly.[16] It took me at least a hundred contractions over a six-hour period to deliver my second child, and all present considered it an "easy birth"! I wanted to smack every last one of them who kept saying that.

This compromise between larger human brain size and the

smaller human pelvic opening is also the reason why human babies are so helpless when born. All other primate babies are born with a brain approximately half the size of an adult brain; human baby's brains are only one-third their adult size at birth. In order for babies to be born with their brain half the size of their adult brain like other primates, the human gestational period would have to be recalculated at twenty-one months.[17] There is no way the baby would be able to fit through the female's pelvic opening with a brain that size. At some point in our evolution, the size of the pelvic opening had to be stopped to allow women to walk upright and the expansion of neonatal brain size had to be accommodated by growth outside the womb. This is why human babies are so helpless for the first year after birth; they live like the embryos they still are in their brains' development.

This happened well over two million years ago and had nothing to do with any snake, apple, or some Tree of Knowledge. Many of us don't consider ourselves religious and roll our eyes at the whole Adam and Eve story, understanding there is much more to the story than we are told. Even in our secular society, where religion does not have the hold on us it had a mere 50 to 100 years ago, we tend to believe we are immune to the psychological influence or implications these stories have on us. But I think we underestimate the impact these stories have on how we view the world and our place in it. Most Western children know of the Adam and Eve story, even if they are not Jewish or Christian. We have to wonder what affect that story has on the self-esteem of a girl or the psyche of boys. The Jewish and Christian "Mother of All Living," as Eve was called, rather than being honoured and respected for giving us life and nurturing us, is instead viewed as the reason for all the ills of the world.

The Staying Power of the Goddess

Christianity wanted to assign the goddess to the past, but despite their efforts, she would not disappear. It seemed that the role and the need for a goddess figure was simply too strong. One of the reasons patriarchal religions have such difficulty eliminating the goddess from the human spiritual psyche is because of the importance of the mother/child bond. This bond forms the basic building block of all animal societies, especially humans. Most infants, both boys and girls, spend their early months in intimate symbiotic association with their mothers. So close is this relationship that psychoanalysts call it "merging" between mother and child.

To the infant who knows nothing about religion, politics, or ancient history, the biological mother is the great Mother Goddess. She is the giver of life and their survival is based upon the will of this mother. She is the giver of everything: life, nourishment, comfort. There is also an element of fear on the part of the child: if mother leaves, that security leaves with her and the baby is left alone. This earthly mother is the original Great Mother Goddess from whom all things emerge. Of course, the mythic figure of the Great Mother Goddess will always be far more than the mere human mother can ever hope to be. The fact remains, however, that the human mother as we know her in infancy will always be at some unconscious level a goddess to her child. This may be the reason why despite numerous attempts by many different patriarchal religions to eliminate the goddess figure from religion, humans still remain hesitant to give her up.

The cult of the Virgin Mary is an example of this. It's interesting how the Catholic Church termed the worship of Mary a cult but named the worship of Jesus a religion. Mary is the unrecognized Mother Goddess of the Christian tradition. As the Christian forefathers ordered the repression of the goddess cults, the people deprived of their goddess turned to Mary instead. Portraits from the end of the fourth century and the beginning of the fifth century show Mary seated in the same position as the Egyptian Isis with her son Horus, or wearing the mural crown of the Cretan Cybele, or sitting on the moon like Diana. It had taken less than a century for Mary to take over the role of these remaining goddesses at the time of Christianity. Joseph Campbell's introduction to Mary's mythic tradition sums it up:

> It is simply a fact—deal with it how you will—that the mythology of the dead and resurrected god has been known for millenniums to the Neolithic and the post-Neolithic Levant...The entire ancient world, from Asia Minor to the Nile and from Greece to the Indus Valley,

abounds in figurines of the naked female form, in various attitudes of the all-supporting, all-including goddess...And so it came to pass that, in the end and to our day, Mary, Queen of Martyrs, became the sole inheritor of all the names and forms, sorrows, joys, consolations of the goddess-mother in the Western world.

The Church fathers recognized the threat Mary posed and they denied her powers possessed by previous goddesses. She did not have any influence over fertility, agriculture, hunting, or childbirth. All they allowed her to do was give birth to a son she was impregnated with through the word of God. In the New Testament, Mary's significance is entirely secondary. She appears very infrequently in the Gospels and when she does, she plays a completely subordinate role to her son.

The Christian forefathers tried numerous times to wipe out the worship of the Virgin Mary by encouraging the worship of her son. Mary's worship, however, reached a height in the Middle Ages and early Renaissance from the eleventh to the fifteenth century. Between 1170 and 1270, for instance, in France alone, over one hundred churches and eighty cathedrals were built in her honour. She was constantly celebrated in the poetry and music of the troubadours and was a popular subject of paintings by artists. The Church eventually had to acknowledge Mary's rapidly rising popularity among the common folk. In medieval times, the Vatican proclaimed August 15th the Feast of the Assumption in her honour—the same day Pagans had honoured the Goddess Artemis in pre-Christian times. The Protestant Churches never accepted the worship of Mary to the extent the Catholics did. From Martin Luther, the father of Protestantism, came the instruction "Ye shall sing no more praises to Our Lady, only to Our Lord."

Honour Thy Mother?

Pregnancy puts females at a disadvantage from a survival aspect because pregnant females require an enormous amount of resources to support and compensate for the growth taking place within them. The human female requires 75,000 calories to bring the baby to its birth stage and then an additional 500 to 600 calories each day while nursing the baby.[18] When you think that the average caloric intake for a person is 2000 calories per day, the realization of the resource needs of the pregnant or nursing woman becomes apparent. With the added care a newborn human baby needs, it is understandable that a woman needs a support network around her for the baby to survive. After all, she needs more resources at a time when she is least able to get it. This is the initial reason for the division of labour that usually takes place in all cultures from prehistory to today.

Some people say this division of labour based on gender is inherently sexist. I think we are missing the point when we say that. It may not be fair, I concede that, but it is not inherently sexist. It evolved for purely practical reasons. It is not the actual division of labour that is sexist; instead, it is the values we attach to the respective roles that are sexist. When a society values masculine roles more than feminine roles, and when men are given more rights and freedoms than females, you can call that what you wish but I would label it sexist. If as a society we view feminine traits as less valuable than masculine traits, we belittle womanhood. If we belittle womanhood, we can't help but belittle motherhood.

It is no surprise that many women do not see motherhood as a worthy objective in life. Why should they when society doesn't value it either? Modern women have been caught in the conundrum of the battle between career and family. It seems that no matter what a woman chooses to do, stay home with her kids or go back to work, it is never the right decision. If she goes back to work, she is neglecting her kids. If she stays home, she has quit the fight and is now just a "mom." Women have even sometimes become their own worst enemies. At times, the debate between "stay at home" moms and "working" moms seems more like a battle than a debate. This divide-and-conquer strategy is not new and by taking part in the battle, women undermine themselves, both as women and as mothers.

Religion and society have tried to send out the message to honour our mothers and fathers but the value and the rights they assign to the female say the complete opposite. Why should the child honour the mother if religion and society dishonour the female? It is only when our society recognizes and respects the value of motherhood in the same way it respects and values the worth of the professional lawyer or successful entrepreneur that Mother's Day will be more than a consolation prize.

The Making of Modern Mother's Day

It is ironic that considering the low esteem in which the Greeks held motherhood some historians claim the predecessors of our Mother's Day holiday was the ancient Greek spring festival honouring Rhea, the wife of Cronus and mother of the important Olympian Greek gods and goddesses Hera, Poseidon, Hephaestus, Pan, Hades, and Zeus. In Rome, the most significant Mother's Day–like festival was dedicated to the worship of Cybele, another mother goddess. Ceremonies in her honour began some 250 years before Christ was born. This Roman religious celebration known as Hilaria lasted for three days from March 15th to 18th. The festival began as a solemn occasion as the Mother Goddess mourned the death of her son. The mourning then turned to wild joy when the Mother Goddess rescued her son from death and the underworld through her power, strength, and love.

Christianity appropriated this pagan festival and instead of celebrating the power of a mother's love, the Church tried to sell it as a day to honour a person's "Mother Church." This new Mother Church festival called for people to visit the church of their baptism and provide that church with offerings and gifts. This idea never took off with most folks; instead, the festival moved over into honouring real live mothers. Wow, what a radical thought! In the 1600s, a growing number of people were moving away from home to find work and earn money. Since they were only allowed one holiday a year, it was on the fourth Sunday in Lent that people went home to see their mothers. This was called "a-mothering" and thus the custom of Mothering Sunday was started. A special "mother's cake" was often brought along.

When the first settlers came to North America, the Mothering Sunday tradition was not continued, mainly because their mothers were on the other side of the Atlantic and too far for them to go "a-mothering." In 1872, Julia Ward Howe, who wrote the "Battle Hymn of the Republic," suggested the idea of a Mother's Day as an attempt to reserve a day for peace after the hatred and discontent of the civil war.

It is Anna M. Jarvis, however, who is considered the woman who originated Mother's Day as we know it. She created the day to honour her departed mother. When she was young, her mother mentioned the unfairness of the multitude of memorial days dedicated to men considering there were none for women and/or mothers. When the little girl grew up, she went on to lobby for just such a day. In 1907, Anna Jarvis and her friends began a letter-writing campaign to gain the support of influential businessmen, congressmen, and religious leaders (all men mind you!) in declaring a national Mother's Day holiday. The first Mother's Day observance took place in honour of her mother, Anna Reese Jarvis. It was held at Jarvis' request in Grafton, West Virginia and in Philadelphia, Pennsylvania on May 10, 1908. Jarvis supplied white carnations, her mother's favourite flowers, because she felt they represented the sweetness, purity, and endurance of motherly love.

Jarvis continued to write letters in support of a national Mother's Day to be held on the second Sunday in May, and by 1909, almost every state was celebrating this day. On May 9, 1914, President Woodrow Wilson signed a proclamation declaring the second Sunday in May as Mother's Day in every state. It did not take long, however, for the holiday to become the materialistic commercialized day we all know. Anna Jarvis, disgusted by what had flourished from the original holiday, filed a lawsuit to impede the Mother's Day festival. She was even arrested for disturbing the peace at a gathering of wartime mothers who were selling carnations, Jarvis' symbol for motherhood, to raise money. "This is not what I intended," Jarvis said, "I wanted it to be a day of sentiment, not profit."

Anna Jarvis never married or became a mother; instead, she spent most of her life mothering and caring for her blind sister. Towards the end of her life, she bitterly stated that she regretted ever having created Mother's Day. She died alone in a nursing home in 1948 at the age of eighty-four.

Mother's Day is celebrated in many different countries all around the world. Although it is celebrated in different ways and at different times of the year, the purpose is the same: to say thank you to someone who nurtured you and cared for you at a time when you needed it. While we, like Anna Jarvis, might be fed up and frustrated with the commercialization and materialism of the holiday, we have to realize it is up to us whether we go along with it or not. We don't have to spend $60 on flowers and wait in line for an hour at the restaurant, we just have to say thank you and mean it and more than once a year would also be a good idea. Of course, not all mothers are equal and some did a better job than others, but we have to acknowledge that without them, not only would we not be here, we might not even have survived and we certainly might not have flourished.

We also have to remember that mothers are not the only ones mothering. Just because one gives birth to a child, it does not mean one will be able to care for that child and most certainly not all alone. Raising a child is a group effort and there are many people mothering daily who are not the children's biological mothers. Caring sisters, grandmothers, daycare workers, mentors. Anyone who gives their heart and soul to help someone grow into a better and stronger person has played the role of the Great Mother.

Mothers need to reclaim their heritage, value, and prestige as creator and nurturer of new life. Remember that in our role as biological mother, adopted mother, grandmother, or nurturer, we have acted out the role of the Great Mother Goddess and reclaimed her original meaning, value, and strength and each of us in our own way become her.

FATHER'S DAY
The Third Sunday in June

There are a few countries in the world with an official day for children to honour their fathers. In North America on the third Sunday in June, children give their dads the same old presents and attempt to share their feelings and say thanks to them for the role they play in their lives. At the end of the day, we are left wondering, how many socks and how much cheap aftershave can one man use? It's not only the presents that are boring about Father's Day; the history of Father's Day is boring too.

The idea came to a woman named Sonora Louise Smart Dodd, who grew up on a rural farm in the state of Washington. While listening to the first Mother's Day sermon in 1909, Sonora envisioned the idea of observing a day to honour fathers. Her mother died when she was a small child and her father, William Smart, raised Sonora and her five siblings all by himself. Considering the important role her father played in her life, she felt since there was a day set aside to honour mothers, there should also be a special day to honour fathers. Wasting no time, Sonora organized a Father's Day celebration in Spokane, Washington on June 19, 1910. She chose the month of June because it was the same month her father was born.

Over the years, many people continued to spread the idea of

a special day to honour fathers, and while it was quite popular, it did not receive the profile that Mother's Day was able to achieve. Father's Day was only made official in the United States in 1966 when Lyndon Johnson signed a presidential proclamation implementing the third Sunday in June as a special day set aside to honour fathers. But why was Father's Day so slow on the uptake? Maybe it is because few children were sure what they were supposed to be honouring Dad for.

What is the value of a father? Now there is a question that isn't boring. It would be a whole lot easier to talk about the value of Dad if by doing so it didn't feel like it would devalue Mom, and vice versa. It's like there is this ongoing battle between a mother's value and a father's value and if we talk about one, we risk belittling the other. The simple truth is that both parents are important to their children.

It is true that we have an easier time understanding the mother/child bond than we do the father/child bond. The animal world is rife with images of mothers tending and protecting their young, whereas the mammalian father is rarely seen. Mothers gave birth to us, fed us, nurtured us, and even if they only managed to do a crappy job at it in our books, they still played a specific role. What was father's role in our upbringing? The first thought to come to mind is as a provider, but even if he did that to the best of his ability, was that role enough to satisfy the child or the father?

Women get pregnant and give birth, but does this mean they love their children more than fathers do? Mothers are probably more likely to think this is the case but I bet many fathers also believe that the mother/child bond is more important than the father/child bond. Is this true? What really forms our attachments and love for our children? If mothers were not the ones to get pregnant and provide milk for their babies, would their relationship or love for their children be any less than it is now? Do mothers of adopted children love these children any less because they did not give birth to them? Most of us would say no. Sure, biology makes a difference but I think we have let the old Freudian saying "biology is destiny" limit us. It is because fathers have not had, and still do not have, the same opportunity as mothers to develop that ongoing relationship with their children that we have more difficulty pinning down the value of a father.

For the most part of history, fatherhood has been ignored. I know this may seem strange since so much has been written about men's lives and achievements. It is men's public lives, however—their work, political exploits, literary accomplishments, scientific discoveries, and heroic battles—that received all the attention. Their private lives as fathers and husbands, on the other hand, have largely been ignored.

Society's ideas of fatherhood have been, and still are to some extent, about power and authority. To be a father implied power over others, especially women and children. The institution of patriarchy, rule by the father, is our legacy. The chain of fatherhood goes through a long list of authority figures eventually ending at the concept of God. God, and it doesn't seem to matter which "god" we are talking about, is father to all people. Then we move to the idea of kings, who are the father of their people; then we move to the idea of priests who are supposed to be fathers to their community. Finally, we come to fathers themselves. Those who might be on the lowest rung of society's ladder at least get to be head of their family. The father was the moral pillar for the family, the disciplinarian, and since women were isolated from public life, the father was also the family's representative to the outside world and the representative of the outside world for the family.

Fathers even got to play the role of God within the family. Even when a father wasn't physically around or involved in the day-to-day upbringing of his children, his presence was felt. Just like God (and Santa Claus), Daddy knew if you were bad or good (usually because Mom, a sibling, or the hired help ratted on you) and there were consequences for not living up to Dad's expectations. Fathers were given the right to decide their children's futures: whether they married, and if so, to whom they were married; whether they were sent to the priesthood or convent; what profession they took up; whether they were sold into slavery; and even whether they lived or died. Fathers at different points in history were allowed to sell their wife or children into slavery, physically abuse them, and even murder them without legal repercussions.

Strangely enough, with all the authority society granted to them to govern as head of the family, fathers were discouraged from developing anything but an authoritarian role in the family. From the sixteenth century right up to the twentieth century, society tried to convince men that partaking in the nurturing and day-to-day duties of parenthood would cause them to lose their masculinity. A popular image in the seventeenth century was of a man looking after children and being beaten by them. At this time in France, men were offered a picture of a very sad-looking man nursing a baby while his wife primmed herself in front of a mirror for a night on the town.[1] Even up to the 1950s, it was widely asserted that the children of so-called "submissive fathers" (i.e. father's trying to take on a more nurturing role) would mess up their children's sexual identity and cause girls to lose their ideas of femininity (as if they were their ideas!) and, even worse, would turn their sons into homosexuals and schizo-phrenics. Many fathers might have seemed cold and detached when, more often than not, they only acted that way, not felt that way. Both children and fathers lost out in this arrangement.

The question that comes to my mind is "why?" What could be so horrible about nurturing and showing your emotions and love for your children that would warrant such propaganda? Why did society want to control men's use and understanding of this per-fectly normal human function? What is it that society gains by not allowing men access to that part of their psyche? Well, a lot.

It wasn't that society feared fathers had no interest in caring and nurturing their offspring or even that they would find the experience unappealing; the fear was that they would enjoy it and be unwilling to give it up. Society was able to control women by limiting their access to financial resources, independence, and societal influence. Men, on the other hand, were not restricted in this manner, so society needed to find another way to control them. Now, don't get me wrong, I am not a proponent of anarchy, and let's face it, part of living in a society means there has to be some level of societal control. Without it, cities and even large groups of people or tribes would never be able to coexist. But societal control also has a dark side, and during the ages it had some not-so-endearing motivations.

People in positions of power benefit when society has drones; they need to exert control over people to turn them into useful drones. In her book *Fatherhood Reclaimed*, Adrienne Burgess sums it up:

> Men have been urged to keep at an emotional and physical distance from infants so they would be cut off from their tender, nurturing feelings, so that they would be alienated from themselves. This has helped to condition them to blind obedience, has fitted them to undertake exhausting and debilitating physical work, and has prepared them to be an army-in-waiting in times of peace and to kill and be killed in times of war.

Father As Breadwinner

As family life switched from rural, at-home, farm work into city living and factory jobs, a father's influence in the everyday activities of the family diminished even more. His work took him far from home and in many cases he would be away in the city while the family remained on the farm or often only made it home so late the kids had already been sent to bed. Women were increasingly isolated from this outside "working world" and became even more responsible for all childcare duties. Father was still ultimately responsible for acting as moral head and family disciplinarian, even though in practice he wasn't home enough to do so. Many mothers helped fathers keep their reputation as the disciplinarian as any kid who heard the old "just wait till your father gets home" could attest to. While that disciplinarian threat still worked on many kids, it further limited the role a father could have with his kids. I am sure there were many dads who came home hoping to spend some time playing with their kids or just spend time with them only to have to dish out punishments instead. This kind of ruined the night for both the dads and the kids I am sure.

As the role of fathers became more limited to being the breadwinner, his ability to be a good provider also determined his value and worth as a man. After the depression and the Second World War, the pressure on men to be good providers increased.

It was no longer enough to just keep the family off the welfare line because the ante for the good provider badge kept getting higher and higher—the nice three-bedroom suburban subdivision in the cul de sac, the new appliances and gadgets, the second car to allow the wifey to get out of the suburbs when hubby was not around. The list kept getting longer and "keeping up with the Joneses" became a moral obligation. This linking between a man's self-worth and his ability to be a good provider helped create the consumerist lifestyle we know today.

Everything seemed hunky-dory in the 1950s as people were presented with an image of the average family in American sitcoms such as *Leave It to Beaver* and *Father Knows Best* and mothers seemed happy and proud to be the suburban housewife and mom. It's not surprising that after a decade of watching these shows most people thought their families were inadequate and abnormal. The 1950s sitcom was an attempt to keep men and women in their respective roles: father as provider and mother as nurturer. While we tend to think of the 1960s as the decade of social change, the 1950s were the decade when the seeds for that social change were planted.

During the Second World War, women took the place of men in the workforce. When men returned from the war, women were told they should go back to being the housewife and mother as the men were going to return to their jobs. Many women began to question these preconceived roles society had laid out for them and realized they were getting a bum rap. This is not surprising since raising children provided personal rewards but it was not a role valued by society. The role of breadwinner had, and still has, far more value and recognition than nurturer. Sure, women had control of the everyday nitty-gritty care of the family and therefore were usually in a better position to develop a more intimate relationship with their children, but in exchange for that privilege (this isn't sarcasm because I do think it is a privilege) they payed a price. Women lacked any real power as society defined it. They had little economic freedom or independence, little political influence, and whatever control they exercised in the household depended on the very few legal rights (never mind the lack of enforcement of their few existing rights) available to them to protect themselves from the aggression of their partners.

Few people would deny that women were discriminated against and it is easy to understand women's interests in moving into the men's world where they hoped to have access to some of the resources, independence, and recognition they saw that came with these positions. What was not as obvious was that while women were kept in the role as nurturer and men kept in the role as breadwinner, men also experienced discrimination. I know many of you might be saying *hah!* at this point but bear with me. Being male had many advantages as far as society was concerned. Economics were valued higher than nurturing; masculine traits were valued higher than feminine traits; males had far more rights, authority, and decision-making power than females. It was such a privileged position that no one stopped to think about the costs, but everything has its cost and this was no exception. Men faced discrimination in the sense that they were not allowed equal access to a close loving relationship with their children to the same extent women were.

If this was the case, why was there no corresponding men's movement such as the women's movement? Why didn't men have their own battle cry calling for an end to the discrimination preventing them from achieving a better relationship with their children? Why didn't men demand they be given the right to work less and spend more time caring for their children? I think one of the main reasons men did not complain about their lack of access to a nurturing relationship with their children was because you don't fight to get access to a position that is considered to be lower on the social ladder than the one you already have. Fathers took solace in the fact that even if they were unable to communicate with their children or show their affection, love, and respect, it was only because they were playing the role society expected of them as the strong father figure.

The Fall of Fatherhood's Image
The image of fathers as the wholesome but distant provider presented in 1950s sitcoms such as *The Adventures of Ozzie & Harriet* and *Father Knows Best* seems distant from reality not only because it was unrealistic but also because we compare it to the

image we have of fathers today. It has become politically correct to demean men by making them out to be incompetent contributors to maintaining the home and family. One only has to think of the numerous commercials where the mother leaves the father in charge of the dinner or laundry and the poor sod has no idea what to do and completely messes up the whole thing. If a commercial portrayed a woman being so incompetent in the workforce, imagine our reaction to that. We seem to believe that since it was okay for men to stereotype women in the past, it is now okay to stereotype men. The father figure, far from being the wise head of the family, is now portrayed as the incompetent family freak sideshow.

Why the drastic swing in the pendulum? A part of fatherhood's fall can be attributed to the loss of the father's mystique as breadwinner as women moved into the workforce and gained more economic clout. Maybe booting fathers from their pedestal is an attempt to remove some of the inequality that existed between men and women for so long. Maybe it has more to do with the increased societal disapproval of authority figures, blind obedience, and patriarchy and recognizing the damage it caused by perpetuating racism, sexism, wars, and the overall status quo. More than likely, it is a combination of all the above factors, plus a few more. One thing is for certain, though, from the 1960s to the present, the role of father has repeatedly been questioned.

It is not that we have lowered our aspirations towards authority, we all still fight to get a piece of that authority pie. Yes, it is still the case that the old hierarchical structure is well and strong in our society. What has changed is the societal disapproval of our rank on the ladder being based on to whom we were born and what sex or colour we are, rather than what we have worked for or earned. It would be idealistic and naive not to realize that these factors still play a large role in helping or hindering people in their climb up the social ladder, as they most certainly do. But we no longer choose to passively accept that a person's right to a social ranking is based on what sex that person was born, the colour of their skin, or what part of the class structure they were born into.

As women have refused to be relegated to the role of dependant and instead have moved into the workforce en masse, men have lost their exclusive role of provider, leaving them looking for a new role in the family.

With so much change taking place in the roles of men and women in the outside world and mothers and fathers in the familial world, many groups calling themselves pro-family lament what they view as the demise of fatherhood. They place motherhood on a pedestal and call for a return to the family values of the past. They place motherhood on a pedestal, however, not to give women more rights, privileges, and honour but rather to keep women in what they view as their place: at home with the kids while daddy brings home the bacon. These so-called "pro-family" groups idealize the roles of the past without recognizing the costs that mothers, fathers, and children have paid for that strict role polarization. These pro-family groups would have us believe that our children's disillusionment with the world or even their delinquency is due to mom going out of the house to work and the kids' not having anyone to watch over them when they come home from school.

These same pro-family groups warn us of the demise of society and blame all present social ills on the change in respect for authority and morality. But it's their idea of what they call authority and morality that has changed in society, not the actual principles. No one can say we don't have social problems but there are real positive social changes taking place. Change is scary for people. Whenever we are scared, we tend to fall back on our idealized version of the way we think things were. We may have lost our respect for those in positions of authority who we feel are not acting responsibly with the powers they have been granted, but is that a bad thing? We have more awareness of human rights, are less tolerant of prejudice, sexism, and racism, and are more aware of our individual rights and needs. We are less willing to let society dictate what it expects from us and are more likely than in the past to decide what we want for ourselves. That does not sound like the demise of family values to me.

It is understandable that people are scared of the outcome of the many changes taking place in the roles of men and women and the corresponding changes taking place in the roles of mothers and fathers. With mothers taking part in the role of breadwinner and fathers not taking an equal jump into the role of nurturer, the high rates of divorce and single parenthood, and the dangers of drugs and violence in our children's lives, it is easy to get scared. But to try to go back to the "way things (never) were" is not working for change for the better, it is fighting change at all costs.

Single moms and dads have received an overwhelming amount of attention, both good and bad, in the new family structure. Single parenthood is often used as an explanation for why kids go bad. That there are also many kids from so-called intact families who also go bad does not seem to diminish the public scapegoating of single parents and, more specifically, single moms. It is not some inherent weakness on the part of single moms and dads that makes raising kids alone more difficult but rather as noted fatherhood expert Michael Lamb writes:

> Children who grow up with only one parent are raised by a person who lack somebody to back them up, to give them time away from parenting, to share both the burdens and the enjoyable aspects of being with and raising children. And that sense of being overwhelmed as a single parent translates into difficulties in parenting which also has an effect on children's development.

This is a far cry from the idea that families who are going it alone without a mother or a father are not good families. While they have extra challenges, they usually find their own special way to overcome their challenges. They often put extra effort into extending their family by creating their own community to support them and their children thus providing kids of single parent homes something that the nuclear family is less likely to work for.

If these pro-family groups were really interested in improving family life they would be better off trying to figure out how family life can be better integrated with working life. Children have been increasingly separated from their parent's livelihood and our parental roles have become increasingly isolated and forever in conflict with our professional lives. In order to be truly pro-family, these groups should work towards helping both mothers and fathers gain a better balance between family and career and on changing society's value and respect for children.

The "New" Father

Despite all the lamentations about the demise of fatherhood, there has never been as much interest in the role of the father as there is now. There is a definite renewed interest in this forgotten man. Fathers are now able to be involved in the family in more ways than they were in the past. Yes, it is still generally the case that fathers do way less housework and childcare than mothers do, but today's fathers are much more involved in the family than were men of a generation ago. In a poll conducted by *Newsweek* magazine, 55% of men interviewed felt that parenting was more significant for them than it had been to their own father, and 70% said they spend more time with their children than their fathers did with them.[2] This increased involvement of fathers, in the form of hands-on care as well as emotional availability, is one of the most significant social trends to affect present and future families. To some extent, society has altered its definition of masculinity and has somewhat legitimized the need for more involved fathers. What is even more exciting is that fathers are finally defining for themselves how they want to be involved with their children and not letting society alone dictate their acceptable role. Our next challenge as a society is to allow them the tools and the flexibility to make that goal a reality. Especially since it isn't easy for fathers to reach that goal. Many factors still inhibit a father's ability to create and maintain an active role in bringing up his children.

Up until the last few decades, men were not encouraged, or even allowed, to see their babies being born. Men were considered too psychologically weak to witness the birth of their child. Many people felt that the father's seeing his baby being born would make him unable to relate to his partner in a sexual way ever again. Modesty is not meant to be part of the birthing process and if couples live in an atmosphere of sexual modesty, as many did in the past, then a father's presence at the birth of his child would have been a very uncomfortable experience for both the mother and the father. The major reason for men's growing presence in the delivery room is less modesty and greater sexual openness. I can't help but snicker at the old movies showing a honeymooning couple having sex where the woman is dressed in a honeymoon gown that fully covers her body except for an opening at her genital area. I know it is hard for us to imagine modesty taken to such ridiculous extremes but that was the way things happened for many men and women. If our sexual climate were still like that, there would be no way women would be comfortable letting men into the delivery room. Thankfully for men and their children, the greater sexual openness between a man and a woman has allowed mothers to invite fathers into the delivery rooms.

Nine out of ten fathers attend the delivery of their babies these days. You may wonder what the big deal is. It's not like they just got an invitation to the Oscars or a Nobel Peace Prize, but the overwhelming majority of fathers who take up the invitation report being deeply moved by the experience of childbirth. But being at the birth can be a mixed blessing—the father knows even less than the mother about what is going on and it is difficult for anyone, but especially men, to be in a position of helplessness and watch as his loved one endures a painful experience. Things can even get traumatic if there are complications. Despite all this, fathers consider their child's birth to be a miraculous event that is rated by men as one of the peak experiences of their lives and as a time when they feel an intense commitment that brings them closer to their partners and their children.[3]

While birth may have been a bonding experience for mother, father, and baby, what comes after is likely to drive a wedge into that bond and sets up mothers and fathers for the old role polarization. Although hospitals have made an effort to welcome fathers in the delivery room, the continuation of that welcome is lacking post-delivery. It must be hard for fathers who feel this intense bonding with their baby and partner to then be excluded when the mother and baby get moved to the maternity ward. Little effort is made to make fathers feel welcome and involved here. When I was moved up to the maternity ward after the birth of my first child, the baby and I had a place to sleep but all that was available for my husband was his winter jacket on the floor.

Granted, the hospital staff is already overworked and it probably seems to them like fathers just complicate matters. It is, after all, the maternity ward, but it would not be too much work to provide fathers with a more welcome feeling post-delivery than there often is at present. The impact that this small effort would have on the lives of fathers and their children would far outweigh the costs. There is some movement in that direction and many birthing centres have delivery rooms that are also recovery rooms where the mother and father can spend the next 24 to 48 hours together bonding with their baby.

To make it even harder for the father to get a hang of the whole baby thing, his work commitments and/or the constant presence of the mother does not allow him the luxury of time alone with the baby. This is a real pity for both baby and dad. I remember how much I fumbled with my first baby, how long it took me to change a diaper, or get her to sleep. I was horribly inexperienced despite all the effort I made to prepare myself for taking care of a baby. Thinking back, I am very glad I was able to have the opportunity to have the time alone with my daughter to get the knack, without having someone breathing down my neck telling me how I was doing it wrong and taking over. Many fathers are not able to have the luxury of that unsupervised learning time. "We were amazed," exclaimed the research team Cowan & Cowan when they observed couples in the weeks following their baby's birth at how little time fathers allowed themselves for uncertainty and how quickly mothers stepped in if father or baby looked uneasy.[4]

Another researcher Charlie Lewis found that some men, recognizing their wife's need to feel in control, actually held back from doing things for the baby when they would have loved to do more. Lewis found that very often when fathers withdrew, it was because they felt incompetent, not realizing that many of the moms felt that way too. Babies have a knack for making parents feel incompetent. The Cowans also found the more the father withdrew, the more their partners picked up the slack. The more their partners picked up the slack the more incompetent the father felt and the more he withdrew, causing the mother to do more...and so the vicious cycle begins.

One in three new fathers suffer depressive bouts and at about six weeks, 5% are quite seriously depressed, with the most depressed fathers having wives who are overly involved with the babies. The usual interpretation of paternal depression is that the father is jealous of the attention his wife is showing the baby and frustrated by his reduced sex life. Some researchers, however, are beginning to challenge this stereotype of the depressed father. According to some new studies, it seems probable that in many cases, a father's dissatisfaction or depression might actually spring from his disappointment at his potential to be an active parent who instead has been disabled or handicapped. It has been observed that depression in most fathers lifts when they gain skills and confidence and feel themselves capable of caring for their infants. Men who felt supported and encouraged by their wives in finding their own way of doing things and were not constantly supervised were not depressed and soon developed a strong connection to their infant.[5]

Who Is This New Father?

Images of fathers in the media and in public policy debates would lead one to believe that there are but two types of fathers: the new-age nurturing father who is as comfortable in the boardroom as he is in the nursery and the "deadbeat dad" who doesn't bother to give either his time or financial support to his children. The reality is that most fathers fall somewhere in between the two extremes. While fathers are spending about the same amount of time with their children as they did in 1983, they are, however, spending more time at work than they did twenty years ago. In a survey, over one-third of fathers with young children were reportedly working more than fifty hours per week in 1998, a 6% rise in working hours over the previous decade.[6]

Even when both parents work full time, moms still spend twice as much time with the kids as dads. The perception that mothers are more important than fathers profoundly influences the day-to-day behaviour of working mothers and fathers. While mothers who work exceedingly long hours make the time to spend at least an hour per working day interacting with their children, fathers do not. Fathers are much less likely to rush home from work in order to snatch half an hour with their kids before bedtime. But it's not that fathers don't love or value their kids, it's because fathers don't value themselves at home.

Unfortunately for most fathers (and mothers too), their career demands are greatest when their children are young and need them the most. By the time a father's career demands let up and he is finally free to try and form a relationship with his kids, the kids have already figured out how to get along without him and have moved on to their own friends and their own lives. Many fathers who do manage to have a successful career and a successful family life have one thing in common: they rarely have a consuming hobby, play many sports, or are actively involved in the community. These working fathers, like so many working mothers, seemed to focus a period of their life on just two main areas—their work and their children.

We all aspire to achieve something in life that goes beyond children. It is important for us to have a dream, but should it be done at the expense of those closest to us? Many people chase the dream, thinking it will benefit their family only to realize that the price of the dream is the family. How do we manage to find a balance between providing for the family's material needs while not neglecting the family's emotional well-being? Sure, money is important and it is great to be able to provide our children with material comforts and greater opportunities in life, but no amount of money can replace the time and attention children need from their parents.

Marriage and Parenthood – Time for a Change?

Most couples are getting married and having kids for different reasons than they did in the past. They are no longer getting married in order to have sex with the person they love and they are no longer having children as an inevitable consequence of having that sex. We might not think our parenting responsibilities are linked with our marriage commitments but for centuries marriage was the only socially acceptable domain of parenthood. This is no longer the case.

Perhaps under this new reality, marriage should be viewed as a legal/symbolic agreement between a man and a woman with procreation taken out of it. If we socially and mentally separated the institution of marriage from the institution of parenting, it may reduce the incidences where a marriage breakdown turns into a parental breakdown. Most parents rationally recognize that their commitment to their children extends beyond the breakdown of their marriage, but emotionally, in some ways, couples also see a marriage breakdown as an end to their responsibility to support their partner's role as parent.

Perhaps we can widen the separation between the institution of marriage and the institution of parenting by providing parents with a new parenting ceremony. The couple could make a public commitment promising that no matter what the outcome of their marriage they both agree to support to the best of their abilities each other's role as parent. I am not saying this would eliminate ugly custody battles. After all, getting married does not mean you will never get divorced. What it might do is help foster parental roles and responsibilities beyond just the relationship between the parents. Such a parenting ceremony might make parents more inclined to remember their commitment to their children and to each other as mother and father, even if they are no longer a couple.

The New and Improved Father – Charting New Territory
At the heart of the parenting battle is that dilemma that both mothers and fathers feel judged in their role as parent. We need to stop this father versus mother gender battle. All this judgement is based on some romanticized version of a "normal" family. There is no such thing as a "normal" family.

Fathers no longer have the exclusive role of breadwinner and provider and there is no longer a magical role for fathers just because they are men. Yes, being a father is far more complicated and challenging now than it was in the past but it can also be more rewarding and fun.

Some might say this is the worst of times for fatherhood but it can also be regarded as the best of times for fatherhood. No longer is the history of fatherhood being written for fathers. Instead, it is the fathers of today who are writing their own history. There are so few uncharted territories left on this earth that it might seem like there is nothing left to explore, but on a personal level, fathers are the new explorers. They and their children are on a voyage to discover and redefine what fatherhood is all about. What is even more exciting is that fathers of today are no longer allowing society to determine how they should or should not be involved and are deciding for themselves how they want to be involved. The opportunity now exists for families to find their own strategy that works for them and allows each of its members to access and enjoy all the different options and opportunities the family and the world have to offer.

SUMMER SOLSTICE
JOHN THE BAPTIST DAY
June 24th

Not many people know about a holiday called John the Baptist Day that falls on June 24th and coincides with the summer solstice holidays of days past. What makes the obscurity of this day strange is that it used to be one of the biggest and most widely celebrated of holidays. All over the world on the same night of the year, huge bonfires made out of very flammable wood (sometimes they were even soaked in tar or other locally available flammable substances) would alight the night. All over Europe, bonfires would be lit in valleys, on hillsides, and on mountain peaks to honour this momentous occasion. It must have been a beautiful site to go out on one of Europe's numerous lakes or rivers and see hundreds of fires on the hillside reflected another hundred times in the water. It was the equivalent of a continentwide fireworks show.

What is this summer solstice (or Midsummer Day as it was also called) really all about and why did people celebrate it? Summer solstice is the longest day of the year and therefore the shortest night of the year. It is the time of year when the sun reaches its climax and inevitably begins to make its journey back to longer nights and shorter days. It is hard to think of this day as the beginning of the decline of the sun, since it is at this time of the year when we are definitely feeling the sun's strength and power and hopefully will continue to feel it for a few months more. We inevitably realize, however, that these days will not last forever. Although it is a time of warmth, abundance, and fertility when the days are long and nature is at her peak, it is also the point after which the days begin to get shorter again and darkness increases. The sun has reached its height and is about to begin its journey away from the northern hemisphere towards the southern hemisphere.

The word *solstice* comes from the Latin word *sol stetit*, meaning, "the sun stood still." The sun takes this rest at only two times of the year—the summer solstice and the winter solstice. This is why the summer solstice was celebrated come sundown on the 23rd of June and all throughout the day of the 24th even though it falls on the 20th or the 21st. The length of the day remained at its height for three days until on the night of the 23rd when it would begin its journey back to the other half of the world.

One of the oldest summer solstice celebrations took place in ancient Egypt at the temple of Amen-Ra, whose foundations date back to about 3700 B.C.E. On the days of the summer solstice a beam of light would illuminate a sanctuary in the temple's interior for about two or three minutes during which the brightness would reach a peak and then begin to subside. This not only enabled the Egyptian priests and priestesses to calculate the length of the solar year with a high degree of accuracy but it also enabled them to recreate the yearly passage of the sun in one day. From the sun's darkest point at the winter solstice, to its rise throughout the next six months reaching its height at summer solstice, then to its inevitable decline back to its darkest point at the winter solstice.

No discussion of the summer solstice would be complete without mention of Stonehenge, which is located in southwest England. We seem to equate Stonehenge with the Celtic priests called Druids, but Stonehenge was actually built by pre-Celtic people around 2800 B.C.E. We know little of these pre-Celtic people because they were absorbed into the invading Celtic culture sometime around 1000 B.C.E. We do know that they built this huge monument in honour of the sun and the moon and they had an advanced understanding of astronomy. Astronomers have discovered over two dozen solar and lunar alignments these ancient builders of Stonehenge incorporated into its structure. Stonehenge is one of the most popular gathering spots for the few remaining modern-day summer solstice festivals.

This celebration of the sun's climax was one of the most ancient universal festivals. The custom of lighting bonfires at midsummer was practiced from Iceland and Scandinavia to the middle of Europe, the Mediterranean, and all the way to the Caspian Sea. It was also common in North Africa, which is surprising since the Islamic calendar is a lunar calendar and independent of the movements of the sun. This means it is likely that North Africa's midsummer festivals probably predate their adoption of Islam. It did not stop there, summer solstice rites were also indigenous to the first peoples of North and South America.

So what happened to these solstice festivals? Winter solstice traditions can still be found in modern Christmas and New Year's celebrations but the ancient summer solstice rites have virtually disappeared. In Europe, there are only a few countries— mainly Sweden, Finland, and Lithuania—where the bonfire at summer solstice is still alive. As mentioned earlier, Stonehenge also sees some action come summer solstice but nothing that would compare to the gatherings of days past. In North America, it is only so-called "new age" groups who continue with the bonfires and celebration that marks the point of the sun's height. Although ancient summer solstice festivities were more popular and even more flamboyant than winter solstice festivities, Midsummer Day has become the forgotten and neglected festival. Why?

In ancient China, the solstices were believed to be occasions that brought the divine masculine and feminine principles into ritual focus. The ancient Chinese believed that at sunrise on the winter solstice, the yang (masculine) principle was born and commenced its six months of ascendancy. It is more than a coincidence, I am sure, that Christians also celebrate the birth of the divine male child at the same time of year. The summer solstice ceremony, on the other hand, celebrated the earth, the feminine, and the yin forces. According to ancient Chinese Taoist traditions, the most propitious time to worship the Earth Goddess was the early morning of the summer solstice and the ancient Chinese observed the summer solstice in ways designed to stimulate the earthy, feminine, yin forces.

That there is no longer any corresponding Midsummer Christian festival of the divine feminine is a good indication of the degree of imbalance between the masculine and feminine principles in our society. We tend to make the mistake of thinking masculine means male and feminine means female. Our masculine and feminine principles represents attributes inherent in all humans and are not in the least limited by gender. The problem is we have not been allowed to develop these attributes in ourselves in a way that truly reflects who we are or who we want to be.

The feminine traits of birth-giving (both in terms of life and creative energy), nurturing, patience, and wisdom are undervalued and equated with weakness, passivity, and subservience. While the masculine traits of protection, defence, and decision are overvalued and equated with strength and action. Our ability to develop our personal attributes has been limited by society's need to relegate us into the either/or category instead of the more balanced approach of developing all these attributes so we can call on the best one for a particular circumstance or situation.

When we really come down to it, which character attributes fall under the feminine umbrella and which fall under the masculine umbrella are really quite arbitrary. They could easily be switched around and it would not matter in the least. We have all spent too much time and energy comparing attributes and trying to come to a conclusion on which is better than the other. What we fail to see is that each character attribute has its strengths and weaknesses and where one may be appropriate in a certain situation, it would be wholly inappropriate under a different circumstance.

We all have our biases on which attributes we feel a stronger affinity for—they are what help us develop our personality. I have always had a preference for decision and action over patience and contemplation. I associated patience with passivity and with the idea of passivity came the idea of watching the world pass me by. I had no intention of waiting around and allowing others decide how I should live my life; I just went ahead and did what I wanted to do. While this resulted in some fun experiences, a lot of the negative consequence of my actions could have been tempered had I valued the feminine quality of letting some things go their course rather than having to undertake the masculine action of directing the course. If we always jumped into action in every situation, we would fall into the trap that Maureen Murdock, author of *The Heroine's Journey*, calls "premature ejaculation"—moving to action too soon because the pain and anxiety of waiting to see what would happen would be too much to bear.[1] If we immediately jump into action, we don't allow situations to resolve themselves or allow ourselves the therapy of thinking through our actions before we undertake them. It seemed to me my options were either/or and I never realized you could do both. It may very well be that wisdom and enlightenment is based on knowing which attributes to call upon under certain circumstances.

Instead of encouraging such lofty ideas of wisdom and enlightenment, society taught that men were limited to the masculine traits, lest they be labelled effeminate, and women were limited to the feminine traits, lest they be labelled unfeminine. Instead of each man and woman developing these traits within themselves, they expected their partner to compensate for them. Men asked women on dates because it was unfeminine for a woman to take action for herself, leaving her at home waiting on a phone call dependant on someone else to make the first move. Guys always had to deal with the anxiety of making the first move and risking rejection. Since we have been limited in our ability to develop these traits within ourselves, in many ways we fail at being complete human beings. Not only is our society imbalanced, so are we as individuals.

As our society slowly begins to give credit and value to many of the feminine traits that were looked down upon in the past, people are beginning to recognize and remedy their masculine/feminine balances. Maybe the time has finally come for summer solstice to be pulled out of its resting place in the old attic trunk, brushed off, and finally invited to the party again.

According to James Frazer, author of *The Golden Bough*, ancient healers also viewed the summer solstice as the time of the year when the feminine earth energies were at their height. It was considered the day of all days for gathering the wonderful herbs by means of which you could combat fever, cure a whole host of diseases, and guard yourself and others from sorcerers and their spells. It was believed the healing properties of herbs reached their greatest power just before dawn on the 24th of June with the morning dew still on them.[2]

Modern Western medicine tends to scoff at the medicinal value of herbs even though many of our modern-day drugs are based on the active ingredients in plants and herbs. In pre-industrial Europe, most healers were women and the lore passed down from healer to healer included methods for collecting and extracting natural herbal painkillers, tonics, antispasmodics, and remedies for fevers, indigestion, contraception, and infections. In the twelfth century, a woman named Hildegard of Bingen wrote a manual of herbal and other natural healing methods. In her manual she listed the healing properties of 213 plants and 55 trees. Thankfully, she took the time to write her knowledge down in a book and her work now forms the basis for modern Western herbalism.

Shortly after its publication, the Inquisition began and during the next four centuries, millions of women and men were executed for "witchcraft"—this often simply meant having the knowledge and engaging in the practice of traditional ways of healing, or failing to live and act as instructed by the powers that be at the time. What was saved by the survival of Hildegard's manual is likely only the smallest remnants of the ancient knowledge of the medicinal value of herbs that must have existed prior to the Inquisition. With these healers, the knowledge and experience of the healing properties of many plants also went up in smoke.

One of the herbs believed to be especially potent at the time of the summer solstice was the herb now known as St. John's wort. It blooms around the time of the summer solstice putting out masses of bright yellow flowers that resemble the sun. In keeping with this sunny disposition, many swear by its use as an antidepressant. Another herb called verbena was supposed to be gathered after sunset on Midsummer Eve and was believed to strengthen the nervous system and relieve stress. Other summer solstice herbs were mugwort, chamomile, geranium, thyme, rue, chervil seed, giant fennel, and pennyroyal.

When Christianity spread throughout Europe, the midsummer festival on June 24th became St. John the Baptist Day. Christian symbolism was attached to many of the pre-Christian rites associated with this day. The bonfires were renamed "St. John's Fires" since John's mother said she would notify her cousin (who we now know of as the Virgin Mary) of his birth with a bonfire in front of her house. In addition, since Jesus once called John "a bright and shining light," religious officials saw this as good enough reason to say the bonfires now symbolized John instead of the sun. The herbs that were picked on this day for their healing powers were renamed St. John's herbs.

The religious festival of John the Baptist had importance for all the Catholics of Europe, but it was especially popular for those in France when on the night of the 23rd of June the King of France would himself light a huge bonfire. With the French colonization of Canada, the French brought the festival to the New World, but by then it had become a very pious and solemn religious event. By the end of the nineteenth century and the beginning of the twentieth century, the annual festival was starting to be celebrated with more fanfare, and processions and festivities were held in Montreal and Quebec City. In 1925, the Quebec legislature, seeing this day as a vestige of French culture in an increasingly English-dominant society, declared the 24th of June a provincial holiday.

As French nationalism increased in the second half of the twentieth century, John the Baptist Day became linked to nationalism rather than religion. In 1976, the Parti Quebecois (PQ) swept into power on a platform of having a referendum that would allow people the chance to vote on whether to stay part of English-speaking Canada or try their hand at a new French-speaking country. In 1977, the PQ saw *le jour de fête de Saint-Jean Baptiste* as a wonderful opportunity to drum up some nationalism and June 24th became its official national holiday (same as July 1st in the rest of Canada and July 4th in the United States). The name of the holiday was changed to *La Fête Nationale,* and twenty-five years later, June 24th is still the biggest street party in Quebec—and Quebec still hasn't decided if it wants in or out of Canada. In most other Catholic parts of the world, John the Baptist Day festivities are at most marked by a special mention at mass or the odd bonfire kindled every now and again.

But who was this guy named John the Baptist anyway? John was Jesus' second cousin. John's father was a Jewish preacher by the name of Zachariah and his mother, who was named Elizabeth, travelled all over Judea with her preacher husband. Elizabeth was unable to get pregnant despite numerous animal sacrifices and prayers. Then lo and behold, by the time Zachariah was almost senile and Elizabeth was post-menopausal, an angel appears to Zach and tells him that Elizabeth will soon be with child. Zach is so surprised by this meeting and announcement that he loses his voice and has to explain his encounter with the angel Gabriel to his wife in writing. Elizabeth, upon reading what was in store for her, laughed in hysterical disbelief and then wept herself to exhaustion. The story goes, much to Elizabeth's surprise and pleasure and to the shock of fellow villagers and family, Elizabeth did indeed become pregnant and John was the result. A few months later, Elizabeth's cousin Mary announced that she was also visited by Gabriel and was told she was to become pregnant with a divine child sent upon her by the Lord himself.

Not many people believed Mary became pregnant without sexual intercourse and since her husband, Joseph, was of an advanced age people's tongues started wagging about the greatest sin a wife could commit. No, it wasn't murder but adultery rather. Mary decided to move in with her cousin Elizabeth since people in that village were apparently more willing to buy the story. According to Christian storytelling, John was born on June 24th and Jesus was born six months later on December 25th.

Since Zach was already into his seventies when John was born and Elizabeth was on in years as well, John's parents died when he was still young. After his parent's death, John spent his twenties living as a hermit, clothed in camel's hide and surviving on wild honey and locust beans. When John turned thirty he began to preach about the unfairness that God's chosen people should be in bondage to the pagan Romans. He spent years preaching by the River Jordan about the coming of a Messiah who would free all those who repented their sins and allowed John to baptize them in the River Jordan. John's talk about a Messiah and freedom was not an anomaly, there were preachers travelling throughout Judea berating people's heathen ways and promising all sorts of freedoms and miracles if they would just change their ways. The Romans tolerated all these preachers as long as they kept their preaching confined to simple spiritual matters. If, however, any talk of rebellion or insurrection against Rome was voiced then the preacher had better run for the hills and not let the Roman authorities catch him, lest he become just another head on a stick.

John, for some suicidal or idealistic reason, did not stick to the safe stuff. He instead saved his most venomous words for the Roman appointed ruler of Galilee, Herod Antipas and his wife Herodias. Herodias was previously married to Herod Antipas' brother Herod Philip and had a daughter with him named Salome. When Philip had died, Antipas divorced his wife and married Herodias. To us this seems like something out of a soap opera and can make for some awkward (and interesting) family reunions but it was not unusual for that time and culture. There was a Jewish priestly law that encouraged the brother of a deceased husband to marry his sister-in-law. John the preacher considered this arrangement incestuous and condemned what he considered their whorish ways. John must have had a decent following among the peasant folk that made Herod fear a backlash if anything happened to John because his preachings only landed him in the dungeon rather than a beheading as would have been the norm.

John refused to stop his preaching and he continued to spew venom on Herodias and Herod even from the dungeon. While he may have been a thorn in the side of Herod, he really got Herodias' goat. She did not understand why her husband did not just behead him. Despite repeated attempts to get John lopped, Herod would not do it. Along comes Salome into the story. Considering she is an obscure biblical figure who is mentioned in only a few lines of the bible, it is quite ironic the impact she has made on our minds and imaginations. Her infamy comes from causing John's execution.

At his birthday party, Herod asked Salome to dance and promised her anything in his kingdom if she would oblige him. She must have been quite the dancer or he must have been quite intoxicated. Whatever the reason, Salome consulted with her mother on what she should ask for. Herodias, seeing her opportunity, encouraged her daughter to ask for John's execution. Whether Salome was a reluctant participant, an active participant, or perhaps simply doing something to help or protect her mother, we will never know, but it would not be unheard of for a daughter to try and protect her mother from venomous words. Since it was considered the right of royalty to decide who lives and who dies, the calling of an execution would not have been an unusual occurrence.

After her dance, Salome is said to have asked for John to be beheaded. According to the story as we know it, Herod was very reluctant to go along with that request and would rather have given her half his kingdom instead of John's head. But since he did promise her anything she wanted, he decided to save face, honour his promise, and off came John's head.

The Bible never says which dance Salome performed but it seems to be ingrained into our minds that she performed the Dance of the Seven Veils. This idea is due to the play called *Salome* by Oscar Wilde published in 1894. The Dance of the Seven Veils was considered to be very erotic. The dancer would cover her body with seven veils and as she danced she would slowly remove each of the veils. Nowadays we think of it as a mere striptease when the Dance of the Seven Veils actually depicts the myth of the goddess Inanna's descent into the underworld to visit her sister, Ershkigal.

Ershkigal was mourning the death of her husband so Inanna decided to visit her and provide her with some comfort. Inanna starts out on her journey by putting on all her royal paraphernalia and leaves instructions with her loyal servant Ninshubar to wait for three days and if she has not returned to call upon the Gods for help. As she tries to enter the underworld, she discovers that her sister will not give her any special treatment; she, just as every one else, must give up one of her possessions at each of the underworld's seven gates. Each of these possessions (which are represented by the veils in the dance) are symbolic of the illusions we use to protect us in the earthly world.

What these illusions are is open to individual interpretation. Some people think they represent the seven deadly sins; others think they represent our earthly illusions of class, position, ego, wealth, that we use to enhance our survival and position; others think they represent the "isms" (such as racism, sexism, ageism) that limit our humanitarian evolvement; and still others think they represent the seven different chakra points in the body. Whatever they are, they apparently have no place in the underworld. We have to go down there naked, as just us, and hope it is enough to see us through.

Unfortunately for Inanna, her sister does not give her a warm welcome and is not touched by her attempt to provide comfort. Ereshkigal instead fixes her sister with the eye of death and speaks the word of wrath against Inanna, striking her dead and hanging her on a hook to rot. Why the rude welcome, you might ask. Well it is because the descent into the underworld is never easy and/or safe. It has inherent risks associated with it and most would be glad to avoid it at all costs. This descent into the underworld, however, is something every one of us must at some stage of our life endure.

Yes, we can put it off and hide from it or deny its existence but the journey is more or less inevitable. It may be precipitated by the death of a loved one, an illness, a divorce, a loss of meaning in life, abandonment by a loved one, a near-death experience, disillusionment with society, and umpteen other reasons including the mid-life crisis or the empty-nest syndrome. These are all situations and circumstances we would like to avoid and would be happy to dismiss from our lives. But try as we might, they will have their day.

And so, just as seasons have their cycles, people have their cycles too. We can't always be accommodating, pleasant, fun, patient, loving, and cheerful—we are human. We all go through a period in our lives when our perception of ourselves and the world is lowered. It is an inevitable part of human existence. Some people are so scared of this phase; they will try to do anything to get out of it and at any cost. Then there are people who recognize it as an inevitable phase and see that the healthiest course is to allow themselves to experience this lowering of the mood so they can turn inward and figure out what is causing them to feel down. Only by doing this will they be in a position to determine the best course of action.

This is no easy journey, and bravery is essential. It also requires people to develop their masculine and feminine attributes because they will need to call on both of them to help themselves get in and out of the underworld. If they only rely on their masculine attributes, they will never make the journey because they will be so busy doing things and taking action that they will never take the time to turn inward and face themselves. They will remain in a state of perpetual motion and cut themselves off from their emotions so that they can remain in a state of limbo, thinking everything is okay. Meanwhile, no matter what they do, they still cannot stop themselves from feeling disquieted, disillusioned, or outright depressed. If they rely only on their feminine attributes, they will be able to begin their journey and will have an easier time gaining access to the underworld but they risk not being able to make the decisions and take the actions needed to get themselves out of the underworld.

We might think that allowing ourselves to experience these thoughts and feelings leads us to this state called depression, but this is because we see depression as an unnatural and unacceptable state to be in. But if we saw it as a difficult yet inevitable phase in our lives, and one designed to help us address certain issues and circumstances in a way that will lead to our long-term fulfilment, then we might be more inclined to prepare ourselves and make the journey. Yet most of us would rather have the instant gratification of eliminating these unpleasant disturbing thoughts and feelings and continue on with our lives without disruption.

There is little difference between making the journey and not making the journey in terms of depression—both leave us feeling depressed. If we take this risk, however, we have the potential for getting out of this phase of our lives instead of just remaining in the limbo of disillusionment and depression because we were unwilling or afraid to take the chance. This place of limbo is not an easy place to be in, especially for a long time, and people inevitably look for an escape from this state via constant busyness, emotional denial, or increasingly popular antidepressants.

Our worst fear in undertaking the journey to the underworld is that we will be destroyed just as Inanna was left to rot on a hook. And, unfortunately, there is usually a point when we will feel like all has been lost and everything indeed has turned to shit. But remember that Inanna was not foolish enough to go down there without some support. She left her loyal servant with instructions on what to do in the event she did not return, and we would be wise to follow that example. Whether we call on some part of our inner strength we did not know we had or rely on an outside guide or helper to help us make our journey back (or, even better, a combination of both), we need to make sure we have done everything we possibly can to ensure we have something to help us if we get stuck down there.

When Inanna fails to return in the prescribed time, Ninshubur goes around to try and enlist the help of the gods. She goes to Enlil, the highest god of sky and earth, and to Nanna, the moon god and Inanna's father, but both refuse to meddle in the ways of the underworld. But does Ninshubar give up? No, she goes on to Enki, the god of waters and wisdom, who sets about rescuing Inanna when he hears Ninshubur's plea.

From the dirt under his fingernail Enki makes two creatures, neither male nor female (they could even represent our masculine and feminine attributes). He gives them food and drink to bring to the underworld and tells them to grieve with Ereshkigal. Since they are so small they manage to slip unnoticed into the underworld and practice a feminine form of therapy on Ereshkigal. Women repeatedly complain about men's quickness in providing them with solutions to frustrations or problems they are having with family or work instead of just listening and empathising with sympathetic feedback. Allowing a person the time to voice their frustrations or pains and playing the so-called passive listener is a feminine characteristic that has not been highly valued. Enki's little creatures don't try to convince Ereshkigal that she should let Inanna go or that she should just get over her grief and get on with it; they do not provide her with solutions, they simply listen to her lamentations and repeat them back to her with empathy and compassion. She is so grateful for what they have given her that she blesses the creatures and offers them any gift they desire. They ask for Inanna, feed her food and water given to them by Enki, and they all make their way back to the earthly realm.

I know it might seem strange to start out talking about summer solstice only to end up on the topic of depression. What could one possibly have to do with the other? Summer is not depressing— the snow is all gone, food is plentiful, and the sun warms the earth and our lives. It is a time of abundance, warmth, and fertility. What could one of the easiest and most joyous times of the year for the northern hemisphere have to do with depression?

Sure, the sun is at its height and daylight has reached its annual supremacy, but that passes. The sun has begun its journey to the southern hemisphere and we are on our way from the supremacy of the day to the supremacy of the night. Our ancestors found meaning in the irony that at the peak of light and life at the summer solstice there is the seed of death, darkness, and decay. For many cultures, it must have seemed that the sun was now on its journey to the underworld and they wanted to do everything in their power to encourage the sun to come back from there as well.

We in the modern world know the sun has not sunk into the underworld but is actually making its transitions to its height in the southern hemisphere and will inevitably make its way back to us. While we might have more knowledge of the sun's cycles than our primitive ancestors, they might have had a better understanding of the meaning of these events as a reflection of the cycles of their lives. Winter solstice as a time of darkness signalled a time of death with the hope of rebirth. The summer solstice signalled fulfillment of that rebirth tinged with sadness since we know that fulfillment must end.

If you think back to the best day of your life, you will probably remember that at some point during that day you felt a tinge of sadness when you realized this day and this feeling would come to an end. We don't want it to end because we would love for it to last forever, but we realize it can't. It would be nice to forget about gravity sometimes too. Try as we might, we know what goes up must come down. By accepting this as an inevitable cycle, however, we can more fully appreciate the heights of our lives. We can also better deal with the lows because we know that they don't last forever either. Hope will rise again. Life becomes a bit easier and a tad more exciting when we realize nothing is ever totally gained and nothing is ever totally lost.

LAMMAS

August 1st or the first Monday in August

Many of you are probably asking, "Lammas, what the hell is Lammas?" On the first Monday in August there is a public holiday whose origin few know anything about. In Ireland, Scotland, and Wales, it is simply called a bank holiday (as if the banks really need a holiday) and in Canada it is called a provincial holiday (as if that tells us anything). In the United States it has been done away with completely and there is a real dry spell in long weekends between the 4th of July and Labor Day. Back in our agricultural days, however, there were two harvest festivals: one before the harvest, called Lammas; and one after the harvest, which we now know of as Thanksgiving. It makes sense to us that there would be a post-harvest festival. Being fortunate enough to have produce to carry one through the long cold winter is definitely something to celebrate, but why a pre-harvest festival?

On the Celtic calendar, Lammas—along with Beltane (May Day), Samhain (Halloween), and Imbolc (Groundhog Day)—was known as one of the four major Celtic festivals. August 1st was the first day of autumn for the Celts. This might seem premature to those of us who are still intent on enjoying the hot hazy days of August, but back in the time of our agricultural ancestors this date would mark the beginning of the hardest work they had to do—the backbreaking work of bringing in the harvest. Their time to enjoy the heat and warmth of the sun was over. Getting all of the harvest in and packed, stored, cooked, salted, etc., before winter was a race against time; no wonder they felt the need to celebrate before all the hard work began. First, they wanted to thank their deities and/or fate that there was actually something to harvest. Second, I'm sure it didn't hurt to have one last fling with summer to provide the enthusiasm to get through the hard work, until it was time to finally celebrate again.

This pre-harvest feast of Lammas was originally called Lughnasadh by the Celts, who named it after their Celtic deity Lugh, the god of light. Many people think this early August celebration was to celebrate Lugh's death but he did not actually die (mythically speaking) until the autumnal equinox. On closer inspection of the Celtic legend, it is not Lugh's death this festival celebrates. Instead, it marks the feast Lugh decreed be held each year at the beginning of the harvest season to honour his foster mother, Tailtiu. Tailtiu was the Mother Goddess to the Fir Bolg, the first human inhabitants of Ireland (the pre-Celtic people of Ireland). After the defeat of her people by the Tuatha Dé Danaan (the Celtic conquerors), she was obliged to clear a vast forest for the purpose of planting grain. She died of exhaustion in the attempt. It is really her funeral and sacrifice that was being celebrated with games, competitions, and feasts.

One of the common features of these "Tailtean games," as they became known, was the "Tailtean marriages." They were rather informal marriages that lasted only a year and a day (until next Lammas) at which point the couple would decide to continue the arrangement or stand back-to-back and walk away, thereby dissolving the marriage. Parish priests did not approve of this marriage arrangement and usually did not perform these trial marriages. They were instead performed by a poet, bard, or priest or priestess of the old religion and were very common up into the 1500s. According to Madeleine Pelner-Cosman in her book *Medieval Holidays and Festivals*, a prize (a pig) was offered to any of the couples who had decided to stay together after their trial period and could convince others they had not regretted their marriage in any way, at any time. As if!

Several sets of couples would stand in front of twelve people who made up the jury. A judge would preside over the contest and ask the couples questions. He would present absurd scenarios of "what if...your spouse brought the dog into the dining area, which scared the cat, who jumped onto the table and turned over all the banquet food spilling it all over the guests, was there no jealousy, joylessness, or jangling (loud complaining)?" The couples would then compete to come up with the most creative story explaining their gladness that their wonderful, considerate, compassionate partner caused this unfortunate incident. The pair deemed worthy to "bring home the bacon" was the couple considered to be the most imaginative liars.

As Christianity made its way to that part of the world, the festival became less about feasts, games, and battle competitions and more about getting people into church. The festival known as Lughnasadh became known as Lammas, which isn't such a bad thing considering how hard its predecessor was to pronounce and spell. The name Lammas is thought to have come either from "Lugh-mass"—mass held in Lugh's honour; or from "loaf-mass"—since it became the ritual for loaves made from the first ripe grain to be placed on the church altar as a sacrifice on the first Sunday in August. To this day, people in parts of the British Isles still decorate churches with sheaves and corn dollies on Lammas. Another theory is that the name derived from "lamb-mass" because it was the time of year when worshippers would bring a live lamb as an offering to the church. The old tradition of paying honour to the gods and goddesses of the harvest by setting aside some of the freshly harvested grains in honour of them eventually evolved into giving it to the landlord. Lammas became one of the four traditional times of the year for tenants to pay their rent.

Bread has always played a part in harvest celebrations. Pre-harvest festivals were not only a Celtic tradition. Early to mid-August marked the beginning of the harvest season for all of Europe and there were many rituals and celebrations held to honour the generosity of the gods and goddesses for allowing a bountiful harvest. If the harvest wasn't bountiful, then there was a lot of appeasing and sacrificing to do in order to make up for whatever people had done to displease the deities that brought about this punishment.

Another day linked with old pre-harvest festivals is the Feast of the Assumption of the Blessed Virgin Mary, which is a public holiday still celebrated all over southern Europe on August 15th. The Virgin Mary requested that all the apostles be present at her death, and the message reached them miraculously even though they were scattered all over the world. Only Saint Thomas, who was late, missed the final gathering at her deathbed. Arriving after the funeral was over he was so filled with grief and regret that he asked to have the tomb reopened so he may have one last look at her body. The tomb was empty—proof they took to mean that rather than being subjected to the usual process of decomposition, Mary's body had been assumed into heaven where it was reunited with her soul. In Christian art, Mary's body is usually shown being carried up to heaven via the power of angels. Since Christianity did not consider her to be divine in her own right she did not have the power to do such a thing on her own. Jesus, on the other hand, was always portrayed rising up to heaven by his own power and divineness.

Even though this day is supposed to commemorate Mary's body's ascent to heaven, it has kept much of its pre-Christian harvest rituals and symbolism. Many Assumption shrines show Mary wearing a robe covered in ears of grain. It is also likely that the date was chosen to replace the old Greek and Roman harvest festival in honour of the Great Goddess of the Grain, who was known as Demeter in Greece and Ceres in Rome (she is the origin of our modern word *cereal*), held at this time of the year. It is still customary in the Orthodox Catholic Church for worshippers to make offerings of new wheat to churches on August 15th.

In many agrarian communities, the first and the last harvested sheaf of grain was treated with special honour. In pre-Christian times, a priest or a priestess, who would lament its death and thank it for its sacrifice by paying honour to the goddess who allowed it to grow, would cut the first sheaf. In Christian times, this honour went to the father of the household.

The whole family in their best clothes would go out into the fields; the father would take off his hat and take a sickle to the wheat and turn it about his head clockwise thanking God for his blessings. The last sheaf of grain was constructed into a corn dolly or a corn maiden. This figure was braided into the form of a woman and represented the harvest spirit. The doll was often saved until the spring when it was ploughed back into the field to consecrate the new planting and ensure a good harvest. In other traditions, the corn dolly was fed and watered throughout the winter then burned in the fires of Beltane to ensure a continuation of good growth. The tradition of making corn dollies is still practiced in Europe at this time of year and in North America during Thanksgiving.

Lammas was also the traditional time for craft festivals. The craft guilds would elaborately display their wares throughout the country. It makes sense that this would be market time. Since bartering used to be the currency of choice for most of our medieval ancestors, this was the time when the artisans could barter their goods for food that would help get them through the winter. If they had held their fairs earlier in the year, nobody would have had much to trade, and if they had held it later in the harvest time, few would have had the time to attend in their rush to get their bounty put away before winter came. The atmosphere of these markets must have been very similar to the fairs and corn roasts that take place throughout the country at this time of year.

Many of us do not go out and cut our own grain anymore, and the closest we get to a pre-harvest festival ritual is writing our grocery list. Even though we may not celebrate a harvest festival called Lammas anymore, this time of year still celebrates our harvest—the rewards of our hard work over the past year—it is just that our harvest has changed. August is our prime vacation time and we probably think our vacation time originated at this time of the year because it is perfect for camping and backyard barbeques and to otherwise enjoy the short hot season. For those who live and work on farms, however, August is not vacation time. Their vacation, if they were lucky enough to get one, would be in the dead of winter if there were nothing to do. August is the time for hard work.

Back in the time of the industrial revolution, many men left their farms to go work in factories in the city, leaving their wives and their children to do the work on the farm. Many of the factory workers who were lucky enough to still own or lease land would have needed to take time off of their factory jobs to go back to the farm and help with the harvest. Factories knew they were going to lose at least half their workforce in August and many smart ones would have closed down or significantly reduced production in order to deal with this loss of labour.

Although there is a dry spell in long weekends for the United States, August is still our harvest time where we reap the rewards of our long year of hard work and take our two weeks' vacation. While this is not a bumper crop, considering our European and Australian counterparts get six weeks of vacation, it is still better than nothing and we intend to enjoy every moment of it.

While we still have the nice warm nights, there is a little tinge of the coolness of fall poking through every once in a while. Just enough to remind us that summer and our vacation will not last forever and we had better appreciate every moment. It's not that we are in denial that it will end—we realize it will—but we have gotten to the point where none of that matters anymore. We do not waste our energy lamenting the passage of time; we do not let our fears of the coming winter, the year of work, or even what the future holds cloud our thoughts. This is our time and we are not going to let the past or the future interfere. For at least one time of the year, we make sure we get the chance to experience what it is like to truly live in the present. Now that is a harvest worth celebrating.

LABOUR DAY
The first Monday in September

We take for granted that there is a day of the year dedicated to paying respect to the workers of the world, and we know it has not always been easy for them. We learn in school how atrocious the working conditions were during the Industrial Revolution. Men, women, and children made to work sixteen hours a day; at least six days a week; no safety protection; no compensation should you get hurt on the job because the owner of the factory was trying to save a buck or two; no protection from harassment and physical or sexual abuse; and to top it off, no one seemed to think the worker deserved anything more. This wasn't as bad as slavery because they were at least paid and could look for another job, but other than that, it wasn't all that different.

What is not part of the school curriculum is how we got from the working conditions of the Industrial Revolution to where we are now. Did the factory owners finally realize they were treating their workers little better than livestock, were greedy, and saw the error of their ways? Intuitively, we realize this was not the case. Workers had to fight to get the rights we now take for granted. It was not an easy fight and many people paid a heavy price to achieve the rights that workers have today. Why isn't this fight taught in schools? Wouldn't that be a logical follow up to all the lectures on the working conditions during the Industrial Revolution? It would, but I guess the people in charge of school curricula were worried about the possible repercussions of teaching teenagers how to fight authority. Teenagers are always being told what to do and what not to do and adults represent (or at least they like to think they do) the authority figure. If workers had successfully refused to accept conditions they believed were unacceptable, maybe teenagers could successfully take on some of the conditions imposed on them that they deemed unacceptable.

When people realize they can band together to fight something they view as unacceptable, it makes them feel they have more control over their lives. The best way to disempower a person is to take away their sense of control by making them think, *this is the way it is and this is the way it will always be and there is nothing I or anyone else can do about it*. Well, the fight for labour rights shows us that in spite of those who benefit from a meek populace that thinks this way, people working together can make a difference.

But do we think of all that stuff when we think of Labour Day? No way; we think about what we want to do on the last long weekend of summer—or the last weekend of freedom before school—and where we want to go and with whom we are going to spend it. There is too much fun to be had to waste time on the plight of workers during the Industrial Revolution. But Labour Day is not only a last fling with summer; it is also about the fight with authority and society for control of your own life. That is a fight worthy of at least one day out of the year.

Although Labour Day is celebrated on the first weekend of September in the United States and Canada, most of the rest of the industrialized world commemorates labour's fight on May Day, held on May 1st. May Day as a day for labour began in 1886 when national strikes were held all over the United States and Canada on May 1st, calling for an eight-hour day. Why did May 1st lose favour in North America? Well, here is another story we are not taught in schools, but what a story it is!

These nationwide strikes did not have a happy ending. In Chicago, where over eighty thousand workers marched in support of shorter working hours, the police, getting a little too keen on their need "to serve and protect," let loose on striking workers, killing two of them and wounding several others. A few days later, another demonstration to protest police violence was held in Chicago's Haymarket Square. During the protest, a bomb exploded and seven police officers and numerous protesters were killed.

To this day, the question of who threw the bomb has not been answered. Did a protester throw it at the police? Did a police officer drop it in his haste to retreat from workers that were charging at him? Either way it happened, figuring the old eye-for-an-eye form of justice, someone had to pay the price. Authorities arrested and tried eight people considered to be leaders of the local labour movement in what was the O. J. Simpson trial of the nineteenth century. They were not tried on exploding the bomb, or even murder, since six of them were apparently not even at the protest. Instead, they were tried for conspiracy since labour unions were illegal at the time. All were found guilty—four were hung; one committed suicide in jail; and the remaining three were freed years later when public opinion turned against the trial.

A few years later in 1889, a congress hosted by world socialist parties was held in Paris, France. They voted to support the U.S. labour movement's demand for an eight-hour day and declared May 1st an international working-class holiday. Many American unions did not want to be linked to the May 1st date since it was so closely associated with the Haymarket Martyrs (as the eight people mentioned above became known) and many unions facing an anti-union climate wanted to distance themselves from the whole incident. The movement for a national Labour Day did not stop, however, and labour unions were lobbying state governments for a designated day for labour throughout the late 1880s and early 1890s. In September of 1892, union workers in New York City took an unpaid day off (a nice way of saying a strike) and marched around Union Square in support of a national day for labour.

In 1893, a strike against the Pullman Company broke out when the company was caught in the nationwide economic depression. Orders for its train sleeping cars plummeted and George Pullman was forced to lay off hundreds of employees. Those lucky enough to be kept on had to endure wage cuts even though the company housing rental payments that were deducted directly off their paycheques remained the same. Their take home pay plummeted and workers walked out demanding lower rents and higher pay. The American Railway Union (ARU), led by Eugene V. Debs, came to the workers' cause and railway workers across the nation boycotted trains carrying Pullman cars. Some rioting, pillaging, and burning of railroad cars ensued and the strike instantly became a major political hot potato.

U.S. President Grover Cleveland, dealing with many very nervous railroad executives and interrupted mail trains, declared the strike a federal crime and taking no chances deployed twelve thousand troops to put an end to the strike. Violence erupted and two strikers were killed when U.S. marshals tried to disperse a crowd in Kensington (near Chicago again). But with thousands of troops at his disposal, President Cleveland quickly brought the strike to an end. Eugene Debs went to prison, his ARU was disbanded, and Pullman employees had to sign a pledge promising never to unionize again.

With the use of such heavy-handed tactics, the appeasement of the nation's workers became a top political priority. Who says governments can't accomplish things quickly if it is to their benefit? In the immediate wake of the Pullman strike, legislation for a national "day for labour" was rushed through both Houses of Congress, the President quickly signed the bill and Labour Day was born.

In an effort to distance it from the more radical Labour Day of May 1st, the date chosen for the "day for labour" holiday was the first Monday in September. Not all unions were quick to accept the new date and many saw it as a cop-out where governments could make speeches regarding all the gains that had been made and make no mention of all the gains that were thwarted or that needed to be made. These "more radical" unions continued to celebrate Labour Day on May 1st but their efforts to do so were continually undermined.

At the turn of the century, the difference between the two holidays was exaggerated and the press emphasized May Day celebrations as being for militants, hooligans, and immigrants, while Labour Day in September was for the hardworking American worker. It became more and more difficult for unions and groups to get permission to hold marches on May Day. In 1919, police and anti-labour rioters attacked May Day participants, and many socialist and communist party offices in numerous cities were destroyed. As time went on, the increased anti-communist senti-ment and fear of socialist revolution in America led to the media labelling May Day as a "commie" event and between the Cold War and McCarthyism, May Day labour events dwindled to nothing.

We realize Labour Day for us today has little to do with the struggle of labour to achieve some level of personal control. Progress has been made, and while it is a pity that the people who fought the good fight and paid a price for it probably never lived to see the rewards of their efforts, we should say thanks to them—not only for improving the workplace but for improving society as well.

Many people would say we have forgotten all about the mere worker. We should seriously take into account how the world changes and how labour unions are not exempt from change. I find it very interesting when unions buy into ownership of the companies they work for. I think it is still too early to judge how well that strategy works and I can see how there might be some conflicts of interest, but I have to admit that I find it a very inter-esting change and one that I hope will be positive for all those involved.

Although we all make the mistake of taking for granted the gains made in the labour movement, we would be wrong to say that Labour Day no longer plays a role in reminding us about the role of the worker. It is just that the demands of the average working-class person have changed. Labour Day has become more about our leisure, and if there is one recurring demand on the lips or minds of the average modern worker it is for more leisure time.

Essentially, leisure time is really about finding a better way to balance our work life and our personal life. Perhaps our modern-day worker's protest is to take advantage of this last weekend of summer to remind ourselves of our priorities in life. While our employers would like nothing better than to have us think we live to work, Labour Day reminds us that the reverse is true—we work to help us live. Keeping our priorities in check helps us pursue what is really important to us and this gives us personal control over our life. Labour Day reminds us that we never hear anyone on their deathbed say, "I should have spent more time at work."

Friday the 13th

A black cat crosses your path, you walk under a ladder, you break a mirror, so what!? What does this have to do with bad luck? Well, a lot if you let superstitions hold some sway over you, and let's face it, most of us do. We would like to believe we are not superstitious but most of us would be surprised to realize the role superstition has in directing our actions and behaviours. Have you ever been extra careful around a mirror for fear of having seven years of bad luck; knocked on wood; been afraid not to pass on a chain letter; avoided opening an umbrella indoors; blessed someone when they sneezed? Chances are you have. It is nothing to be ashamed of, but you may be curious as to how these superstitions originated.

One of the best-known superstitions is the fear of Friday the 13th. What is it about these two factors that gave this day such a bad reputation? After all, it is even the subject of a hugely successful horror movie series! Although Friday the 13th is not a genuine holiday in the traditional sense, it does cause an awful lot of commotion. Almost all of us have used the date of Friday the 13th to explain why something went wrong. Because of its erratic schedule of appearances every year, there will never be fewer than one, nor more than three days on which Friday the 13th falls and there is no particular month in which it creates its excitement and anxiety. Examples of the taboos for both Friday, but especially the number 13, are endless. Everything has a story, so to get to the root of this superstition we must first look at the two elements separately. As it turns out, both Friday and the number 13 have a fascinating past.

Friday

What could possibly be so bad about Friday? Most people look forward to Fridays because it is the end of the workweek for many, hence the ever popular slogan TGIF (Thank God it's Friday). Friday's ill-fated day in superstition is believed to result from the belief that it was the day of the week on which Eve tempted Adam and Christ was crucified. Among the activities viewed as taboo to do on a Friday are: setting sail on a ship; moving house; beginning any new work; writing a letter; knitting; starting a journey; and, believe it or not, cutting your nails. In both England and America, the custom to hang criminals on a Friday earned it the reputation of Hangman's Day. It would seem, however, that one activity offers some promise on a Friday: sleeping. The thought is, if on Friday morning you wake from a wonderful dream and you want it to come true, you merely have to tell a family member about the dream that morning and— presto—it becomes a reality.

Not everywhere does Friday have this dubious distinction. Friday just after noon is the time for Islam's prayer Jumu'ah and on this day after sundown is the Sabbath of the Jewish lunar calendar. Scandinavian pagans, Hindus, Scots, and Germans consider Friday to be a most propitious day for a marriage or courting because they consider it a day favouring fertility. Their more favourable view of Friday is a result of its history before Christianity.

Friday is the only day of the week named after a woman. The others pay homage to either male Scandinavian gods (Woden, Thor, and Tiu) or celestial bodies (Saturn, Sun, and Moon). Friday was named after the Norse goddess Freya who represented fertility and sexual love. She is strongly associated with spring, birds, and cats. Romans named the day *dies Veneris* after Venus, their own version of the Freya goddess. Ancient fishermen did not set sail on a Friday out of respect for Freya because she was considered Goddess of the Sea. This tradition is still practiced by many sea folk today, except their reason for not setting sail on a Friday is now due to a fear of bad luck rather than reverence for an ancient goddess. To make the history of Fridays even more interesting, it turns out fish were often eaten on Friday as fertility charms in honour of Freya. It seems the Catholic habit of eating fish on Friday was pagan in origin.

The Number 13
The number 13 has an even more special place in superstition. The fear of its effects has even been given a scientific name, *triskaidekaphobia*. (More specifically, a fear of Friday the 13th is called *paraskevidekatriaphobia*.) You've probably have noticed that buildings avoid numbering the thirteenth floor and airlines avoid using the number in tracking their flights and in numbering their seat aisles. The number 13 is rarely found on offices or shops and even less frequently on the rooms of a hotel or guesthouse. Apparently, in some cities, such as Paris, scarcely a single house exists with that ill-fated number. They get around this by designating the property twelve bis (twelve twice).

The main reason given for 13's ill omen is its association with the Last Supper, attended by thirteen—Christ and the twelve Apostles. According to tradition, if a gathering of thirteen is held, one member of such a group—the first to rise from the table—will die before the year is out. Reportedly, an organization in France exists solely to provide a last-minute party guest so thirteen people are never at a dinner party! Again, as was the case for Friday, not all cultures share this dislike for the number 13. For example, the Chinese have no aversion to the number 13 because its literal meaning is "alive." Their taboo number, however, is 4 because it sounds like the word for "dying" or "death."

Two conflicting calendars were in use during most of the early Christian era in Europe. The Church's official solar Gregorian calendar and their later solar Julian Calendar (the one we use today) and the peasant's unofficial lunar calendar. When the number 13 is examined in a little more depth, a strong pagan and even stronger female pattern emerges. Much of paganism centres around Mother Nature and within this context the moon is vital. The moon and female fertility are also closely connected.

The connection is so strong that it is generally believed calendar consciousness developed first in women because the natural menstruation of their bodies correlated with the moons phases. The lunar cycle is approximately 29.5 days long. With 12 moons in a year, that would make the year 354 days long, 11 days short of a solar year. Without artificial lighting at night to mess things up, the human female fertility cycles tends to become synchronized with the moon's phases with the fertile time coming at the full moon. According to a study published in the December 1987 issue of the journal *Human Biology*, women whose menstrual cycle coincided with the moon's cycle tended to be most fertile.[1]

Friday the 13th

So when Friday is combined with the thirteenth day of the month, we have a double dose of pagan symbolism and female significance. Up until the Middle Ages when pagans continued to celebrate symbolic pagan days, Friday the 13th was thought to be especially lucky because it combined the goddess' sacred day with her sacred number. As a result, Friday the 13th was a celebration and festival day for many pagans.

While the New Testament rationale for the dislike of both Friday and the number 13 is often used as the explanation for the bad luck associated with Friday the 13th, it is, in my opinion, a little superficial to create such a strong taboo, especially when one takes into account the pre-Christian history of both Friday and the number 13. After all, the Last Supper was certainly not the only time Christ gathered with his disciples and there were always thirteen of them. No one suggests these earlier events were unlucky. Based on the historical view of 13 at the time of Christ, it consistently shows 13 as a lucky number, and this probably played a role in determining how many disciples there should have been. The same goes for the New Testament rationale for the dislike of Fridays. The crucifixion of Christ is the foundation of Christianity—this holy day is afterall called Good Friday.

What seems to appear, after one reviews the history, is that the modern taboo of Friday and 13 (and especially the two together) is the result of the Christian manipulation of earlier pagan beliefs.

This is far from the only pagan celebration day Christianity has changed. Both Christmas and Easter are old pagan holidays, where many of the pagans' traditions continue to be practiced, only without the understanding of their true origins. But Friday the 13th is different from these other plagiarized holidays because the Christians turned what used to be a day of celebration of female strength and power into a day of fear and taboos.

In trying to understand why they would try to do such a thing, one should keep in mind that for the first couple of hundred years after Christ and the birth of Christianity, Christians were forced to practice their religion in secret for fear of persecution. This may explain why they linked their Christian celebrations with pagan celebrations to avoid being discovered. Their inability to practice Christianity in public during this time probably resulted in their dislike of pagan religions, the dominant religions during the time of the Christian persecution. In turn, this led to their persecution of pagan celebrations when Christianity became the dominant religion.

It is not surprising that this took place. After all, most conquering nations try to destroy or change the customs of the conquered. This is, however, inconsistent with the teachings of Christianity where tolerance and "turning the other cheek" is encouraged. In actual practice, the Christians of the time realized they would be much more successful in suppressing some pagan celebrations if, instead of trying to eliminate the holiday, they focused their energy on changing the meanings behind the celebrations to those of Christianity. Other holidays, such as Friday the 13th, they suppressed by convincing people that unfortunate things would happen to them if they celebrated on those festival days.

We need to take the history of Friday and the number 13 into account and look at them afresh in order to see them in a more positive light. Australians have one interesting way of looking at this day. Sales of Australian lottery tickets go through the roof on Friday the 13th. Maybe they try to defy the odds by taking on the jinx of bad luck, or maybe they realize that things are rarely what they seem on the surface. Ideas, superstitions, and cultural symbolism exist for numerous different reasons, but it is usually based on the evolution or manipulation of beliefs or customs predating them. It is important for us to question the origin of these customs to make an informed decision on whether we want to partake in the custom, challenge it, or just ignore it.

HALLOWEEN
October 31st

Halloween is a mutt—a wild and rambunctious mutt. No pure-bred ailments and neuroses for this holiday. Our present-day Halloween is a mix of many different cultures: a Celtic and Roman harvest/death festival; a Christian death festival; and a contemporary spooky, crazy, playful, and commercialized death and candy festival. Sometimes the mutt that is Halloween is not considered worthy of adult appreciation and it is left for kids to play with. It hasn't always been this way and it need not be now. Halloween has a lesson for all who choose to indulge in its history and symbolism, or who just take the risk of befriending it.

Many different cultures have had their chance to influence and mould this holiday to suit their own purposes and wishes. This may have changed the holiday over time but it hasn't dampened its richness of symbolism and rituals. Halloween is not considered one of the major religious holidays so its flexibility allowed it to change and serve many different centuries, cultures, and even age groups. It has something for everyone; all we need to do is recognize that.

Most parents consider Halloween a time when they have to spend a lot of money on candy and junk food and also deal with their own sugar-pumped kids. Kids thank their lucky stars that

Halloween exists, where else would they get a candy stash lasting them a month or two? Next to Christmas, and maybe even more than Christmas, it has become very much a kid's holiday. Although kids have taken over the festival, it serves more purpose than just to secure a candy stash for kids. Halloween is a death festival, and no matter which century, culture, religion, or age group, death is something everyone has to deal with.

In our present society, we try to protect our children from the idea or prospect of death. Rationally, we realize we cannot isolate them from the death of a family member, friend, pet, or animal found on the side of the road or in the woods. Especially when we consider most fairy tales and Disney movies perpetuate the topic of death to children. Try as we might to gloss over death and deny its existence, our subconscious knows it is out there waiting. While most people claim public speaking is their greatest fear, death often runs a close second. All things considered, it is the greatest unknown and we fear what we don't know, and denying death's inevitability only makes us more afraid. Halloween can help people deal with these basic fears and apprehensions regarding death and can serve to bring the fear of the unknown to the surface in a fun and rather playful way.

Many cultures celebrated their festival of the dead at this time of the year. It seems logical they would as this time signifies the death of nature. Perhaps this is why so many of these celebrations focus on thankfulness, providence, and honouring of the dead. Fall, in its colourful display, is Mother Nature's last dance. All the crops have been harvested, the air grows colder, and darkness descends.

The Celtic Festival of Samhain

Halloween has its origins in what was called Samhain (pronounced *sow-en*), a Celtic harvest/death festival. *Samhain* means "summer's end" and that is what this festival signified: a change. Samhain was also the eve of the Celtic New Year. Their year ended and began at sundown on October 31st. With our current Western view of the world of good/bad, ending/beginning, birth/death, all being total opposites, it might seem strange having a New Year festival and a death festival rolled into one. But to the ancient Druids, Celts, and Anglo-Saxons it seemed perfectly appropriate since they viewed time and life as cyclical. Their gods and goddesses each contained positive and negative attributes; death was followed by rebirth and life, and all endings were also new beginnings. Although a death festival, Samhain was not a sorrowful festival. Death was considered as only a part of the cycle of life.

Samhain was thought to expose a crease in time—a fissure between summer and winter, between life and death, between the old year and the new year. The ancient Celts believed an invisible layer existed that separated the world of the living from the world of the dead. At sundown on the last day of the year, this veil grew to its thinnest point, allowing the living and the dead to make contact with one another. It was a time to honour and welcome dead relatives, show hospitality, tend gravesites, open burial cairns, and release the dead spirits and air out the inside of their tombs. Souls of the dead were thought to revisit their relatives to experience a bit of the warmth and security of the hearth. Apparently, spirits of the dead wanted familiar surroundings and loved ones around them before the long dark winter, which I guess was dreaded just as much by the dead as it was by the living.

The Romans Commeth

In the first century B.C.E., the Roman Empire invaded and conquered Britain and Gaul (France at the time). Although the Romans were unable to eliminate the Celtic festival of Samhain, they did bring with them their own festivals and customs. The Roman harvest festival of Pomona, which honoured their goddess of fruit and trees, was also held in late October. This was where Halloween's association with apples and nuts and fortune-telling comes from. Pomona was also the time when the summer stores were opened for winter consumption. Over the years of Roman rule, the customs of the Celtic Samhain and the Roman Pomona festival mixed, becoming one major autumn holiday. The Romans had their own festival of the dead called Feralia. It was originally celebrated on February 21st and its main purpose was to give rest and peace to the departed. Elements from Samhain and Feralia eventually began to merge because the two festivals were very similar to one another.

Although the Romans did not seem to care much about the merging of the Celtic and Roman festivals, the Roman emperors began to feel threatened by the Druid religion. According to Edna Barth in her book *Witches, Pumpkins, and Grinning Ghosts*, the Roman emperors were disturbed because many of the Roman soldiers who remained in England adopted the beliefs and the customs of the Druids and the Druid religion's influence was becoming a bit too popular in Rome. In the year 61 C.E., Seutonius (the Roman Governor of Britain) ordered the destruction of all the groves where the Romans stated the Druids performed human sacrifices. The Druid religion was banned and the Druid priests were systematically murdered. This, however, did very little to curb the celebration of Samhain among the country people.

Was Human Sacrifice Really a Part of Samhain and the Druid Religion?

Now we are brought to the question we can't help but ask: Did the Druids really sacrifice people at Samhain? Scholars are sharply divided on this account with about half believing it took place and half doubting its truth. Most of the so-called "evidence" proving the Druids practiced human sacrifice is based on what their enemy, the Romans, told people of the Celts' practices. Both Julius Caesar (d. 44 B.C.E.) and Tacitus the Historian (d. 120 C.E.) told numerous tales of the Celts' human sacrifices. An objective historical account can't really be derived from that.

The claim of the practice of human sacrifice has long been used by certain powers as one of the most common strategies to villanize groups perceived as threatening. The Hebrews used it on the Canaanites and the Phoenicians to justify taking over their lands. The Romans used it not only on the Celts but also on the Christians, who, as it was suggested, used to get together to sacrifice and eat little babies. This helped the Romans in justifying the persecution and torture of the Christians.

According to Nora Chadwick in her book *The Celts*, other than the Roman accusation of Celtic human sacrifice, there is little archaeological evidence in Celtic stories and mythology to justi-

fy the claim of human sacrifice. The only reference to human sacrifice in Celtic literature or mythology relates to an evil race of
giants said to inhabit portions of Ireland before the coming of the
Celts. These giants demanded the sacrifice of two-thirds of the
corn, the milk, and every first-born child of the Fir Bolg (the
fourth wave of invaders to Ireland). The sacrifice was supposedly offered on the occasion of Samhain. Incidentally, it is said the
practice was ended in the battle of Moy Tura, which also took
place and was won on Samhain. According to J. C. Cooper in his
book *Dictionary of Festivals*, traces of human sacrifice ceremonies
may possibly be interpreted from the Welsh Black Sow ceremony
in which everyone ran downhill shouting "the black sow take the
hindermost," with the last being the victim. The black sow represented the spirit of cold and death.

The claim of Celtic human sacrifice might only be propaganda, or it might have been an embellishment of the practice of animal sacrifices, which was a big part of Samhain. Being pastoral
and agricultural, the Celts correlated their seasons according to
the needs of their cattle and sheep rather than simply the agricultural season. The year was divided into summer, when the herd
was led out into far off hills, and winter, when they were brought
back home again.

When the flock was brought back for the winter, it was also a
time of killing the livestock thought to be too weak to survive the
winter or even just to cull their numbers so there would be
enough feed to last the winter. Animals were slaughtered and
their meat smoked and/or salted down for the winter. The
Samhain slaughter was used as an opportunity to express thanks
to the pagan gods and goddesses for the harvest, the hope of an
easy winter, and the rebirth of nature in the spring.

Even in the off chance the Celts did practice human sacrifice,
let's be careful not to be too self-righteous and label them barbarians and demons. As Nora Chadwick points out, "the Romans
themselves had only just abolished human sacrifices not long
before Caesar's time." During the Roman persecution of the
Christians, Christian religious leaders encouraged their followers
to sacrifice themselves for the cause of Jesus Christ. I think this
falls pretty close to the concept of human sacrifice. Imagine how

parents would feel today if the leaders of a new religion encouraged their followers to sacrifice their lives for the good of the cause. It can be argued human sacrifice is still practiced by almost all cultures via war, massacres, genocide, and terrorism.

The Christians Cometh

Once Christianity took control of the Roman Empire in the fourth century, it declared a holy war upon paganism and all the rites and symbols associated with it. The rites and worship of the Celtic religion were outlawed and all those who continued to practice it were persecuted. The Christian missionaries tried this strategy for centuries and still had little success in suppressing Samhain and converting the Celts. The Christian Church then tried to eliminate the Druidic celebration by offering All Saints' Day as a substitute. In the eighth century, the Church moved All Saints' Day, which was originally held in May, to November 1st, the date of the festival for Samhain. The reason the Church needed an All Saints' Day was because it honoured so many martyrs and saints by assigning them each their very own day. Eventually, the Church ran out of days because there were fewer days on the calendar than saints to venerate, so it decided to incorporate them all into one day.

As hard as the Catholic Church tried to discourage the Celtic people from practicing the ancient Samhain rites, over the centuries the rituals, dances, feasts, and fires of the Samhain celebration still retained a more loyal and enthusiastic following than the Christian replacement of All Saints' day. The Catholic Church recognized it needed something less abstract and cerebral than a holiday honouring saints nobody really knew or cared about. In the eleventh century, the Christians claimed the continued practice of the heathen Samhain festival for the Church by creating another festival called All Souls' Day, which was offered for people to pay respects to their ancestors. All Saints' Eve (October 31st), All Saints' Day (November 1st), and All Souls' Day (November 2nd) turned into the festival of Hallowmas. The eve of October 31st was called All Hallows' Eve. Eventually, laziness won out (as it always does) and the word became Halloween.

Ironically, as the Christians established All Saints' Day and All

Souls's Day in an attempt to eradicate the heathen death festival of Samhain, it did so by virtually duplicating it. The pagans believed that honouring their long-departed ancestors would pacify the dead so they would not haunt the living. The Christian celebration of All Souls' Day is based on the belief that offering prayers for the dead will benefit the souls of the departed. By making the two festivals so similar, the Christian Church was able to hold onto its newly acquired "followers" by allowing people to continue a festival they had celebrated long before becoming Christians.

Dining with the Dead

The tradition of welcoming the dead home to the hearth on Samhain can be considered the origin of the trick-or-treating custom. It was believed homesick spirits would be out on Samhain Eve roaming the mortal world and were likely to seek the warmth of the hearth fire and the company of their living kin. Families placed small offerings of fruits and vegetables outside their homes to show their hospitality and retain the favour of passing spirits. Many families would lay out the dinner table with their best china and a huge feast of food before retiring for the night. It was considered a bad omen if the dead did not partake of the feast. People believed this meant they had lost the favour of dead relatives who were believed to serve as their advocates in the spirit world. Who actually partook of the feast is anyone's guess, but a possible explanation will be provided a bit further along. Many families would also leave out toys and sweets as an offering for their dead children who were thought to return to them each year on this night.

This tradition of dining with the dead continued into the Christian Hallowmas tradition and reached elaborate heights even in non-Celtic Europe, especially in Southern Europe. In Sicily, children were led to believe that the Halloween gifts they received (usually sweets and small toys) were brought to them by the spirits of dead ancestors who rose from their graves each year on this day to mingle with their living descendants.

In the fourteenth century, many Christian families also prepared feasts for the dead, but on All Souls' Day. One of the most notable would take place in the city of Salerno, Italy. Families would prepare an elaborate banquet and lay it out upon a finely decorated table. Then all the family members would leave for church where they would spend the entire day praying and singing hymns to the dead. The unattended house was deliberately left open to enable the spirits to enter and feast upon the offering of food and drink. It was taken as a bad omen if the dead refused to partake of the family's hospitality, for this indicated the dead's disapproval and the possibility that they would work evil deeds on the family. The only spirits known to partake of the feast, however, were thieves and beggars from the surrounding villages. It seems like a fair trade to me; the family who offered the feast got what they wanted and the beggars and thieves probably got their best meal of the year. Regardless, the Catholic Church banned this custom in the fifteenth century because it felt threatened by its pagan undertones.

Demon Worship

Halloween is a holiday that has fallen victim to numerous misconceptions and many people today regard it as a night of demonic mischief, doing evil deeds, and unholy terror. How did Halloween become viewed as something so evil? The answer lies somewhere between our own natural human fear of the coming cold of winter, death and the unknown, and the negative stereotypes and propaganda created and exaggerated by the early Christian Church and perpetuated by some modern-day Christian anti-pagan groups and the media.

During Samhain, a Celtic deity known as Lord of the Underworld gathered together the souls of all the people who died during the previous year and had been confined in the bodies of animals while waiting for their chance to enter the underworld. With their sins expiated they would be free to begin their journey to the Celtic underworld of Tir-nan-Og where they were awaited. Keep in mind that the Celtic Lord of the Underworld was not considered anything similar to our Christian understanding of the Devil and the Celtic underworld was nothing like the Christian perception of hell. The Catholic Church created the Devil and hell image in an attempt to get the public to believe all the people practicing this paganism were evil emissaries of the newly devised Devil figure.

By the Middle Ages, the Christian Devil had been assigned horns, a forked tail, and cloven hooves and resembled a mixture of many of the pagan fertility gods, including the Greek Pan and the Celtic Cernunnos. These fertility gods might have been mischievous at times but in no way were they linked with evil. With the advent of Christianity, the gods of the old world were bastardized into the demons of the new religion in the Church's early efforts to convert the pagan population. As a result, the horns, hooves, and goatish beards of the old horned gods became the attributes of the newly Christian-designed Devil.

After continuing to try without much success to rid the public of their liking for Samhain, the early Christians tried to convince people these Samhain spirits of the dead were actually delusions sent by the Devil. Due largely to their efforts, the Celtic underworld eventually became associated with the Christian hell. Furthermore, the concept of honouring the benevolent spirits of loved and departed relatives gradually gave way to fears about evil spirits and witchcraft. Even though the Christians tried to pass off All Souls' Day as a replacement for Samhain, there was a catch. On All Souls' Day, prayers were offered to the dead and the dead fell into one of two groups. Those who died as Christians were now in Heaven and posed no threat to the living. People who were not Christians at the time of their death were in purgatory or hell and, according to Christian thought, these souls returned to earth on All Hallows' Eve to haunt the living.

Although some cults and Devil worshippers may have adopted Halloween as their "favourite" holiday, the association of Halloween with the Devil did not grow out of Celtic beliefs but rather through Christian misrepresentation. We should not allow the original intention of Halloween, as a day to honour and pay respects to dead relatives and ancestors, to become forgotten and it certainly should not be considered evil.

How Halloween Came to North America

Halloween was not widely observed in North America during the first few hundred years of settlement. It was only when the potato famine hit Ireland in the 1840s resulting in thousands of Irish immigrating to North America that Halloween made its way over. The majority of the Irish were relatively recent converts to the Catholic religion when compared to the English and French and they still retained many of their old customs and rituals. The pagan symbolism of these customs and rituals ruffled the feathers of many religious groups in North America at the time. Halloween's popularity, however, especially among the young, outweighed the chagrin of the Puritan and Christian opposition and numerous early attempts to have the celebration banned proved futile. This opposition to Halloween continues to this day in the United States. Every year before Halloween, schools across North America end up rehearsing this recurring debate over the possible negative influence on children of celebrating this holiday.

There is no doubt people want to protect kids but we have to ask what it is we are protecting them from. Is it the fear that celebrating Halloween will turn these little angels into Devil worshippers, or are we trying to protect them from the idea and understanding of death and its place in the world? As is usually the case with kids, they often understand far more than adults give them credit for. Halloween might be better used as an opportunity to talk about the changes of seasons and the changes of life. But let's not make it all morbid and serious, Halloween is about dealing with these issues in a fun and joyful way. Kids have made this holiday something for themselves and it is unlikely they will give it up easily. So let's join them in the celebrations and try and protect them by making their fun and games as safe as possible.

Halloween in Mexico and Central America

Halloween as we know it, with bobbing for apples and trick-or-treating, is unknown in the countries of Mexico and Central America. There was little emigration of Irish to these countries and so the Celtic influence was nil or minimal. These countries, however, do celebrate a festival of the dead that is a blend of the Catholic All Souls' Day festivity and remnants of the tradition of the local Mayan and Aztec festival of the dead practiced amongst the local population prior to the arrival of the European Christians.

In Mexico, the festival of the dead, instead of beginning at sundown on October 31st like Samhain and Halloween, begins at midnight on the first of November. The Day of the Dead is a joyous fiesta and national holiday honouring the dead. Cakes and cookies in the shapes of skulls and skeletons are displayed in nearly every bakery window on this day and street vendors can be found selling dancing skeleton marionettes, coffin-shaped jack-in-the-boxes containing skeletons, skeleton-shaped jewellery, and other macabre items. Bread of the dead (*panes de muertos*) is a traditional food that blends this holiday's association as a harvest festival as well as a festival honouring the dead. The bread, shaped like people or animals, is decorated with brightly coloured icing or with coloured sugars. According to tradition each loaf represents a dead soul.

It is also a custom for Catholics in Mexico to prepare a special supper for the spirits of deceased loved ones. The food is set out on the best tableware and blessed by prayer. After a period of time to allow the dead to partake of the food in spirit, the non-dead family members happily feast on what remains. It is also a tradition at this time of year to tend the dwelling place of dead relatives. Graves are tended and cleaned, flowers are left, candles are lit, and hymns are sung. Another custom associated with the Day of the Dead is to scatter yellow marigold petals from their ancestor's burial site to the front door of the family's house. According to folklore, the yellow marigold is a flower of the dead. It was believed to possess magical qualities offering protection against evil spirits.

Holiday Symbolism
Fire
Fire was a big part of the Samhain festival. The Celts would extinguish all fires and relight them from a common source. The symbolism of this act was replicated for the Christmas yule log. There were three main reasons for big bonfires on this day. The first was a purely practical matter. There was always a lot of vegetable matter and refuse that needed tidying up and burning before the winter. Second, it was done to scare away any dead

spirits intending harm. Apparently, benevolent spirits would be glad to hang out around the bonfire and join in the festivities with the living but dead souls intending harm were afraid of the fire and would stay away. Third, cattle and sheep were driven between the bonfires. Driving the animals around the bonfires was supposed to get rid of any evil influences but it also served the practical purpose of fumigating the animals against parasites. The smoke from the bonfire would kill many of these parasites, which was important since they weaken the animals. And since animals were brought into close proximity of each other for the winter, parasites were more likely to spread to entire herds thereby increasing winter mortality rates and maybe even wiping out entire flocks.

Although they are not a part of the North American Halloween tradition, bonfires are still common in Ireland and form the main part of the British celebration of Halloween called Guy Fawkes' Night.

Apple Bobbing and Divination

The inclusion of apples and nuts and their use in divination during Halloween is a remnant of the Roman harvest festival of Pomona. Nuts were symbols of life and fertility, being the seed from which new fruits grow. Apples were also considered fertility symbols and were used in divination. In some parts of England, Scotland, and Ireland, the night of October 31st was called Nut Crack Night. Young people put pairs of nuts named after certain couples into the fire. If the pair burned to ashes together it meant the couple could expect a happy life together. If they cracked or sprang apart it meant quarrels and separations were inevitable. If only it were that easy to find the right mate.

Dunking for apples was a marriage divination. The first person to bite an apple would be the first to marry in the coming year. In another game known as Snap Apple, boys would take turns trying to bite an apple turning on a rope at the end of a stick. The first to succeed would be the first to marry. Girls pared apples on Halloween trying to keep the peel in a single unbroken strip. They would then swing it three times around their head and throw it over their left shoulder. The fallen peel was supposed to fall into the shape of the initial of their future husband's name. People would also peel apples to see how long their life would be. The longer you could peel the apple without breaking the peel, the longer the person's life was destined to be.

Costumes

It is believed people dressed up on Halloween as spirits, ghosts, witches, and blackened their faces with the bonfire ashes to protect themselves. The Druids believed the spirits of the dead returned to the world of the living each year. Most of these spirits were benevolent, some were mischievous, and still others possessed a genuine evil streak and delighted in bringing harm upon vulnerable humans. For protection, the white-robed Druids who led the sacred rites of Samhain would wear masks upon their faces to disguise themselves as spirits. They believed this would trick the wandering dead into thinking they were also spirits rather than flesh-and-blood mortals. The general populace, fearful of being recognized by the spirits of their ancestors, would also disguise themselves, often by wearing clothes of the opposite gender. This confusion was apparently enough to prevent their lonely ancestors from taking them back to the otherworld for company. I guess the spirits' IQs must have decomposed along with their bodies.

It wasn't only from the dead that people needed protection; more often than not, the living posed a far greater threat. During the time of the Druid and pagan persecutions and during the days of witch hunts, people wishing to practice the old customs and religions wore masks and dark robes. Their attire concealed their identities from the spying eyes of those who might turn them over to the local witch hunter.

Trick-or-Treating

The true origin of the custom of trick-or-treating goes back to the Samhain festival when offerings were left out for wandering spirits. Then some time in ninth-century Scotland, a custom called "souling" appeared. On November 2nd (All Souls' Day), poor Christians would walk from village to village begging for soul cakes made out of square pieces of bread with currants inside.

For each soul cake a person received, they had to promise to say prayers on behalf of the dead relatives of the donor. Originally, costumes were not part of the "souling" custom, but after a few centuries, instead of just beggars going door to door, children started to get in on the custom. Then in the seventeenth and eighteenth centuries when religious persecution reached its zenith, many people took to wearing masks and robes as a means of protecting their identity while still taking part in the festivities. This custom became known as "guising." Dressed to look like ghosts, ghouls, and other supernatural beings, these "guisers" would parade from house to house begging for apples and nuts, singing traditional folk songs, and filling the night with songs and dance to intimidate malicious spirits and keep all evil at bay.

Another reason these guisers might have wanted to keep their identity a secret was because many of them, if refused a treat, would retaliate with a prank of some sort. These tricks often looked like supernatural forces were behind them. A favourite prank used in rural areas involved dismantling a piece of farm equipment and reassembling it on a rooftop. Other common pranks included doors being unhinged or latched so they could not be opened. Brooms and other tools left outside were found in the most unlikely places such as on top of the church steeple. Bells were rung continuously. Chimneys were filled with turf so the smoke would back up into the house. Bottles were smashed so it sounded like windows were broken.

Taking advantage of the belief that all matter of supernatural and inexplicable things were supposed to happen on this night, children and youths also saw this as their opportunity to play pranks on people who were unpopular. The message behind these and other attacks on domestic security was the importance of exercising caution at this time of year when everyone is vulnerable to the forces of death and destruction. Just as Samhain was the time for people to secure their farm and animals against the coming winter, Halloween pranks served as a reminder that nature would not be kind to those who failed to take the necessary steps to prepare themselves for a long cold winter.

The actual phrase "trick-or-treat" is considered to be American in origin and it dates back to the 1930s. In 1930s North

America, people who offered candy to Halloween visitors were genuinely concerned with protecting their homes against pranksters.[1] But the custom of playing tricks on Halloween declined in popularity over the years, and by the 1950s, most children had no idea what kinds of pranks they were supposed to play—they just wanted the candy.

All was fun and games until the 1970s and 1980s when the tampering of Halloween candy became a part of Halloween. The fear of pins, needles, and razor blades being found in trick-o-treater's loot became an issue. Kids used to be invited into homes and served homemade treats in the form of freshly baked cookies and caramel-wrapped apples. Nowadays, kids wait on the outside doorstep and are followed door-to-door by their parents who scrutinize their candy stash with their x-ray vision. Which brings us to the question: Is this tampering a real threat or an urban legend?

In all the instances of tampering with Halloween candy that could be traced back to a specific person, it was always some kid intent on freaking out his little brother or his parents or anyone else who would pay attention to him with his idea of a neat little holiday prank. Pranking has always been a part of Halloween and most of the kids who engaged in tampering never really consider the ramifications of their actions. The urban myths surrounding kids innocently biting into their candy stash and onto a razor blade are greatly exaggerated.

According to many of the media reports that come out around Halloween, you would think every neighbourhood had some poor little innocent tyke getting their mouth cut open by a razor blade in his chocolate bar. Joel Best and Gerald Horiuchi, authors of *The Razor Blade in the Apple*, tracked about eighty cases of sharp objects in food incidents from 1959 onwards and found more than 75% of reported cases involved no injury and detailed followups in 1972 and 1982 concluded virtually all the reports were hoaxes concocted by the children or parents.[2] Only about ten instances culminated in even minor injury, and in the worst case, a woman required a few stiches. In the aftermath of the 1982 Tylenol tampering murders, there was a sudden jump in the number of Halloween treat tampering the likes of which had never been seen before, or since.

That whole year, not just Halloween, was a bad year for the tampering of foodstuffs and medicines.

The tales of some evil madman handing out poisoned chocolate bars to all these adorable little kids dressed in their costumes has been around for decades. The thought is a frightening one and it is sometimes enough to stop parents from allowing their children to go out trick-or-treating. Many parents take their little ones to parties instead of door to door. This is ironic considering the only incidence of Halloween poisoning having the slightest smidgen of truth to it is the case when fifteen children and one adult became ill after eating candy and cakes supplied at a school Halloween party. Some newspapers reported that angel dust (PCP) was found on the food and others stated all tests for drugs turned up negative. Whether this was a true Halloween poisoning or a random case of food poisoning we still don't know. Every other incident which was thought of as a random Halloween poisoning turned out to be an act targeted at one particular child, an accidental poisoning, or a death caused by something other than poison.

Halloween is about facing up to our fear of death and that is why I think these urban myths have so much sway and influence over us. It is a pity that kids and parents have to deal with the fear of tampering and poisonings but we should keep in mind the reality of this fear. This is not the first time, nor the last, where we are worried about something happening to us that is very unlikely. It makes us feel more secure to worry about dying in ways we are very unlikely to die because then we feel we have more control over our life than we really do. Kids have a far greater risk of getting hit by a car as they cross the street to go to school than they do of being hurt by tampered Halloween candy.

I remember the most wonderful thing about Halloween for me was not only the candy (okay, I admit it was mostly the candy), it was also that feeling of owning the street and the night on Halloween. Everywhere outside you saw teenagers, kids, and their parents walking around and woe to the fool who was stupid enough to drive their car over 20km per hour down the street. The streets and the night belonged to people—more important, to kids—on Halloween and it was wonderful and empowering.

Jack-O'-Lantern

The tradition of carving the jack-o'-lantern is well over two thousand years old. The origin of the jack-o'-lantern can be traced back to Ireland where hollowed out turnips rather than pumpkins were carved with faces to serve as handheld lanterns. They were used not only to help light the way for those travelling the dark roads on Halloween but also to scare away mischievous or evil earthbound ghosts. It is believed faces were carved in the turnips to give the jack-o'-lantern the look of a head. The Celts believed the head was the most sacred part of the human body for it housed a person's immortal soul.

The phrase "jack-o-lantern" was used to describe the mysterious phosphorescent lights that sometimes appear in swamps, bogs, and marshlands after sunset. This mysterious phenomenon is called will-o'-the-wisp in the United States; corpse light in England; foxfire in Ireland; and witch fire in Africa. This natural phenomenon is caused by methane gas produced by the decomposition taking place within the swamp but it is understandable how its eerie glow can strike fear into people. It was believed to lull people into a hypnotic state causing them to try to find the source of the light, thereby bringing them into the heart of the swamp where it was likely they would get caught in the bog, be unable to escape, and were never heard from again.

The curious name of the jack-o'-lantern appears to reflect the Church's early efforts to link Halloween and its pagan customs with the fearful Christian Devil. Jack is another name for the Devil, especially in England. According to European folk legend, the mysterious jack-o'-lantern light is a wandering soul that has been turned away from both heaven and hell and is condemned to spend eternity earthbound, restless, tormenting, and scaring humans. This belief comes from an old Irish folktale that attributes the invention of the jack-o'-lantern to a stingy, nasty, drunkard named Jack.

Disliked by everyone, Jack was in his usual pub drinking alone on All Hallows' Eve when the Devil appeared in front of him to claim his doomed soul. He talked the Devil into having a last drink with him before taking him to hell. Upon finishing his drink, Jack informed the Devil that he was too broke to pay for the drink. He asked the Devil if he would be kind enough to change himself into a sixpence to pay for the drink and change back to his true form afterwards. The Devil, who in many other stories seems to have a real naive streak, went along with the idea. As soon as the Devil transformed himself into the sixpence, Jack snatched the coin from the tabletop and deposited it into his coin purse, which had a silver latch in the shape of a cross.

Rendered powerless by the cross, the Devil was trapped and very furious with Jack. The Devil made a deal; if Jack would set him free, the Devil promised to give Jack another year. The Devil kept his promise. And Jack, realizing he had a new lease on life, at least for a year, decided to mend his ways. For a time, he was good to his wife and children and tried to make amends with his fellow villagers, attend church, and be charitable. But as the memory of his close call with the Devil diminished, his patience with this new way of life soon ended and Jack slipped back into his old ways.

The next All Hallows' Eve, the Devil, who had been looking forward to this time, approached Jack again and demanded he accompany him. Jack, being quite the swindler and not keen on spending the rest of eternity in hell, tried to pull another trick on the Devil. Jack distracted him by pointing to a nearby apple tree, trying to convince him an apple was just what the Devil wanted. Jack offered to hoist the Devil up on his shoulders to reach it. Why the Devil would fall for this when according to all the stories I heard he could be or do anything he wanted, I don't know, but I like the story because it gives the Devil more character. You have to find such naivety or stupidity (it all depends on the way one looks at it) endearing. Anyway, the Devil fell for Jack's trickery again. When Jack had the Devil hoisted up in the tree, he quickly took out his pocketknife and carved a cross in the tree trunk. The Devil, who was downright angry and humiliated this time, promised Jack another ten years of peace if he released him. Jack, on the other hand, insisted the Devil never bother him again. The Devil agreed and was released.

About a year later, Jack's body gave out on him and he died. He tried to make it up to Heaven but, of course, those doors were closed to him. He then tried for hell. The Devil, still angry and humiliated, told Jack he was not welcome in hell and threw a piece of lighted coal from the fiery pit of hell at him. Jack put the piece of coal in a turnip and created a lantern. He used this lantern to illuminate his way as his lonely restless spirit wanders the earth in search of a final resting spot.

Before making their way over the Atlantic to the New World, the Irish did not have time to pack their turnips but luckily they found something far bigger and better to take their place: the humble pumpkin. Uncarved, pumpkins serve as a symbol of the harvest and are often displayed on front porches until Thanksgiving. Carved and illuminated by a candle, they are symbolic of death and the spirit world.

Halloween certainly has a spooky element about it. The air is cold and it seems as though the light and warmth of the sun has disappeared from our lives. As you walk around at night, the trees have been stripped of their visible life and their branches look like claws reaching out for you. The decaying carcasses of their leaves are all around as the wind blows them, making them sound like footsteps following you down the street. Your rational mind tells you it is all in your imagination but you can't help but stop and look around on many cold and windy October and November nights to make sure no ghost or goblin is following you.

All your nerves are on high command with simultaneous feelings of excitement and apprehension, similar to the phenomena when people watching a horror movie cover their eyes to avoid the scary parts but inevitably peak through their fingers. There is something within our psyche that makes us fascinated with the feeling of fear. Why else would so-called "amusement" parks have rides that scare us half to death, and why are they so popular anyway?

I still remember the most popular houses on Halloween night were not only the ones with the best candy but also the ones who really decked their yards out with all sorts of spookiness—coffins that opened as you walked by; scarecrows on front porches that looked lifelike with someone hidden in the bushes who would just delight in making the "person's" head fall off and roll on the ground as unsuspecting trick-or-treaters came to the door; and recordings of ear-piercing screams played at random to make the hair on the back of your neck stand up. Kids would run away from those houses only to reappear a few minutes later to do it all over again.

Humans have a fascination with fear and death and it is good to understand why. It isn't some morbid fascination as many people think it is and it doesn't lead to evil. In our society, we try and deny death its due—we ignore it and try to diminish its power over us. But our subconscious knows it is there and will find ways of offering death its rightful contemplation and honour. Fear makes adrenaline pump through our bodies, heightening all our senses and energizing us. Fear of death works in a similar way and Halloween is a time to remember there is a cycle to life. While on an individual level it may seem like an ending; on a larger scale, an ending is always a new beginning. By honouring the meanings and purposes of Halloween, we can enhance the experience of life for the other 364 days of the year. As the saying goes, "Without the realization of death, how can you ever experience the joy of life?"

Guy Fawkes' Night

The 5th of November

The celebration of Guy Fawkes' Night is England's version of Halloween. People often wonder why the British left it to the Irish to bring the festival of Halloween to North America. Didn't the British celebrate Samhain as the Celts and Scots surrounding them did? The Celts, Britons, and Saxons of England did have their Day of the Dead festival just like others around them. That is until southern England became the hot spot of two millennia of religious battles, persecutions, crusades, and other forms of religious madness.

What did those in southern England do to deserve such dishonour? With so many different peoples trying to gain control of this area, it was simply a matter of being in the wrong place at the wrong time. In just the first millennia C.E., the Romans, Britons, Normans, Celts, Norse, and Scots, to name just a smackling of tribes, fought for control of this small but apparently very tasty piece of land. Anyone who has ever spent a winter there would wonder what they wanted it for in the first place, but want it they did.

With the Romans and Christians having conquered every other part of Europe, England became their biggest challenge. Much effort was put into converting all the different pagan cultures to Christianity. Most of those who stuck around decided to convert to Christianity to make their lives easier and those who were unwilling to convert headed for the outskirts to escape persecution. As the second millennium C.E. came around and there were fewer pagans left to persecute, the different Christian sects started to turn on each other.

So, do the British celebrate Halloween? The answer is somewhere between a yes and a no. No, they no longer celebrate a holiday called Samhain or Halloween but, yes, they still partake in the traditions and customs associated with festivals of the dead. It's just that in England's case, the religious undertones were traded in for political overtones. The religious fighting must have been really bad if politics became easier to celebrate than religion.

First, let's start with who this Guy Fawkes guy was and what he did that resulted in his effigy being burnt to a pulp in hundreds of bonfires all over England each November 5th. Guy Fawkes and his friends conspired to blow up the House of Parliament and all its inhabitants. I'm sure it was not the first time people thought about getting rid of their politicians but this was an awfully ambitious undertaking and you may wonder what possessed Fawkes and his friends to resort to such drastic measures.

About a hundred years before Guy Fawkes was born, King Henry VIII broke away from the Roman Catholic Church and the power of the Pope and created what he claimed to be a new and improved religion called the Church of England. When Henry ascended England's throne in 1509, he showed the promise of what a great king could be. He was pious, handsome, athletic, musical, and scholarly.

Henry married Catherine of Aragon, six years his senior, and together they tried for a son. After several stillborns, Catherine delivered a girl they christened Mary. At the age of two, Mary was betrothed to the eldest son of the king of France. More stillborns followed and Henry and his advisors grew increasingly anxious because without a male heir, his throne would pass through the marriage of his daughter Mary to the king of France. At that time, the Catholic Church ran England and it was immensely rich and powerful. Our present-day idea of separation between state and religion did not exist in those days. The Church was the State and the State was the Church.

When Henry first took the throne, he was a devout Catholic and was therefore completely against the newly emergent Protestant religion led by Martin Luther and John Calvin, which hoped to do away with the corruption inherent in the Roman Catholic Church. Henry's pro-Catholic attitude began to change, however, when it became apparent that his sweet and loyal Catherine was not going to produce a royal son. Even though the Roman Catholic Church forbade divorce, Henry expected his royal position would get him the necessary papal approval. In anticipation of his expected freedom, Henry wasted no time in knocking up his seventeen-year-old mistress, Anne Boleyn. Powerful enemies of Henry were hard at work in Rome, however, and advised Pope Clement VII to deny Henry's request for a divorce, which the Pope did. Without the Church's approval for his divorce, his mistress' child would be illegitimate, therefore having no right to the throne.

Henry's advisors proposed a solution to his little predicament; he could excommunicate the entire Roman Catholic Church and replace it with a new religion with him as its head. An added bonus of this coup was that the Crown would then be able to confiscate all the Church lands in England and distribute it how they saw fit. As can be expected, a whole bunch of loyal nobles became even more land wealthy. In 1532, Henry broke with the Vatican and established the Church of England. He banned Catholicism and ordered every subject to swear an oath of fealty to him as the head of the new Anglican Church.

His mistress-turned-wife, Anne Boleyn, having failed to give him his much sought after son by giving birth to a daughter, named Elizabeth, was beheaded. Upon his death in 1547, Henry's six serial wives had yielded but one male heir—the sickly Edward VI who managed to hold the throne for a measly five years.

During his kingship, Edward brought Protestantism into England and created a divide between the Catholic Anglicans and the Protestant Anglicans. To further mess things up, when Mary, the daughter of Catherine and Henry, followed Edward in ascending the throne, she, being a devout Catholic, reversed the earlier Act of Succession and all previously confiscated lands were returned to their old owners. Mary instituted a Catholic reign of terror. From that time onwards, people suffered greatly for their religion depending on the faith of the ruling monarch. The Anglicans, Protestants, Catholics, Anabaptists, and Puritans, all fought for control and the ability to dominate and persecute others. This went on for at least two hundred years, except for a brief period of relative peace and prosperity when Elizabeth, Anne Boleyn's child, was crowned in 1558.

This was the environment Guy Fawkes and his friends were living under. Fawkes was born a Protestant in York in 1570 and was the son of a wealthy lawyer. After his father's death, Fawkes inherited much of the estate and he became wealthy at a young age. As time went on, he became more and more interested in the Catholic faith and eventually became a member of the religion. He joined the Spanish army to fight in Belgium against the Dutch. This may seem strange, an Englishman joining the Spanish army to fight in another country altogether. But the Spanish Catholics hoped that helping the English Catholics fight off the Dutch who had invaded England, they would be able to take over the monarchy of England and claim it for the Roman Catholic Church once and for all. Fawkes was a good soldier and quickly rose in rank to colonel despite the fact he was only in his twenties. It was while he was in the army that he became somewhat of an expert in the use of gunpowder. In those days, very few people knew how to handle this dangerous stuff.

Colonel Fawkes was not the one who came up with what became known as the Gunpowder Plot. The daring idea of blowing up the House of Parliament and its resident politicians was devised by a group of Catholics in England who had grown desperate with the way they were being treated. When Queen Elizabeth I died, James VI of Scotland, the son of Henry and Catherine's daughter Mary, inherited the throne and became James I of England. Although James himself held no personal grudge against the Catholics, he was young and easily influenced and allowed his ministers to push him into putting pressure on Catholics by penalizing members of the religion. His ministers feared a Catholic uprising might succeed in replacing King James I with a Catholic monarch.

Robert Catesby, another Protestant-turned-Catholic, began devising the gunpowder plot in 1604 in an attempt to put an end to the persecution of the Catholics "with one blow." Thomas Wintour and his brother Robert were next involved and they all worked on Guy Fawkes to get involved. Catesby impressed on Fawkes how important it was they had a man who was well versed in the properties of gunpowder and how this was such a rare and valuable skill. Fawkes was so honoured and impressed at being asked to take on such an important task that he readily agreed without much thought of the consequences. And, boy, were there consequences!

As more people became involved in the plan, they managed to rent a house next door to the House of Parliament. The idea was to tunnel through the wall of the house into the Parliament building and pass the barrels of gunpowder and combustible fuel needed to make the explosion effective through the hole in the wall. The walls of the house proved very thick and the task of tunnelling through was very tiring and frustrating. At one time, a loud rumbling noise seemed to come from the room to which they were trying to gain access and they were afraid the tunnel was going to collapse and come crashing down upon them. It was Fawkes who told them it was only the coal merchant moving his stock from one room to another. They approached the coal merchant and found that he owned the room directly beneath the State Chamber of Parliament and they managed to rent it from him for a short period of time. They must have thought this was a stroke of luck, as they were able to put down their shovels and axes. All they had to do now was sneak in all those barrels of gunpowder under the cover of darkness.

The opening of Parliament was fixed for October 31, 1605, but King James postponed the occasion a few days later to November 5th so he could attend a hunting party in the North Country. This really threw a wrench in the conspirator's plans with the air being so damp and misty, as the air tends to be in England especially at that time of year. Fawkes was worried the gunpowder might get too wet to ignite. To cause further problems, fights started to break out among the group of plotters because many had friends and relatives in Parliament and did not wish to see them killed, but the group decided nobody was to be warned about the impending plot. On October 26th however, a letter was sent to Lord Mounteagle telling him not to be present at the opening of Parliament on the 5th of November. The sender was thought by some to be Francis Tresham, one of the gunpowder plot group who was the brother-in-law of Mounteagle. In the note were the words: "Though there be no appearance of any stir, yet I say they shall receive a terrible blow, the Parliament, and yet they shall not see who hurts them."[1]

On the morning of November 5th, a party of soldiers searched the House of Parliament and found Guy Fawkes hiding in the room with the explosives. He was arrested and later interrogated by King James and his councillors, who, for some reason, took the whole plot quite personally. Other conspirators were overtaken fleeing the city. Fawkes and seven others were taken to the Tower of London where they were questioned and tortured to reveal the names of others in the plot. Apparently, Fawkes was a brave man and did not squeal on anyone. After a brief trial, Fawkes and his companions were found guilty of treason and were executed on January 31, 1606, opposite the building they had planned to blow up. Their execution was not simple and clean—no firing squad or simple hanging for them. Instead, the prisoners were hung, drawn, and quartered. This means they were hung, disembowelled, and left to die a slow and very painful death.

In 1606, one year after the attempted Gunpowder plot, King James declared November 5th a national holiday. This holiday was used by the people as a method to incorporate some of the older Samhain rituals back into their lives—with the two most popular customs being the bonfires and the fireworks. At sundown, Guy Fawkes' Night was a time for bonfires to be lit all over England. It is supposed to be symbolic of Fawkes' execution even though we know he wasn't burned at the stake. The bonfires on Guy Fawkes' Night are symbolic of the earlier Samhain/New Year bonfire festivities, as was the burning of effigies.

It isn't only Guy Fawkes who receives the honour of being the most represented effigy. The burning of effigies started long before Fawkes was born. In the Middle Ages an effigy of a fool or a jester was burnt in many parts of England. The fool possibly represented a god named Ak. As the Lord of Misrule, his name had become rendered as "Jack" in such mischievous mythical spirits like Jack Frost, jack-in-the-box, and jack-o'-lantern. Ak was likely the equivalent of the evil Nordic god Loki who was the trickster of the gods and an effigy of him was burnt each year at this time to stave off his unruly influence during the cold days ahead. But throughout the crazed witch-hunt days, it was an effigy of a witch that was burnt and Queen Victoria is said to have observed many a witch-effigy burning with great delight. During Protestant reigns, the Catholic Pope was a popular effigy. Effigies of Napoleon were burnt during the Napoleonic Wars, the Czar during the Crimean War, the Kaiser during the First World War, and, of course, Hitler during the Second World War. Since then, England seems to have reverted back to good old Guy Fawkes.

There is a good reason why these bonfire and effigy rituals reappeared after their banning during the Reformation. According to Jean Harrowven in her book *Origins of Festivals and Feasts*, the reason this holiday remained popular with the common folk was because it provided them with a way to voice their grievances without fear of being punished. The heavy tax burden placed on small landowners; the starvation wages of the farm workers; the inhuman conditions imposed on factory workers during the Industrial Revolution and later; and the suppression and victimization of the poor in general resulted in looting, damaging of property, and general bad behaviour on the 5th of November.

This day was for people who felt disempowered most days of the year to regain a sense of control and influence over their lives, even if it was only symbolic. While the political and religious conditions in England are different than they used to be, the feeling of mayhem and destructiveness is still played out via the building of bigger and longer-burning bonfires around England. What other major city in the world allows their population to build huge bonfires with old furniture et cetera in the middle of the city?

Guy Fawkes' Night is not Halloween as North America knows it, but it serves a purpose for the psyche of the culture and it goes to show that despite political manipulations and control, people will find outlets for their old customs and traditions if they serve their needs and feelings.

REMEMBRANCE DAY
November 11th

Remembrance Day is celebrated in Canada, the United Kingdom, France, and Belgium on the eleventh day of November.[1] We know Remembrance Day is marked by a moment of silence to commemorate those who died fighting wars, but why was the eleventh day of the eleventh month at the eleventh hour chosen as the time to honour our dead?

At 5 a.m. on November 11, 1918, Germany surrendered to the allied forces when German public official Matthias Erzberger accepted the armistice terms presented by Allied Commander-in-Chief Ferdinand Foch of the French army in a railroad car in Compiègne, France. The demands of the armistice, which were to become effective at 11 a.m. on that day, included the withdrawal of German forces to the east bank of the Rhine within thirty days; immediate cessation of all warfare; and surrender of the German fleet and all heavy guns with no further negotiations until the signing of the peace treaty.[2]

The armistice became effective at eleven o'clock on the eleventh day of the eleventh month, and as the guns fell silent on the Western Front in France and Belgium, four years of bloody hostilities ended. The symbolism of the number eleven may simply be a coincidence—we will never know for certain—but it is also possible that people chose or maybe, just maybe, it was inexplicable fate.

It makes sense why we and so many other cultures pay honour to our dead at this time of the year. The harvest is over, the fields are empty, the trees have lost their leaves, and the death of nature surrounds us and reflects back to us our own mortality. The old spirit of Samhain/Halloween reflects the spirit of our modern Remembrance Day. The Germanic people of Old Europe celebrated their Day of the Dead on November 11th and for the Celts who followed the Julian calendar, Samhain fell on November 11th. When the old Roman Julian calendar was revised and replaced by the Gregorian calendar (which we now use) ten days were eliminated from the year making what would have been November 11th, November 1st.

As the Christians in northern Europe became more numerous and influential the "Old Samhain" festival that took place on November 11th became the festival of Martinmas. It was celebrated in honour of Saint Martin of Tours. The custom and traditions associated with Martinmas were very similar to the festivities surrounding Samhain. There would be a bonfire in every street, much feasting, drinking, storytelling, plays, and games. The yearly pre-winter slaughter of animals that could not be housed throughout the winter was also a big part of Martinmas. Households killed many farm animals and sprinkled their thresholds with the animal's blood. The tradition of slaughter is still preserved in the British custom of killing cattle on St. Martin's Day.

Saint Martin – The Reluctant Soldier

Martin was born in the Roman province of Pannonia, now part of modern-day Hungary, around the year 315 C.E. His father was an officer in the Roman army and his mother was a follower of the old Roman gods and goddesses. Young Martin yearned to learn everything he possibly could about this new Christian religion so when he was barely ten years old, he secretly went to the house of a priest and begged for instruction. A few years later, Martin was drafted into the Roman army. This caused him much dismay because Martin considered himself a pacifist. He was so reluctant to become a soldier that he had to be held in chains until he was inducted into the Roman army. After the chain incident, he seemed to have a change of heart and decided to be a soldier that best emulated the life of a monk. He decided to fight for the principle of helping others regardless of what side they were on. He was considered a bit of an odd man and lucky for him his time in the Roman army was during a rare period of peace and religious tolerance in Europe.

You might wonder what it is he did that got him recognized as a saint. It was the warm and highly decorated uniform of a Roman officer that first got him noticed. When he was about twenty years old, he was riding home one bitterly cold night when he saw an exceedingly old and poor man who was almost without clothes and close to freezing to death. Martin jumped from his horse, took off his luxurious cloak, and cut it in two with his sword. Wrapping one half around the beggar, he returned the other half to his own shoulders and rode off. You might be thinking, as I was, that if he were a real saint, he would have given that old man his entire cloak. As it turns out, by this time, Martin had pretty much given away most of his nice and warm officer dregs to other poor beggars and did not have all that much to keep himself warm. He might have been a generous man, but he wasn't stupid enough to let himself freeze to death.

After ending his military career he finally got to live his life as the monk he wished to be since childhood. According to legend, in 372 C.E., he was trying to live his quiet monkish life in Tours, France; he was hiding from the city's officials who were trying to provide him with the honour of the consecration of the city's bishop. The honking of the geese gave him away as he hid in the bushes and he was reluctantly appointed. Geese still pay the price for ratting on Saint Martin. Goose is frequently the main course at St. Martinmas Day feast dinners.

St. Martin is said to have died on November 11, 397.

"The War to End All Wars"

In its modern inception, our Remembrance Day used to be called Armistice Day because it was specifically set up to commemorate those who fought and died in World War I. Few people were left untouched by this war which marked the advent of modern warfare. The human cost of World War I far exceeded previous wars. About ten million soldiers were killed in the fighting and at least another seven million civilians died because of the war.

The First World War was nicknamed "the war to end all wars" and it was thought to be the last war humankind would fight. There was a period of enlightenment and idealism following World War I that led people to believe that humankind had finally learnt its lesson from its past misdeeds and the futility of war was thought to be one of those lessons. Coincidentally, in numerology, the number 11 represents a need to contend with difficulties and the struggle between vice and virtue. It is also related to the qualities of intuition and patience and is highly idealistic.

The Great Depression eliminated a huge amount of that postwar idealism and what wasn't destroyed by the Depression was eliminated when World War II broke out in Europe in 1939, a mere twenty years after humans had "learnt their lesson" from World War I. Not surprisingly, for many years following the Second World War, celebrations of the 1918 ceasefire received little attention.

Starting in the early 1950s, many countries changed the name of Armistice Day to Remembrance Day to acknowledge that this day was now meant to honour all those who were killed in the Boer War (1899–1902), World War I (1914–1918), World War II (1939–1945), and the Korean War (1950–1953). We humans were kept busy with warfare in the twentieth century, and that doesn't even include the Vietnam War or numerous other skirmishes and close calls, not to mention our insistence on building up a nuclear arsenal to wipe us all off the face of the earth. What were we thinking? What are we thinking?

As much as we would like to think of war as a simple case of us fighting on the side of good against the forces of evil, war, just like life, is not as simple as good and evil. We tend to want to blame Germany for starting the First and Second World Wars; they did push the issue by going after France in the First World War and then again with Hitler's power-hungry grab at all countries surrounding Germany in World War II. Germany, however, cannot be blamed for creating the European atmosphere in which war was a probability. The first decade of the twentieth century in Europe reads like a nasty game of *Axis and Allies* with all these empires building up their armed forces, making alliances and then breaking them, and then going in and taking whatever they thought they could get away with. It was not simply one nation doing this, but several of them. This isn't the greatest environment in which to build stability and trust.

When the Germans lost the First World War and had to sign the armistice treaty on November 11, 1918, the resulting Treaty of Versailles was extremely hard on Germany, not to mention unrealistic. Along with many other conditions, Germany had to accept the sole responsibility for causing World War I and was required to pay vast reparations they could never afford. The humiliation the German people felt at having to submit to the armistice conditions and the economic liability of these reparations did much to set the climate of public discontent, blame, and nationalism that brought Hitler to power. While I do think that Hitler was one of those people we can consider evil, we shouldn't blame all the atrocities of the Second World War on him alone. The settlement that helped bring an end to the First World War unfortunately planted the seeds that grew into Hitler's plot to teach Europe a lesson. His placement of blame on the Jewish people for all the ills of Germany provided the minds and hearts of the nation's humiliated and discontent populace with a scapegoat.

No matter which era, which war, or even who started it, the real battle that allows people to fight wars is not fought on a battlefield but in people's hearts and minds. The origin of the word *propaganda* is Latin and means "congregation for the propagation of the faith." This originally referred to a committee of Roman Catholic cardinals set up in 1622 with the aim of spreading the Roman Catholic faith around the world. Later, *propaganda* came to mean the spreading of not just religious beliefs but of any ideas or principles. "Propaganda, propaganda, propaganda," Adolf Hitler is supposed to have said in 1923 after he had failed to seize power in Germany, "All that matters is propaganda." During wartime, the real battle for all sides is to win people's hearts and thoughts by convincing them that one side is right and certain of victory while the other is evil and bound to lose. Without achieving this there is little chance of getting people out on the battle-field and certainly even less of keeping them there.

Wartime propaganda is used by all sides to keep people fighting—and dying. While it would be so much easier to have just one person or one country to blame for allowing such a waste of life to happen, the fact remains that we all have to accept some responsibility. The first casualty of war is the truth. Yes, many of us go unwillingly into the battle, but no one can force us to believe one side or another's simplistic good/bad version of events. We allow ourselves to believe and in that way we allow ourselves to be used.

The Remembrance Poppy

While most war movies focus on the perceived glory and honour in war, most war poetry portrays the waste of human life surrounding war. When people think of Remembrance Day the image that comes to mind most frequently is the poppy. Poppies are the flowers that bring us opium, morphine, and heroin. In ancient times, poppies were sacred to Morpheus, the god of sleep. But what does the poppy have to do with Remembrance Day? Well, besides the fact that drugs were always welcomed by soldiers to help them pass the time or escape the physical and emotional pain of battles, the poppies worn on this day also mirror the vast poppy fields that grew on the site of the old battle-field of Flanders and many other battlefields throughout France and Belgium. Poppy seeds lie dormant until disturbed and there were many dreadful disturbances during the First and Second World Wars throughout these areas of Europe. The sight of seeing beautiful poppies sprouting on the same battlefields where dead bodies had lain earlier moved Lieutenant Colonel John McCrae, a Canadian doctor who fought in both the Boer War and the First World War, to write the following poem:

> In Flanders fields the poppies blow
> Between the crosses, row on row,
> That mark our place; and in the sky
> The larks, still bravely singing, fly
> Scarce heard amid the guns below.

We are the Dead. Short days ago
We lived, felt dawn, saw sunset glow,
Loved and were loved, and now we lie,
In Flanders fields.

Take up our quarrel with the foe:
To you from failing hands we throw
The torch; be yours to hold it high.
If ye break faith with us who die
We shall not sleep, though poppies grow
In Flanders fields.

For me, Remembrance Day holds a warm feeling of continuity, knowing that we are taking time to pay respect to our ancestors at the same time that many others before us took time to pay respect to their dead. Our tradition of a moment of silence at 11 a.m. on this day is touching and, when you come to think of it, no small feat. It is hard enough to get a single person to be quiet and allow themselves time for reflection, but to take the time to reflect on our losses in a society that does not seem to ever hold still let alone keep quiet is an achievement. But is it enough?

When we sit back and think of all the battles and wars the human race has fought, it seems like there is some part of being human that makes us want to kill each other. Considering our track record, it seems naive to even think this may not be the case. I would have to say that the lust some people have for power and control and their using whatever means available to help them acquire them is inevitable, but their getting away with it is not. Going to war to stop these people and their supporters may seem like an appropriate response, but is it the only one? Do we really exhaust all other options or do we jump into war too easily because it is what we know and are used to doing? What does each side get out of this power struggle? Do the dead really need to pile up before we can come to a so-called solution to our differences? And, finally, the hardest question of all: Did the death of these people really serve any purpose or was it a total waste of human life?

We can all resort to the national pride and feelings of honour that most governments try to foster on Remembrance Day by telling us that all these people died fighting for freedom and to preserve our way of life, and those who died probably believed they were fighting for that too. But were millions of dead inevitable? Was there no other solution? What errors and manipulations lead us to allow this slaughter? I don't have the answers to these questions but I think they are questions we all need to ask. Remembrance Day is not only a day to reflect on the needless loss of millions of people's lives but also a day to reflect on the actions, errors and manipulations that allowed it to happen in the first place. This might help us reduce the likelihood of it happening again. I think the dead would appreciate that.

THANKSGIVING

Thanksgiving takes place on the first Monday in October in Canada and the last Thursday in November in the United States. While the dates may differ, the spirit of Thanksgiving Day remains the same. The festiveness of sharing a wonderful meal while surrounded by family and friends is something worth celebrating—and celebrate we do. Thanksgiving is one of the most popular holidays in North America. As I am sure you can guess, however, setting aside a day to express gratitude for our bountiful lives did not originate in North America. Of all the seasonal observances, the harvest used to be one of the most important. The harvest wasn't just a matter of food and fun, it used to be about life and death.

In early agrarian cultures, it was thought that the Earth Mother (in later years she became God) controlled the seasons. If the harvest was good, it meant the Earth Mother was pleased and there would be food to last the winter. If the harvest was meagre, it meant the Earth Mother was vexed and needed to be placated. Before the advent of year-round movement of food from one end of the world to our local supermarket, food supply was based on what people managed to reap from the earth by the fall. If it was a disappointing harvest, they knew it would be a long hard winter where they and those around them would be forced to go without and perhaps not even make it through the winter. But if there was a successful harvest, then after completing the hard work of gathering in the crops and storing it away for the winter, there was much reason for thankfulness.

Every culture has some sort of festival marking either the beginning of the harvest or the ending of the harvest, and most cultures celebrate both. The Greeks paid tribute to their Goddess of the Harvest, Demeter, with a nine-day feast. The ancient Romans had numerous harvest festivals including the Cerealia and the October Horse Festival. The Egyptians celebrated Min, the God of Fertility, with an annual harvest festival where the Pharaoh would cut the first sheaf of grain. The Hebrew people have a harvest festival called Sukkoth (The Feast of Tabernacles) that goes on for eight days and involves offering two loaves of bread to the temple. The Chinese have their Harvest Moon Festival, the Japanese pay honour to their numerous agricultural gods, and Hindu women have a ritual thanking their Goddess of the Grain. The Native American people celebrated the harvest for several thousands of years prior to European colonization. The ancient Celts' pre-harvest festival was held at Lammas and their post-harvest festival is now known as Halloween.

Despite all these various harvest traditions, we still believe Thanksgiving was started by a group of people called Pilgrims who made their way over the rough sea to found a new life in a place called Plymouth Colony. Except the first documented European Thanksgiving that took place in North America was almost fifty years before the Pilgrims landed at Plymouth Rock. In the late 1500s, English explorer Martin Frobisher held a formal ceremony in what is now known of as Newfoundland to give thanks for having survived the long ocean journey. In addition to Frobisher's celebration in Canada, the Spanish, French, and the Dutch all had settlements in North America and would have carried out their old observances marking successful harvests at their new home. In the 1600s, Samuel de Champlain and the French settlers who came with him established "The Order of Good Cheer," a group that held huge celebrations marking the harvests and shared food with its Native American neighbours.

Even in the United States there were at least two Thanksgiving celebrations before the Pilgrims had one. In 1607, a group of English settlers led by Captain George Popham met with a group of Native Americans known as the Abnaki near the mouth of the Kennebec River to share a harvest feast and prayer meeting. On December 14, 1619, there was a celebration in Virginia led by Captain John Woodleaf and thirty-nine colonists who had travelled up the James River to a place called Berkeley Hundred where they went ashore and gave thanks.

Still most of us think the first official Thanksgiving took place at Plymouth in October 1621, a year after the Puritans first landed on the coast of New England. They arrived on the banks of the New World in November of 1620 and their first winter was devastating—they lost 46 of the original 102 who arrived on the *Mayflower*. Their luck began to change in the spring when their Native American neighbours decided to teach these Europeans coming to their land how to survive in their new surroundings. I am not sure they would have made the same decision if they had been able to look a few decades into the future.

Thanks to Mother Nature, the Pilgrim's God, the Native Americans, a lot of hard work, and some luck, the Pilgrims had a bountiful harvest in the fall of 1621. Those lucky enough to still be alive after their devastating first winter decided to celebrate this bounty. They held a large celebration to which the Native American Chief Massasoit came with ninety of his men. There is no mention of native women attending the feast. This could be either because the Native Americans did not bother to bring women with them or because the Pilgrim who recorded the event did not think the women worth mentioning; either one is a possibility. Being a considerate guest, Chief Massasoit sent several of his men into the forest and they came back with five deer and numerous wild fowl to add to the feast. The Pilgrims and their Native friends feasted for three days and also held competitions in archery and hunting.

These Pilgrims did not likely think of this feast as a "Thanksgiving" in the sense that many cultures, including ours, now think of it. They did not hold this Thanksgiving feast to thank their God for their wonderful bounty. To these devoutly religious people, a day of Thanksgiving to God would have been a day of prayer and fasting, not a day of playing and feasting. The Pilgrims felt that since many of the festivals and holidays celebrated by Christians were not mentioned in the bible and instead had their origins in pagan religions, they were the work of the Devil and should not be celebrated by "true" Christians. As the Puritans gained political clout in England and New England, they outlawed many holidays including May Day and Christmas and told people that instead of honouring the Devil, they should be honouring God.

It is likely that what we now know of the first Thanksgiving is actually not a Pilgrim tradition but rather a Native American harvest tradition. But the Puritans were willing to be flexible and showed their appreciation and thanks in the manner their Native friends were accustomed to and not necessarily in the manner of which the Pilgrims were accustomed. This shows us the deep appreciation the Puritans must have felt towards their new neighbours who taught them what they needed to know to survive and prosper at their new home.

So what happened to this friendly camaraderie between the Pilgrims and the Natives? How did they go from sharing a festive celebration with the Native Americans to killing them or selling them into slavery? A better understanding of the Puritan ideology and their migration to North America might be in order here. The Puritans were a group of people who grew discontented with the rampant corruption of the Roman Catholic Church (and they had every reason to be critical of the favouritism and bribery that was taking place within the ranks of the priesthood but that is a story in its own right). When King Henry VIII separated England from the Catholic Church and set up his very own Church of England, there was much euphoria and high hopes for this new religious sect. As you can guess, that idealism quickly dissipated and was replaced with anger because many people felt that the reforms of the Anglican Church did not go far enough and had merely replaced a corrupt pope with a corrupt king.

From the time of Henry's succession in 1532, for at least a hundred years, the religious infighting taking place in England between Catholics, Protestants, Anglicans, Puritans, and numerous other offshoots would be enough to make you think that everyone had gone completely mad. Each took turns trying to gain power so that they could then in turn persecute and kill others who disagreed with their philosophy. Many grew tired of this way of life and decided to set out for greener, more tolerant pastures. A group calling themselves separatists or Pilgrims set up camp in Amsterdam, Holland to escape the madness overtaking England.

After having spent a decade there, they decided to establish themselves at a place where they could speak English and so they set off in the *Mayflower* to make their way to the New World with much enthusiasm and hope for the future. Only a few were dedicated enough to attempt this risky voyage and new life, and up until about 1629, there were only 300 Pilgrims living in widely scattered settlements around New England. As word leaked back to England about their peaceful and prosperous life, however, many of their religious cousins calling themselves Puritans decided to join these adventurous fellows. Since all the religious infighting and persecution were still merrily taking place in England, Puritans began to arrive by the boatload. Their numbers rose to 17,800 in 1640 and to 106,000 in 1700.

With the influx of so many people, the debate over ownership of land and the fight for resources became more and more adversarial. In addition, these newly arrived Puritans had attitudes towards the Native people that were far different from the first wave that had come to North America who held their Native benefactors in relatively high regard. The new influx of Puritans mostly saw the Native population as a threat to their way of life and competition for resources and saw nothing in the least immoral about killing them or selling them into slavery. Perhaps many of the first wave of settlers tried to create a more peaceful existence between the new Puritan immigrants and the Native population. Sadly, the number of newly arrived immigrants hostile to the indigenous tribes was just too overwhelming. Those earlier Pilgrim settlers who did not bow to the newer "Puritan" way of thinking were quickly excommunicated and expelled from the Church. Before long, the previously friendly relationship between the Native Americans and the early Pilgrims had degraded into an all-out fight for land, resources, and survival.

The 1621 Pilgrim feast was their first and last Thanksgiving celebration; there is no evidence that the Pilgrims ever continued the tradition. Whether this is due to bad harvests or the deteriorating relations between the Natives and the Puritans as more and more settlers arrived, we do not know. Other Europeans who had settled in the New World held the odd harvest festival here and there across the country but Thanksgiving Day, as a recognized national day to celebrate life's bounty, did not come to fruition until 1789. This is when George Washington declared Thursday, November 26th as a day "we may then unite in rendering unto Him our sincere and humble thanks."

Even after this presidential proclamation, there was no one consistent day of the year when Thanksgiving was held. The reason for this was that in order for there to be a Thanksgiving Day, each year the government had to set a day and ratify it by congressional mandate—sort of like a politician make-work project. Some years they did not even bother; on the years they did, the date moved around from November to December. Some years it was not even held in the fall.

For a number of years before the outbreak of the American Civil War in 1861, Thanksgiving fell by the wayside, with all those politicians having other things to worry about. We can partially thank Sarah Hale, editor of the magazine *Godey's Lady's Book*, for making Thanksgiving a national holiday in the United States. In 1827, she had begun lobbying the President for the instatement of Thanksgiving as a national holiday. After lobbying successive presidents, her dream finally came to fruition in 1863. It was the ending of the Civil War and her persistent campaign that had encouraged President Abraham Lincoln to proclaim the fourth Thursday in November as a national day of Thanksgiving for the whole nation. Even at that late date, the holiday was not nationally accepted, particularly in the South, where it was viewed as another Yankee event intent on eroding their way of life. By the late 1800s, however, the New England harvest festival, which evolved into our modern-day Thanksgiving, was celebrated nationwide.

By 1939, Thanksgiving Day had worked its way into the nation's psyche enough to prompt Franklin D. Roosevelt to permanently set the fourth Thursday in November as a nationwide Day of Thanksgiving. The date of Thanksgiving in the United States was probably set by Lincoln to somewhat correlate with the anchoring of the *Mayflower* at Cape Cod, which occurred on November 21, 1620, by our modern-day Gregorian Calendar—coincidentally, it was November 11th to the Puritans, who were still using the Julian Calendar.

Much like the United States, Canada also used Thanksgiving as a politician make-work project where a Day of Thanksgiving needed to be set by parliament each year. Canada also had decision issues and had been moving it between October and November until 1957 when Parliament finally decided to permanently fix the second Monday in October as "a day of general Thanksgiving to almighty God for the bountiful harvest with which Canada has been blessed."[1] Canada established a harvest festival that falls about a month and a half earlier than the one held in the United States because of Canada's earlier harvest.

Just like all holidays, Thanksgiving has it's own set of traditions and symbols that pique our curiosity. Our modern-day Thanksgiving feast of squash, sweet potatoes, pumpkin pie, cranberry sauce, and, of course, the big stuffed turkey might be what we now call a Thanksgiving meal, but we do not actually know what was on the dinner menu at the one and only Pilgrim Thanksgiving. We do know there were some deer and wild fowl but we do not know if that wild fowl was a turkey as there were many different types of wild fowl that were good eating in those days. Nowadays, turkey is as close as most of us get in our diet to wild fowl. Whether or not it was a turkey that was on that first Thanksgiving menu, there is no mistaking its place in the modern-day Thanksgiving feast. Much to many a turkey's dismay, it is part of the joy of the festivity. Today, Americans eat more than 535 million pounds of turkey every Thanksgiving (that is a pound and a half for every woman, man, and child).

In addition to being given such distinction on this one day of the year (an honour I am sure most turkeys would like to do away with), the turkey was almost chosen as the national bird of the United Sates. After the U.S. won its independence from England, congress debated the choice of a national bird. Benjamin Franklin disliked the idea of the bald eagle because he thought it was a bird of "bad moral character" (it must have been that scrutinizing look eagles are so good at giving). He advocated the turkey as a "true original Native of North America," even though the eagle is just as native as the turkey. The bald eagle won out as everyone knows, either because of its dubious moral character or maybe because the eagle is majestic and really quite beautiful. I am not sure what Benjamin Franklin was thinking because I must say I think the turkey has to be the ugliest member of the entire fowl family. We should, however, thank it for providing us (unwillingly, I am sure) with a tasty feast of plenty—something we often neglect to do.

The horn of plenty, a crescent-shaped horn with food flowing out of it, is a symbol that shows up in many Thanksgiving illustrations. This symbol, like most others, is rooted in myth. According to Greek legend, Zeus gave this horn of plenty to honour a goat named Amalthea. Zeus, who became the supreme ruler of the gods in the pantheon of Greek myth, was the son of Rhea and her brother Cronus. Their father, Uranus, grew tired of his offspring's whining and whinging and decided to shut them away where they could not be seen or heard. Gaia, who was the mother of Rhea and Cronus, did not agree with this decision so she conspired with Cronus to get rid of Uranus. Eventually, Cronus managed to get rid of Uranus by castrating him and sending his privates into the ocean and the rest of him to the underworld.

As what usually happens when conspiracies take place, those who commit them begin to get paranoid that a similar fate is in store for them. That is what happened to Cronus, who tried to protect himself by devouring his children soon after they were born. He managed to get away with doing this to his first four children until Rhea finally got smart enough to send her fifth child, Zeus, off to safety and gave her husband a stone wrapped in infant's clothing to swallow.

Rhea left the baby Zeus in the care of a nanny goat Amalthea. While a goat may seem like a strange guardian for a baby to us, to those who were around before the time of baby formula, a goat was the best animal to have around you when you were handed an orphaned baby and there were no women who were able or willing to breastfeed the baby. The goat may not have been the most reliable caregiver but as a substitute for mother's milk, a goat was a baby's best chance and many a baby were saved from certain death through the hospitality of a nanny goat willing to share her milk. Zeus, wanting to thank his nanny goat, Amalthea, for honouring him with her milk of life, broke off one of her horns (some stories say he knocked it off by accident when they were frolicking in the grass and others say it was upon her death) and filled it with fruit, nuts, and flowers. This was no ordinary goat's horn, however, this was a magic horn of plenty (cornucopia) and no matter how much was taken out, it could never be emptied. According to the legend, in order to show his gratitude to Amalthea, Zeus later set the goat's image in the sky. We know it today as the constellation Capricorn.

The symbol of the horn of plenty was later used to represent the nourishment provided by Mother Nature, who provides the bounty that sustains humans and animals throughout life. While I would bet that most people during good times have made the mistake of taking nature's gifts for granted, our modern-day separation from nature, seasonal changes, and, most important, the process involved in getting us our food supply has made us even more likely to do so. Even with information being provided to us on a daily basis about the havoc we are wreaking on our natural environment, we still continue to hope that no matter how much we abuse or take nature's bounty for granted, she will still provide for us.

Despite our planet's scary aspects, such as floods, tornados, and hurricanes, it is still our only source of sustenance, and if we don't show our appreciation, it begs the question, what is it that we are thankful for? Try it at your next Thanksgiving dinner; ask everyone to share a bit of themselves by saying what it is they are really thankful for. It is surprising how much harder we find it to verbalize our good fortune than we find it to lament what it is that is missing from our lives. Maybe this is because under all our sophistication and rationality we are still quite superstitious and might feel that verbalizing our good fortune will tempt the fates who are just waiting for a chance to take it all away from us.

This superstition does not explain this weird phenomenon I can't make sense of. Why is it that many people who have so very little find more to appreciate than people who have more than they know what to do with? I am lucky enough to belong to the 20% of the world's population who uses 80% of the world's resources and yet I look around me and find people who just want more and more.[2] Having travelled to a few Third World countries, I have been fortunate to see just how lucky I really am. But I have been very confused at how the people in these countries, despite their obvious material needs and wants, seem more happy and satisfied with life than many of the richest 20% of the world.

Poverty is an undesirable aspect of our humanity. Many people who do not belong to the privileged minority would understandably love to get a piece of that pie. After all, I have the ability to choose more options and take advantage of more opportunities than most of the world's population. I have been blessed with the advantage of being able to play a more active role in choosing my course in life rather than those who unfortunately experience the opposite. The underprivileged might desperately try to improve their lot in life but the odds are stacked against them.

All these choices and opportunities that we take for granted come at a price. Many people who are in the same position as I am become paralyzed and unsure of which of the numerous forks in the road to take. This indecision causes many of us a lot of grief, insecurity, and anxiety. Whereas if you only had the likelihood of your life taking one or two or even three different directions then the choice is likely to cause you less anxiety and stress. But despite these uncomfortable feelings, they aren't nearly as bad as living a difficult life of poverty.

Chances are, when you go around the dinner table someone will have the guts to be honest and verbalize what many are thinking: "I would be thankful to win the lottery." Most people think that money will buy them more happiness, and they might be right. Money does buy us the ability to enjoy more of what the world has to offer, and possibly the freedom from the basic day-to-day concern for survival. But let's be honest, money is not what makes us happy. It is this frustrating Catch-22 most of us face: when we have the money, we often lack the time to do what makes us happy and when we have the time to do what makes us happy…well, then most of the time we don't have the money.

This big economic machine called "the market" has seen that

most of us are in this dilemma and has offered to save us by providing us with an alternative. It has sold us on the idea that it is not the things we do in our life or even the people we share our time with that makes us happy but rather it is what we buy that makes us happy. With more money we will be able to have a better house, better car, better spouse, better kids, and a better life. We have bought into this plan, hook, line, and sinker. We can blame the companies that make their profits by getting us on this treadmill, we can even blame television for being so effective at convincing us of it too, but when it really comes down to it, we have to accept responsibility for ourselves. As the saying goes, you can lead a horse to water but you can't make it drink.

In our attempt to offer ourselves more security and control, we have decided to honour this new and powerful "stuff god" and have transferred our loyalties from people to stuff. Let's face it, stuff is more reliable; it does not have its own agenda, can be moved around and set up any way we like, it is still there when we come home from work, and it does not complain about its crappy day or how much of a mess the house is. People, on the other hand, are not quite as reliable. Their unpredictability makes us insecure and fearful of our lack of control, so we collect assets and retirement funds to help assure that we will always be able to buy more stuff and have a place to put it and not be dependant on those around us. But we then feel cheated when even after we have accumulated all the things we are told will make us happy, we still feel unfulfilled and wanting more. This might be one of the reasons for the rampant use of antidepressants in a society that, when looked at with a global perspective, doesn't really have all that much justification for being so bummed-out.

People who have not been given the opportunity or the means to act out their worship of this new "stuff god," either because it is too hard to get or too hard to keep, have not had the luxury of being taken down that road. They still have to rely on people for security and fulfillment. They are more free to be hospitable and giving because they do not have to worry so much about people taking things away from them and also because they realize that one day they might be the one in need of hospitality. They haven't yet been given the opportunity to lose sight of how much fulfillment and happiness we actually get from building and caring for our unpredictable "people" security net in return for a more controllable and secure, but far less fulfilling, "stuff" security net. When you really stop to think about it, the things that we are most thankful for and the source of most of our happiness are not things we can own. Fulfillment in our relationships with people is really what brings us the most satisfaction. Fulfillment in ourselves—who we are and what we can provide to others and how much happiness we can find in the simple act of giving and sharing—that is what really matters.

Maybe this Thanksgiving we should take time away from the bombardment of messages and images all around us telling us how we can buy happiness and instead take some time for ourselves to think how our lives provide us with the most fulfilment. Try it, it really can't hurt, and who knows, you may even be thankful you did.

CHRISTMAS
December 25th

The Christmas holiday is the biggest and most lavish of festivals put on in the Western world. It is meant to be a Christian holiday celebrating the birthday of someone thought to be the Son of God, turned political and religious rebel with a cause, turned scapegoat, turned prophet. Jesus had many good things to say and we can't really blame him for trying to take on the powers that be during his life. After all, if you had a father like his, you would have to do something pretty wild in order to get out from under dad's shadow. Well, lucky (or unlucky) for him, his words, symbolism, actions, fables, et cetera seemed to strike a chord with people and, lo and behold, he even surpassed his father in popularity.

Jesus' rise in popularity, his subsequent fall, followed by the amazing comeback after his death, mirrors the topsy-turvy popularity of our modern-day Christmas celebration. We might think our present Christmas Eve and Christmas Day celebrations are extravagant, but next to the twelve-day Christmas bashes our medieval ancestors put on, we look like a bunch of high-school nerds trying to put on a party nobody wants to come to. Then again, at least we can throw a party better than those Puritan folks who made Christmas illegal.

Christmas is the biggest Christian birthday bash—it's so popular that even those who do not consider themselves religious get into it. Many of you might be surprised to learn that Jesus was not actually born on December 25th. While the Son of God might not have been born into our world on December 25th, this auspicious day does mark the birthday of the sun. You may have suspected it, and you are right, the rituals and traditions we associate with Christmas actually have more to do with winter solstice than Christian doctrine.

Practically all the known ancient sun gods were born on December 25th. It was essentially the festival of the birth of the Sun God from the Virgin Queen of Heaven. The names of these entities varied between regions and cultures but the story was basically the same. In Egypt, he was Osiris or Horus. The priests and/or priestesses would emerge symbolically from underground caves and shrines at midnight announcing "the Virgin has brought forth—the light increases." In Canaan and Palestine, he was Tammuz. In India, he was called Indra. In Asia Minor, he was known as Attis. The Scandinavian goddess Frigga was born on December 25th and her dying and resurrected son, Balder, emerged on Christmas Eve. The ancient Chinese believed that at sunrise on the winter solstice the yang, or masculine principle, was born. Many Native populations from Central and North America also celebrated the birth of the child of the Celestial Queen around the winter solstice.

The winter solstice, however, precedes religious ideology. The solstices are astronomical facts. The winter solstice marks the shortest day and the longest night of the year. Twice a year, once in late June and again in late December, the sun appears to set and rise at the exact same time and in exactly the same place, giving the solstice its name, "the sun stood still." It was marked as a victory of light over darkness, life over death, and growth over decay. It was traditionally viewed as a time for people to celebrate the gradual lengthening of the days and the regeneration of the sun.

Saturnalia

Of all the winter solstice festivals, the Roman celebration of Saturnalia is probably the best known and the one that had the biggest influence on the medieval European Christmas. In Roman times, November was a month of hard work of harvesting and preparing the soil for the spring and there was little or no time for leisure and festivals. But December was the time of the Saturnalia. All the agricultural work had been done and the people were finally able to relax and enjoy themselves a bit more. While the actual festival started on the 17th of December and went for seven days, all of December was consumed by preparations and activities surrounding the most popular Roman festival of the year. The origins of the Saturnalia are obscure but similar types of festivals took place in many different places around the region. Saturnalia's likely precursor was the Babylonian festival of Sacaea, a festival that marked the twelve days of chaos and conflict between the cosmos; good and evil; and summer and winter.

Saturnalia was held in honour of the Roman god Saturn. Saturn was both sinister as the reaper of death and time; and nurturing as a god of agriculture and ruler of the Golden Age. The Golden Age of Saturn was viewed as the utopian time before agriculture when humanity lived in friendship with the animals. The Breton legend of animals being given the gift of speech on Christmas Eve comes from the belief that, before humans arrived on the scene, there existed a utopian period of time when animals possessed the power of speech.

For one week in December, all laws—civic and moral—were suspended. Businesses closed, there was noisy rejoicing, gambling was allowed in public, and festivities could be heard around every corner. Slaves and masters changed places and slaves were allowed unlimited licence. They sat down at their master's tables, wore their master's clothes, ordered their master's around, drank as much as they wanted, and exhibited behaviour that would normally have been punished by imprisonment or death.

A master of ceremony, chosen by lottery, resided over the festivities. His role was to play Mock King and he was given complete and absolute license to do as he wished. His sole responsibility consisted of presiding over the revels and making silly, fun, or downright ridiculous and scandalous demands of his subjects. As you can probably figure, sex and dancing naked were quite popular requests. You can't really be too hard on the guy for being extravagant—at the end of Saturnalia, he was sacrificed by cutting his own throat on Saturn's altar. Although this bloodshed was supposed to symbolize the renewal of life at the winter solstice, it is also possible that the Mock King acted as a New Year's scapegoat as well—by taking his own life, he took with him the sins of the community as a whole.

While Saturnalia's original function was to mark the human idealization of a utopian time when humans were all equal and people lived in harmony with the plants and the other animals sharing the earth. Saturnalia eventually degraded into a week-long spree of debauchery and crime. This is not surprising considering how repressive and hierarchical Roman society was. It was a society made up of a small group of male elites who controlled all the resources, wealth, and held power of life and death over their families and the rest of the population. With so many oppressed people finally given the chance to let off some steam, what did they expect?

The Creation of Christmas

With the Roman army being so effective at conquering nations, a new problem emerged. The Roman Empire acquired so many different languages, tribes, ethnic, and religious groups into its mélange that it began looking for a common thread to better assimilate all these diverse peoples into Roman culture. So many emperors had conducted themselves so foolishly and cruelly that the common people found it difficult to take seriously the previous official dogma that the emperor was the incarnate deity (if they ever took it seriously to begin with). The worship of the sun, however, was a common thread running through many of the cultures conquered by the Romans. Around the year 200 C.E., Emperor Severus identified himself with the sun god named Sol and took the title Invictus (Unconquered) and chose December 25th as the date for the new festival that was to replace the Saturnalia—and *Dies Natalis Invicti Solis* or, as we would say it, the Birthday of the Unconquerable Sun was born.

With so many gods having being born on the December 25th date, it is not surprising that another one soon emerged. This one proved even more popular than all the other gods preceding him and was spread far and wide by the Roman soldiers who worshipped him. The new god was born of a virgin in lowly surroundings and was attended by shepherds. The chief tenants of his faith were fraternity and moral purity with the hope of everlasting life. He performed the usual assortment of miracles—raising the dead, healing the sick, helping the blind see, and making the lame walk. At the end of his time on earth, he and his disciples shared a last supper, which was later commerated by believers in a communion of bread and wine. He was said not to have died but to have been returned to heaven and his followers believed he would come again at the end of the world. His triumph and ascension to heaven were celebrated at the spring equinox. His name was—get this—Mithras.

So close was the story of Mithras to the Christian story of Jesus that the early Church decided to get around the problem by using their old excuse that Mithras and his parallel life was the work of Satan. I wonder how this defence would work in a copyright trial? Mithras, however, predates Jesus by centuries and had a good head start. His followers, who included most Roman soldiers, had allies in high places and his cause was spread throughout the empire. In order to appease his Mithras-worshipping soldiers, Emperor Aurelian decided to consolidate the worship of Mithras with that of Sol Invictus.

As the years passed, a radical Jewish sect calling themselves Christians became more and more effective at brewing trouble for Roman authorities. Emperor Constantine, being politically astute enough to realize that the best way to defuse a movement is to co-opt it, made Christianity the official state religion with himself as its head, naturally. Christians went from being the persecuted religion to being the recipient of public funds that were used to build churches and set up a religious hierarchy. By the end of the fourth century, all the old forms of worship had been banned and Christianity began spreading across the lands.

During the first three centuries since its inception, Christianity held no official celebrations of Jesus' birth. In 354 C.E., however, Constantine fixed the birth of Jesus with that of Mithras and it was out with Sol Invictus and Mithras and in with the Feast of the Nativity. Although we accept the date of December 25th as Jesus' birthday, there is still much controversy surrounding this date. We do not even know the actual year Jesus was born. It is estimated to have been sometime between 12 and 4 B.C.E. Since we know that King Herod died in 4 B.C.E., the events cannot postdate that. The census that drew Joseph to booked-up Bethlehem was issued sometime between 11 and 7 B.C.E. If the "stars in the east" were Halley's comet, as some claim, then that would make it 12 B.C.E. Or, as others claim, if the "stars in the east" were the planets of Saturn and Jupiter in conjunction with Pisces, then that would have made it 7 B.C.E.

The actual date of Jesus' birthday is never stated in the New Testament but scholars all agree that it is unlikely to have been in December. This conclusion is based on the only hint at the date of his birth as told in the Gospel of Luke, which says that the shepherds were outdoors tending their flock. If this was so, then the weather must have been warm at the time of his birth; scholars favoured anywhere from late spring to early fall. December 25th was chosen for the practical purpose of connecting it with numerous pagan practices that centred around the winter solstice and to satisfy the people who were unwilling to give up their earlier beliefs and rites.

Virgins Giving Birth? What's Up with That?
No one can help but raise their eyebrows at the idea of a woman getting pregnant and giving birth and yet still keeping her hymen intact. A doctor friend once told me he did not see what the big deal with the immaculate conception was—each week, at least two girls show up at his office pregnant and claiming they've never had sex.

The priestesses of Ishtar, Asherah, and Aphrodite were called Holy Virgins. The function of such Holy Virgins was believed to be to dispense the goddesses' grace through sexual worship, heal, prophesize, perform sacred dances, and wail for the dead. According to Briffault, children born to these temple women were called *bathur* by the Semites and *parthenioi* by the Greeks—both meaning "virgin-born."[1]

It seems the idea of Mary being a virgin at the time of Jesus' birth arose out of a mistranslation or a misrepresentation of the original text in the book of Isaiah, which did not use the Hebrew word for virgin—*betulah*—but rather used the Hebrew word *almah*, meaning, "a young unmarried woman." While we may think of an unmarried woman as a virgin—before the days when unmarried women were stoned to death for partaking in the pleasures of the flesh—a woman's virginal status at marriage was not an issue. A woman's appeal was enhanced by her sexual experience and even more so if she was able to prove her fertility by already having had children.

The notion that gods or spirits impregnated mortal women was a matter of everyday acceptance throughout the ancient world. In the first century C.E., Greek biographer Plutarch noted among the Egyptians the common belief that the spirit of God was capable of sexual intercourse with mortal women. Even the Old Testament says that the archaic giants (ancestral spirits) were born of mortal women impregnated by spirits that came from God (Genesis 6:4). Numerous heroes and/or saviours including Zoroaster, Sargon, Perseus, Jason, Miletus, Minos, Hercules, and dozens of others were god-begotten and virgin-born.

Mary's impregnation with Jesus was similar to the way many other goddesses or mortal women became pregnant in myths—through an encounter with a divine presence. "And the angel came in unto her, and said, Hail, [thou that art] highly favoured, the Lord [is] with thee: blessed [art] thou among women" (Luke 1:28). This sounds kind of like a biblical way of saying sexual intercourse.

After Christianity was established as the official religion of the Roman Empire, Church fathers tried to discredit all other virgin births by claiming that the Devil had devised them and, just to really mess people up, maliciously made them predate Jesus.

Many Christians have criticized the idea that early Church officials allowed Christianity to become infused with various pre-Christian religious rites, beliefs, and customs. But we can't blame them for taking that route. Just imagine how you would react if you were told that from this day forth you were no longer able to celebrate your special days, whatever they might be. The challenge of taking away the times of the year when people got together, celebrated, and threw great parties would not be easy now and it was not easy then. Many religions tried to eliminate religions that were worshiped previous to them and found that it was a lot easier to change the doctrine than it was to change the associated rites, activities, and festivities. The majority of Christian missionaries who penetrated Western Europe after the decline of the Roman Empire followed Pope Gregory I's ruling that they continue to observe the old pagan customs and infuse them with Christian significance in order to propagate the faith.

The Heyday of Christmas

Anyone who is jaded by our modern-day overindulgence and consumerism associated with Christmas and is searching for the wholesome simple yuletide festivities of days past should not go back to medieval Europe. From the first recorded English Christmas in 521 until the mid-1500s, the Christmas feasting and celebration that took place would make us look like a bunch of nerds and scrooges. Although people went to church, the Christmas mass might be a bit of a shock for us twentieth-century folks. The Mock King or Lord of Misrule would direct the proceedings, especially on the eve of the last day of the festivities, also known as Twelfth Night. People dressed up in masks and costumes and often even in the robes of the priests and sang raunchy hymns, gambled, and drank alcohol on the altar. Twelfth Night mass was a rare opportunity to poke some fun at the Church which was so solemn, serious, and yet powerful the rest of the year.

Christmas was a twelve-day festival that provided many people with a respite from harvesting and sowing and the dreary winter. Huge pageants, masquerades, tournaments, revelries, and feasts took place all over the cities and the countryside. In 1252, King Henry III had 600 oxen killed and served with salmon pie, roast peacock, and flowing wine to all his Christmas guests. In 1377, Richard II had a Christmas feast for over ten thousand people. In 1533, Henry VIII, after making himself the Supreme Head of the Church of England, proceeded to rival all previous kings in yuletide extravagance.

It was not only the royalty who showed such hospitality and

generosity at this time of year. It was expected that the wealthy gentry would open their houses for feasting and celebrating and many rich landowners spent the twelve days of Christmas celebrating in the cities in order to impress the neighbours, improve their social standing in society, and give to the needy and poor.

The Fall of Christmas
Christmas in England continued in the same spirit until the sixteenth century when the protestant reformation toned down the yuletide revelries. Then the Puritans got a hold of it and tried to drive a few nails into Christmas' coffin. The colonists of the Plymouth plantation in the New World tried to stamp out what they considered the "pagan mockery of the observance of Christmas." People were penalized for any frivolity on that day. In 1659, the Massachusetts Bay Colony Puritan Court enacted a law requiring the penalty of five shillings for "observing any such day as Christmas" and an anti-Christmas squad was sent around to break up any yuletide celebrations.[2] In England, Oliver Cromwell also forbade any public celebrations of Christmas.

At first the people tried to disobey, leading to riots and social discontent. After many deaths, however, the Puritans eventually won out. They held their ground until the Christmas-loving Irish and German immigrants in the nineteenth century provided an influx of Christmas spirit into the United States. After almost two hundred years, the Puritan Christmas ban was lifted. In seventeenth-century England, King Charles II, upon regaining the throne, restored Christmas, May Day, and a number of other holidays. Despite their reinstatement, however, Christmas celebrations never regained their previous public displays of revelry and instead donned a social manner centred on family, friends, and home.

The disappearance of many medieval holidays can be attributed to Protestant and Puritan dislike of showy pagan-infused Catholic holidays. A third influence, the Industrial Revolution, which witnessed many companies' unwillingness to cut into profits by sparing workers time off, also played a significant role. With the coming of the Industrial Revolution, all thoughts had seemingly turned toward work, while fun, life, and family took a back seat in the quest for money and progress. In 1761, the Bank of England closed for forty-seven holidays over the course of a year; in 1834, it closed for only four. Employees of the mid-1800s considered themselves lucky to get a half-day off for Christmas. It was this spirit of festivity and giving that probably prompted Charles Dickens to create his miserly character Ebenezer Scrooge in *A Christmas Carol*.

Christmas Side Festivals

Although we call it the Christmas season, with all things considered, our modern-day Christmas is really only a one-day, one-night festivity. Unfortunately for many people, the only legal holiday they get off work is December 25th.

Even though we don't really celebrate them much anymore, there are still remnants of other days that used to be part of the Christmas season. We still observe them to a certain extent but, as with most holidays, we have little understanding of their original meanings and purposes.

Advent

Just as Lent is a period for Christians to prepare for Easter, Advent is a period of preparation for Christmas. The word *Advent* comes from the Latin *adventus*, meaning, "coming" or "arrival." Advent was originally a time for fasting and penance and was observed by Eastern and some Western Churches as preparation for Old Christmas Day (the feast of Epiphany on January 6th). When Rome fixed December 25th as the commemoration of Christ's birth in the fourth century, however, Advent underwent a shift in both time and mood. No longer a period of fasting and self-reflection, Advent became a time of joyous anticipation to better integrate itself into the period of anticipation and preparation.

The only thing many of us know about Advent comes from the Advent calendar that parents give to children to tide them over until Christmas. The calendar originated in Germany and quickly spread to other European countries. It usually consists of a Christmas "house" printed on cardboard with twenty-four small cut-out windows that were opened by folding them back to reveal a miniature picture or symbol associated with Christmas.

It was originally intended to teach the Christian Christmas story to children. The last door or window is opened on Christmas Eve to reveal the nativity scene. Nowadays, it is usually a distraction to hold kids off from driving their parents crazy by continually asking them "how many more days 'til Christmas?"

Boxing Day

In England, Australia, Canada, and many other countries, the day after Christmas is known as Boxing Day. It is now known as the day when people raid the stores to pick up a bargain here or there, or to satisfy their wants left unfulfilled. It used to be called St. Stephen's Day. Stephen was Christianity's first martyr other than Jesus. He went out on a limb and told the Sanhedrin (the Jewish Council) in first-century Palestine that the new Christian law should override the old Mosaic Law. The elders' response was to have him stoned to death by the gate of Jerusalem, which now bears his name. Before meeting his demise, however, the Apostles had appointed Stephen as a keeper of alms for the poor. December 26th became associated with the doling of alms. It was usual to open church alms boxes for the benefit of the poor and sometimes food was doled out instead of money.

The box tradition likely stems from Roman times when money to pay for athletic games was collected in boxes. Amongst the ruins of Pompeii, coin-filled earthenware boxes with slits in the tops have been found. The Romans brought the idea of collection boxes to Britain and monks and clergy soon thereafter used similar boxes to collect money for the poor at Christmas. During the reign of Puritanism in England, when individual Saint Days, Christmas, and all such festivities were abolished, the alms box custom was also eliminated. This caused hardship for some to the extent that the needy and destitute took matters into their own hands. They visited their richer neighbours carrying collection boxes. Tradesmen and errand boys later adopted the idea and began to call on their bosses and their clients the day after Christmas with boxes ready to collect tips.

Epiphany

Epiphany (January 6th) was the first date chosen by Christians to celebrate the birth of Jesus in the eastern part of the Roman Empire. It is likely this day was chosen because it coincided with an important day in Egypt. This date corresponded to the birth-date of their dying and resurrected sun god called Horus or Osiris. The water in the Nile River was supposed to be purest and so it was stored in special containers for use on holy occasions throughout the year. Holy water is still drawn from the Nile by Egyptian Christians and used for the year's baptism and sacraments. The word *epiphany* means "manifestation" or "showing." In the ancient Greek and Roman world, *epiphaneia* referred to an occasion on which a king or an emperor made an official state visit to a city, showing himself publicly to his people.

In the Christian world, Epiphany celebrates Christ's manifestation to the world via his birth, his baptism by Saint John the Baptist, and also two other events—the miracles of turning water into wine and the feeding of a crowd of five thousand—both of which are said to have occurred on this date. It also celebrates the day the Magi visited baby Jesus. In Spain and Italy, presents are exchanged at Epiphany instead of Christmas and the Magi bring the gifts to the children. The period between Christmas and Epiphany is celebrated as the Twelve Days of Christmas. For most of the Christian world today, Epiphany marks the end of the twelve days and an appropriate time to take down Christmas decorations and greenery.

Christmas Traditions

There are so many traditions and customs associated with Christmas that it is difficult to know where to start, but I think Santa Claus is a good target.

Santa Claus

There has been an urban myth floating around that it was the Coca-Cola Company who first created the character of Santa Claus. Although it did not actually "invent" Saint Nick, Coca-Cola was the first to see the advertising potential presented by this roly-poly red-suited man. So if Coca-Cola didn't create him, where did old Saint Nick come from? The origin of our Santa Claus comes from mixing the gift givers from numerous different cultures into something completely new, and yet still pretty much the same.

Each culture had their very own gift-giving character. In the Germanic religion, the chief god Woden (or Odin) rode around on an eight-legged white horse delivering his bounty. For the Dutch, it was Sinter Claus who wore bishop's robes and rode a white horse that flew through the sky. For the Scandinavians, Odin and his eight-legged horse, Sleipnir, travelled throughout the world delivering rewards and punishments. His son Thor, the god of farming and thunder, fought and conquered the gods of ice and snow and was victorious over the cold with his weapon of lightning and fire. He made his home in the far north and his colour was red. The Norse had their goddess of the home, Hertha. Before the holiday feast, a fire of fir boughs was laid on an altar of flat stones in the fireplace in the belief that Hertha would come through the chimney and appear in the smoke to bring the family good fortune.

Christians banned these other gods and goddesses, but only in form. A legend grew around a man named Nicholas who lived during the fourth century in a small town called Myra in what is now modern-day Turkey. He was a wealthy bishop, and very generous and modest as well. He liked to help people in need without drawing attention to himself. Poor people would often find a gold piece or a well-filled purse without knowing from whom it had come. Quite a rarity in any century, it is no surprise he stood out.

One legend attributed to Nicholas helps explain the origin of our modern-day custom of leaving stockings by the fireplace in the hope that they will be filled with goodies. Three daughters, whose father did not have enough money to pay for their marriage dowries, decided to help their father by selling themselves into prostitution. Upon hearing this sad outcome, Bishop Nicholas snuck by their house on three successive nights and each time he tossed a ball of gold through an open window. On the last night, the ball of gold landed in one of the stockings the girls had left out to dry by the fire.

After many more good deeds and/or legends, Saint Nicholas died on the 6th of December in 326 C.E. Some say he was martyred for his faith but others maintain that he was one of the few saints who actually died of natural causes.

More than six hundred years after St. Nicholas' death, Russians carried his legend back from Constantinople and he became Russia's patron saint. From there, his story made its way over to Europe and Scandinavia. Besides being a gift giver, he was also known as a disciplinarian who brought switches for children who misbehaved. His feast day was set on December 6th, and in many countries this is the day, not Christmas, when his presents and punishments are handed out. Martin Luther, in his attempt to expunge any pagan and Catholic influence from the new Protestant religion, tried to substitute the Christ child for Saint Nicholas as the bearer of gifts and moved the day of his arrival from December 6th to December 25th.

The person who brings gifts to children in Italy is known as Befana. According to legend, she is an old woman who offered shelter to the wise men on their voyage to visit the baby Jesus. They encouraged her to come with them but she said she was too busy spinning. She later regretted her decision and tried to make amends by going around the world at Christmas distributing gifts to good children. Each year, she passes through Italy in her continuing search for the bambino Jesus hoping that each child to whom she brings a gift is the one she has been seeking. Children write her letters asking for specific presents. She slides down the chimney on Epiphany Eve (January 5th) and fills their stockings and shoes with toys. Parents of misbehaving children threaten to tell La Befana to leave only pebbles, charcoal, or ashes.

Our modern image of Santa Claus came about thanks to Washington Irving who was inspired to describe him as a chubby little man with an alcoholic nose and a jolly smile being pulled by a team of reindeer. Clement C. Moore, captivated by the idea, wrote the now famous "The Night Before Christmas," published in 1823 with the original title of "A Visit from St. Nicholas." Shortly thereafter, our amalgamated modern-day image of a red-suited, generous, roly-poly, jolly Santa Claus, who lives in the North Pole and is aided by eight flying reindeer and can magically make it down the smallest of chimneys despite his hefty size, was born.

The Origin of "Xmas"

I have always wondered were the term "Xmas" came from. Many people, especially those intent on preserving the holiday's Christian religious roots, regard Xmas as an insult to Christ brought on by disrespect or laziness. Although it does fit better into newspaper headlines, its intent is not to disrespect, but laziness may be somewhat blamed. It comes from the letter X representing *chi*, being the first letter in the Greek word for Christ. Back in the days before photocopiers and the printing press, every document had to be handwritten by well-paid scribes. In order to save time and money, a sort of shorthand was developed for words that were used repeatedly. *Christ* was one of those words. The term *Christmas* is more recent; it is derived from the tenth-century Old English *Cristes Maesse* (Christ's mass).

Mistletoe and Holly

The Druids of ancient Ireland and England worshipped mistletoe, which is a parasitic plant that draws its water and nutrients from the tree on which it grows. To the Druids, mistletoe represented immortality because it retained its green colour throughout the winter, even after it had been cut. We may find this worship strange since the only mistletoe we are likely to see is the one that gets hung up at the Christmas office party—a plastic replica that we either avoid like the plague or strategically wander near in order to take advantage of an appealing opportunity. Those of us who have not been lucky enough to see the real thing will find it hard to understand the weird quality of this green ball suspended amongst the dead winter branches. We might wonder how the tradition of kissing under the mistletoe ever originated. There are two variations of this tradition: one from the Druids and the other from the Norse. Both are great stories.

To the Druids, kissing under the mistletoe and holly originated in the belief that these plants enhanced sexual power. The white berries of the mistletoe plant represented semen and the red berries of the holly were equated with menstrual blood (con-

244 — Gabriella Kalapos

sidered the blood of life). During the winter solstice celebrations, mistletoe and holly were often displayed together and symbolized the divine marriage of male and female, and feminine and masculine. Our seemingly innocent kiss under the mistletoe is a pale shadow of the sexual celebrations that once accompanied the rites of the winter solstice. Just think of the dynamics that this would add to the Christmas office parties of days past! Based on its sexual connotations and its general association with pagan religions, mistletoe was banned from Christmas church decorations until the last century. The Church, with its more puritanical practices, tried to eliminate the custom of kissing under the mistletoe. While unable to do so, they did create a tradition in an attempt to limit its usage; they stated that a berry had to be removed for each kiss, and once all the berries were gone, the tradition ceased to be appropriate.

The ancient Norse also thought mistletoe was sacred and had the tradition of kissing underneath it. The origin of their tradition is less titillating but still a great story. The myth tells of Frigga, the goddess of love, becoming alarmed because her son Balder had a dream of his death. She thought that if Balder, who was the sun god, were to die, then all life on earth would also die. Frigga immediately set to work and made all the animals, plants, and minerals—including fire and water—swear an oath saying they would not harm him. Once the other gods realized that Balder was invincible, they often amused themselves by shooting arrows and stones at him. She did overlook one plant, however—the parasitic mistletoe.

The jealous god of evil, Loki, disguised himself and snuck into a dinner party the gods and goddesses were having. He somehow managed to trick Frigga into admitting her fatal oversight. Loki then tricked the blind god of winter, Hoder, into shooting Balder with an arrow he had secretly tipped with mistletoe. When the arrow struck, the god of light was killed. This goes to show that even the most powerful overprotective mother in the world cannot account for all possibilities. The whole world mourned and all became cold and dark.

At the end of three days of trying to bring Balder back to life, Frigga finally succeeded with her power of love. Her tears of joy became crystallized as mistletoe berries and she began to kiss everyone who passed under the tree containing mistletoe where she was standing as she made a decree: Never again would the mistletoe do any harm and anyone who stood under it would be rewarded with a kiss. This myth also led to the ancient Scandinavian custom that arose whenever enemies encountered each other under the mistletoe. They would lay down their arms and maintain a truce until the following day.

The Christmas Tree

Many people are aware that the Christmas tree is a remnant of the pagan practice of using evergreens to symbolize life in the dead of winter. The worship of trees has always played an important part in the spiritual life of many cultures. Both the ancient Norse and the people of central Asia envisioned the universe as a giant tree with the earth's axis as its trunk, the stars and the moon as lights in its branches, and the underworld lay among its roots. Similar world-tree ideas are to be found among the native people of North and South America, India, China, and many other places.

At the dawn of history, most of Europe—from Northern England to the coasts of the Atlantic and Mediterranean, all the way to the Black Sea—was covered with immense primeval forests. Of these, only a few square miles in Poland still exist today. The temples of the Norse, the Teutons, and the Druids, to name but a few, were not located within trees that were cut down to build temples and churches but rather in the sacred living groves themselves. The divine in all its myriad forms was sung, danced, prophesized, and celebrated in these sacred places. The trees were regarded as full of spirit, and many ancient peoples only felled living specimens out of dire necessity.

The Christmas tree, with its green foliage, has its origins in the very ancient belief that at the time of the winter solstice when all of nature seemed dead, evergreen trees were one of the few remaining signs that nature was still alive. During the winter solstice, the Norse, the Teutons, and the Druids would hold rituals in the woods and decorate the branches of the evergreens with candles, cakes, apples, and other such gifts. Even the Romans held on to a remnant of the ancient respect accorded to trees. They decorated their homes, temples, and statues with snippets of foliage they cut from evergreen trees during their Saturnalia festival, but they did not cut down trees and bring them into their homes.

Although Christmas trees can nowadays be seen everywhere during the holiday season, the cut and decorated Christmas tree as we know it didn't come to America until arriving from Germany in the early eighteenth century. Hessian soldiers put up the first Christmas tree on record in the United States in 1776. They were mercenaries from Prussia (now Germany) hired by King George III of England to fight in the Revolutionary War against the United States.

The Germans had for some time been celebrating Christmas by setting up wooden structures shaped like a pyramid and covering them with branches pruned from evergreens. The Christmas tree is still even more a part of the Christmas celebration in Germany than it is in England and North America. No one in Germany is too poor, lonely, or busy to put up a tree. Unlike North Americans who tend to arrange their Christmas presents around the base of the tree, the Germans consider the tree a gift unto itself. It is decorated in secret and revealed with much pomp and fanfare to the assembled family and friends on Christmas Eve.

The Christmas-loving Germans can also be given credit for introducing the Christmas tree to England. In 1840, Queen Victoria's German-born Prince Albert, feeling nostalgic for his homeland, had a Christmas tree erected in Windsor Castle. Their elegant tree appeared in *Godey's Lady's Book*, the fashionable women's magazine of the time. The idea spread quickly because Victoria and her family enjoyed an astonishing popularity that bordered on religious adoration, and much of what they did was widely emulated.

Christmas Eve

My family, being of Hungarian origin, followed the tradition of beginning Christmas celebrations on Christmas Eve. We would all go over to my aunt and uncle's house, eat lots of food, and, with visions of stuffed cabbage dancing in our stomachs, sing a few carols and wait until we heard some noise coming from the front or back of the house. The kids would then run over each other to be the first one to go out into the yard and grab the booty tastefully packaged in a large black garbage bag. The next few hours would be spent rummaging through that black garbage bag and distributing the goodies with only the flickering lights of the Christmas tree to guide our way. No one wanted to disturb the ambiance of the Christmas tree, it being our source of light in the dark. When my Australian-Canadian husband came upon this scene and saw us opening presents on Christmas Eve, he thought we did it because we were too impatient or greedy to wait until the morning. While that might very well be so, it was not the reason we chose Christmas Eve. In many non-English-speaking European countries, especially in German-influenced areas, Christmas Eve is a much bigger deal than Christmas Day.

Since I have young children who would gladly stay up all night opening presents and playing with their new toys, I have moved over to the Christmas morning tradition. While it is still a whole lot of fun, the lights of the Christmas tree do not have the same affect on me during the day as they do at night. I am look-ing forward to the time when my kids are old enough to stop themselves from breaking into hysterics because they are too tired but don't know how to stop. Then we can bring back the tradition of having family and friends tackle each other on their way to grabbing that garbage bag and distributing its bounty guided simply by the lights in the tree.

The Yule Log

The yule log gets its name from the Norse, who observed a twelve-day winter celebration called *Jòl*, which means "wheel" and refers to the turning of the sun at the winter solstice. Danish invasions of England during the ninth century introduced the Scandinavian term *yule* for Christmas. This pre-Christian, north-ern, yuletide festival welcomed the return of the sun at the win-ter solstice. While the sun is vital to survival everywhere, in northern countries, with their cold and dark winter, the coming of the sun and an increase in light at the turn of the year would have been an even bigger occasion for relief and rejoicing.

The yule log is traditionally burned on Christmas Eve and

throughout the Christmas season. The customary burning of the yule log was spread far and wide from Scandinavia to Germany, France, Switzerland, England, and even among the Slavs. The burning of the yule log is really a ceremony that aims to bring many of the elements of the public display of fire and light into the private home. In its purest form, the yule log is a whole trunk of a tree selected and cut on Candlemas (Groundhog Day) and dried throughout the year. The usual practice was to light the yule log with a fragment of the previous year's log, which had been kept in the house throughout the year in the belief that it provided protection against fire and lightning—a sort of primitive lightning rod and fire detector all in one.

Even up to recent times, bringing the yule log into the house was often accompanied by a great ceremony. The youngest child would pour wine, cider, or ale all over the log before it was placed into the fire. In England and Scandinavia, the yule log was often replaced by a large candle that was intended to burn throughout the entire night.

Gifts

If an alien were to come to earth during the Christmas season, it could be forgiven for thinking that our modern celebration of this holiday was the worship of material goods. Our modern-day obsession with gift giving at Christmas is just one of the things that makes Christmas fun but it is also the main reason we dread the season. No one can be blamed for thinking that Christmas was invented by the retail industry in order to suck us all into paying credit-card bills until the middle of April and beyond.

Although presents have always been a part of New Year and/or winter solstice celebrations, a far different emphasis was placed on the value of presents in ancient times. Egyptians used to give each other small symbolic presents conveying good-luck wishes for the New Year. In ancient Rome, it was customary to exchange cards and gifts on the first day of January. The giving and receiving of such tokens continued for some time in many European countries. The presents, however, were quite different—they consisted of cards, candles, or little charms that conveyed good luck. That is a far different cry from the video games,

DVDs, golf clubs, or $200 running shoes that we are holding out for now.

The commercialization of Christmas is not new. Any time you have a large group of people gathering together, smart people somewhere are going to realize that they can make a hefty profit. What I think has changed, especially for those who don't buy into the whole religious story, is that we have lost an understanding of what the holiday is all about. We don't really see what it provides to our lives or our psyche other than the rush of some retail therapy and acquired goods, although there is something to be said for that rush. It is a whole lot of fun to go out and look for the perfect gift for someone you care about—if you can find it, that is. And things turn particularly sour when you have to waste your time buying gifts for people who are difficult to buy for and you see no reason why you should get them a present, but you don't want to be embarrassed or considered cheap.

The whole gift-giving exchange has become less about what happiness you can provide to others and more about how other people will view you via the gifts you offer. This is why so many families cut back on gift giving for Christmas and only get the kids something. Some exchange presents for adults by pulling names out of a hat, or they might chip in to buy presents for needy children. For those families unwilling to give up the bounty of presents, many have made all the gifts anonymous or from Santa for both kids and adults. This way no one has to attempt to improve their self-esteem or value via their gifts. The families that have attempted this say that the number of presents diminishes but that the presents given are more appropriate to the receiver.

Most people would agree that gift giving, or, more truthfully, gift receiving, is enjoyable. We experience a rush when we receive something we've been pining for. But let's face it, the acquisition of material goods is like sugar. When we satisfy a nagging sugar craving, we feel energized and the feeling of emptiness subsides, letting us get on with our lives. Then twenty minutes later, we feel even more lethargic and emptier than before because we think we should be satisfied. And then we want more. If sweet foods were unavailable, we would be amazed at how much more we would actually appreciate something tasty and healthy that would fill up the emptiness more effectively.

We can't blame the retail industry for seizing the opportunity to make a bundle; if we were in their shoes, we would too. But if partaking in the orgy of shopping costs you financial stress for the next four months, is it really worth it? If it isn't for you, then I can bet it isn't for others around you either. Find an alternative. There are as many different strategies as there are families; the goal is to find one for yours. There might very well be one keener who wants to go all-out because they can afford to or because they are willing to take on the financial stress—let them do what they want. After a year or two, they will see that they no longer need to subject themselves to 22% interest payments. If they can afford to do this and it makes them happy, let them be happy because when it really comes down to it, almost all festivities are about bringing some freedom, enjoyment, and happiness to our lives.

The Quest for the Elusive Spirit of Christmas
In the buildup to December 25th, we hear a lot about this thing called the Spirit of Christmas. We know it has something to do with being kind and giving to those less fortunate than ourselves, but why did this feeling of charity and goodwill come about at this time of the year? Winter solstice festivals used to be about honouring and giving back to nature when she was down and out. The Norse and the Druids used to take offerings in the form of food, candles, and decorations out into nature and place it around the only sign around that Mother Nature was still alive— the evergreen tree. Fruits, cakes, meat, and nuts were placed around a live, standing, evergreen tree. This offering was for Mother Nature when she was going through some hard times, but it was also to be shared by the other creatures in the forest that were also having a rough time. Nowadays, we cut the trees down, bring them into our houses, and give ourselves presents.

While this is a time of year when we all try to be generous to the less fortunate, we have to face the fact that this highly commercialized season is more for the "haves" than it is for the "have-nots." Unless, of course, we are one of the have-nots, in which case Christmas is about trying to forget we are one of them. No easy feat at Christmas time. Maybe this elusive Spirit of Christmas isn't necessarily about this once-a-year generosity toward the less fortunate but rather an understanding of our interconnectedness.

Christmas was the time when our ancestors gave back a bit of what Mother Nature provided for them. They wanted to help her through her hard times so she would thrive in the spring. If nature did not provide for them in the spring, then next Christmas they would be the ones who were down and out. What is the difference between being a have and a have-not? We don't spend too much time thinking about how little separates the rich and the poor—a loving family, good friends, a few tough breaks, a mental or physical illness. The loss of a few positives or the addition of a few negatives can easily turn a have into a have-not

With over six billion people on the planet, realizing our interconnectedness becomes even more imperative. Our separation from nature and from each other is leading us to a time when much of what the earth provides for us might one day cease to exist. Clean air, clean water, clean food is not something we should take for granted. So much of our everyday lives centre around what separates us, not what connects us. This could be why I have always found Christmas rather anticlimactic. So much build up and at the end of it, many of us are left asking, "What was the point of that?"

Maybe the reason the Spirit of Christmas eludes many of us is because we are caught up in the spirit of charity at Christmas rather than the spirit of interconnectedness—that what we do to the earth, we do to ourselves; and what we do to others, we do to ourselves. At Christmas, we are given the chance to realize that the fate of the haves is linked to the fate of the have-nots, that the fate of nature is linked to the fate of humanity. Understanding this allows the Spirit of Christmas to follow us throughout the year and throughout our lives, perhaps even leading us to leave this world a better place than as we found it.

BRINGING THE HOLIDAYS HOME

When I first started researching this book, I thought it would end up being about the origin of our fascinating holiday traditions and be an entertaining and enlightening read. As I started digging deeper to answer all the whys that I felt needed to be answered, I was surprised to find that the story of the holidays was far more interesting, depressing, and meaningful than I could have ever imagined.

Holidays started out as attempts by our ancestors to pass on legacies that kept us in touch with the cycles of the seasons and thereby better ensuring our survival. Then as religion began taking over our holiday traditions, holidays became a way of teaching and reminding people of their particular religion's stories. In today's more secular society, we have to ask, "Besides being able to tell a few interesting anecdotes at the next dinner party I attend, what is knowing the ancient origin of our modern holidays going to do for me?"

What I found fascinating about holidays was their universality. No matter which culture, religion, or time period, people seem to have a need to set aside a number of days of the year as special days—days to take time off from the world of mundane problems and concerns and from the world of making a living and surviving—days dedicated to connecting us to the sacred. While we often think of holidays as days connected to the "holy," for many of us, the main thing we think of as holy is religion. If we do not relate to the religious stories, how can we relate to the holidays?

Holidays are not limited by religious beliefs or lack thereof. Our need for holidays stems from the relationship between holidays and spirituality. Spirituality is a celebration of the sacred. Sacredness is about paying honour to connections—between the cycles of the seasons and the cycles of our lives; people and nature; the individual and the family; the family and the community; and the community and the world. Holidays take us outside of the everyday and bring us into sacred time in order to help us make those connections.

Although the original intention of this universal human longing to acknowledge certain days of the year might have been to add meaning and joy to our lives, it has also been used to manipulate and control us. Religious organizations have recognized the capacity of holidays to effectively deliver their messages and stories and have realized that the stories associated with the holidays can be changed far more easily than it is to get people to give up their holidays.

The purpose of using holidays as a medium to deliver religious history often resulted in the disconnection with people who did not share the religious beliefs. All religions have wonderful messages that if practiced would result in a more caring and connected society but quite often religion also creates a divide between those who believe and those who do not.

I am not surprised that many people, especially women, have difficulty continuing to celebrate religion and in many ways this has resulted in difficulty relating to the holidays. Most of our religious stories, and therefore our holidays, are about honouring the divine masculine, be he called God, Jesus, Yahweh, or Allah. When I watch my son and daughter playing out cartoon or movie stories, inevitably my daughter chooses to play the female characters and my son chooses to play the male characters. In the stories of our holidays that for so long have been tied to the stories of our religions, where are the female characters?

This is the aspect of holidays I find the most depressing. By uncovering the origins of our holidays, we now know that there has been what seems like a conspiracy to downplay the role of nature and the divine feminine in our holidays, our religion, our spirituality, and our history. A part of our legacy was lost when this original meaning and purpose of the holidays was suppressed. I can't help but wonder, was it all done on purpose? If so, why? And, more important, what would the world look like today if the original balance between the divine feminine and the divine masculine, and between nature and people, was still a part of our holiday celebrations?

This lost holiday legacy has created a void; one that materialism has done its best to fill. To a certain extent, commercialism has been effective at changing the focus of the holidays. But from the level of stress and depression associated with our modern-day holidays, we have to admit that the acquisition and even the sharing of goods are not enough on their own to give meaning to our special days.

Holidays are gifts passed down through the ages; they are our cultural relics. For this reason, understanding how holidays have changed over time can help guide us through the journey of adding meaning, value, and purpose to our lives. How successful we are at doing this will determine the legacy we pass on.

What keeps coming to my mind when I think of what the holidays can be found in the book of Ecclesiastes in the Old Testament. You might recognize these lines as they were the basis for the song "Turn, Turn, Turn" performed by the Byrds:

> To every thing there is a season, and a time to every purpose under the heaven:
> A time to be born, and a time to die; a time to plant, and a time to pluck up that which is planted;
> A time to kill, and a time to heal; a time to break down, and a time to build up;
> A time to weep, and a time to laugh; a time to mourn, and a time to dance;
> A time to cast away stones, and a time to gather stones together; a time to embrace, and a time to refrain from embracing;
> A time to get, and a time to lose; a time to keep, and a time to cast away;

A time to rend, and a time to sew; a time to keep silence,
  and a time to speak;
A time to love, and a time to hate; a time of war, and a time
  of peace.

Ecclesiastes (3:1-8)

Intuitively, we understand that there are times of the year and times in our life that call for certain actions or behaviours. The challenge remains: How do we know what time it really is? By connecting us to the cycles of nature, the cycles of our life, the cycles of our psyche, and the cycles of our humanity, holidays can play a role in guiding us toward the appropriate course of action. They are the seeds we need to nurture, tend, and propagate in order to keep us connected to the things in life that we need to understand, feel, and act upon in order to better understand the world and our place in it.

CHAPTER NOTES

New Year's Day

1 B.C.E. (Before the Common Era) is the equivalent of B.C. (Before Christ), and C.E. (Common Era) is the same as A.D. (Anno Domini, or Year of Our Lord). B.C.E. and C.E. are favoured by many scholars who seek to avoid abbreviations that are limited to a specific religious denomination.

2 E. G. Richards, *Mapping Time: The Calendar* (Oxford: Oxford University Press, 2005), 206–219.

3 Harvey Cox, *The Feast of Fools* (Cambridge, MA: Harvard University Press, 1969), 152.

4 Leonard Shlain, *Alphabet Versus the Goddess: The Conflict Between Word and Image* (New York: Penguin, 1998), 224.

5 J. C. Cooper, *The Dictionary of Festivals* (San Francisco: Aquarian Press, 1990), 139.

6 Donald E Dossey, *Holiday Folklore, Phobias and Fun: Mythical Origins, Scientific Treatments and Superstitious Cures* (Los Angeles: Outcomes Unlimited Press), 30.

Groundhog Day

1 Sue Ellen Thompson, ed., *Holiday Symbols: A Guide to the Legend and the Lore Behind the People, Places, Foods, Animals, and Other Symbols Associated with Holidays and Holy Days* (Omnigraphics, 1998), 50.

2 A. W. F. Banfield, *The Mammals of Canada* (Toronto: University of Toronto Press, 1974), 107–109.

3 Pliny the Elder, *Natural History*, Book 28, (Cambridge: Harvard University Press, 1938-42), 78–80.

4 Barbara Walker, *The Woman's Encyclopedia of Myths and Secrets* (New York: HarperCollins, 1983), 643.

5 ibid, 643.

6 Joan Morris, *The Lady Was a Bishop* (New York: MacMillan, 1973), 110.

7 Barbara Walker, *The Woman's Encyclopedia of Myths and Secrets* (New York: HarperCollins, 1983), 644.

8 Barbara Walker, *The Woman's Encyclopedia of Myths and Secrets* (New York: HarperCollins, 1983), 8.

9 Barbara Walker, *The Woman's Encyclopedia of Myths and Secrets* (New York: HarperCollins, 1983), 635.

10 Robert Briffault, *The Mothers*, Vol. 2 (New York: MacMillan, 1927), 444–445.

Valentine's Day

1 For more information on the Roman persecution of Christians, see, Leonard Shlain, *The Alphabet Versus the Goddess: The Conflict Between Word and Image* (New York: Penguin, 1998), 254–257.

2 For more information on the Gnostics, see, Elane Pagels, *The Gnostic Gospels* (London: Weidenfeld and Nicholson, 1979).

3 Leonard Shlain, *The Alphabet Versus the Goddess: The Conflict Between Word and Image* (New York: Penguin, 1998), 244.

4 Sarah B. Pomeroy, *Goddesses, Whores, Wives and Slaves: Women in Classical Antiquity* (London: Robert Hale and Company, 1975), 169.

5 For more information on the worship of a Mother Goddess and matrilineal inheritance, see, Riane Eilser, *The Chalice and the Blade: Our History, Our Future* (San Francisco: Harper, 1987).

6 Deborah Blum, *Sex on the Brain: The Biological Differences Between Men and Women* (New York: Penguin, 1997), 94.

7 Mariette Nowak, *Eve's Rib: A Revolutionary New View of Female Sex Roles* (New York: St. Martin's Press, 1980), 235.

St. Patrick's Day

1 Barbara G. Walker, *Women's Encyclopedia of Myths and Secrets* (New York: HarperCollins, 1983), 774.

2 Máire de Paor and Liam de Paor, *Early Christian Ireland* (London: Thames and Hudson, 1958), 174.

3 See, http://www.answers.com/topic/republic-of-ireland (2002 Census).

4 See, http://nationalzoo.si.edu/Animals/Reptiles/Amphibians/NewsEvents/irelandsnakes.cfm

Easter

1 For more information on the history of the Bible, see, David Norton, *A History of the English Bible as Literature* (Cambridge: Cambridge University Press, 2000).

2 For more information on the historical documentation of Jesus, see, Timothy Freke and Peter Gandy, *The Jesus Mysteries: Was the "Original Jesus" a Pagan God?* (London: HarperCollins, 1999).

3 Barbara G. Walker, *The Women's Encyclopedia of Myths and Secrets,* (New York: HarperCollins, 1983), 188–190.

April Fool's Day

1 For more information on the evolution of our modern-day calendar, see E. G. Richards, *Mapping Time: The Calendar* (Oxford: Oxford University Press, 2005).

May Day

1 Riane Eisler, *Sacred Pleasure: Sex, Myth, and the Politics of the Body–New Paths to Power and Love* (New York: Doubleday, 1996), 134.

2 Elaine Pagels, *Adam, Eve and the Serpent* (New York: Vintage, 1988), 117.

Mother's Day

1 There are numerous books that highlight the worship of a Mother Goddess and the associated political and social ramifications of such worship. I suggest browsing through the bibliography to identify just a few, but for a great reference, see, Riane Eisler, *The Chalice and the Blade: Our History, Our Future* (San Francisco: Harper, 1987).

2 Barbara G. Walker, *The Women's Encyclopedia of Myths and Secrets* (New York: HarperCollins, 1983), 681.

3 Barbara Walker, *The Women's Encyclopedia of Myths and Secrets* (New York: HarperCollins, 1983), 680.

4 Robert Briffault, *The Mothers* Vol.2 (New York: MacMillan, 1927), 445–447.

5 Merlin Stone, *When God Was a Woman* (London: Virago (Quartet), 1976), 11.

6 Joyce Tyldesley, *Daughters of Isis: Women of Ancient Egypt* (London: Viking, 1994), 38–44.

7 Merlin Stone, *When God Was a Woman* (London: Virago (Quartet), 1976), 36.

8 Merlin Stone, *When God Was a Woman*, (London: Virago (Quartet), 1976), 15.

9 For more information on the role of women in Roman society, see, Sarah Pomeroy, *Goddesses, Whores, Wives and Slaves: Women in Classical Antiquity* (London: Robert Hale and Company, 1975), chapter 8.

10 Rudolf Augstein, *Jesus, Son of Man* (New York: Urizen Books, 1977), 298.

11 Barbara G. Walker, *The Woman's Encyclopedia of Myths and Secrets* (New York: HarperCollins, 1983), 623.

12 Homer William Smith, *Man and His Gods* (Grosset & Dunlap, 1957), 263; and Elise Boulding, *The Underside of History: A View of Women Through Time* (SAGE, 1992), 399.

13 Ronald Pearsall, *Night's Black Angels: The Forms and Faces of Victorian Cruelty* (D. McKay Co., 1975), 40.

14 Frieda Hauswirth Das, *Purdah: The Status of Indian Women*. (Vanguard Press, 1932), chapter 1.

15 Leonard Shlain, *The Alphabet Versus the Goddess: The Conflict Between Word and Image* (New York: Penguin, 1998), 114.

16 Sarah Blaffer Hrdy, *Mother Nature: A History of Mothers, Infants, and Natural Selection* (New York: Random, 1999), 165.

17 Richard Leakey, *Origins Reconsidered: In Search of What Makes Us Human* (New York: Random, 1992), 160.

18 Sarah Blaffer Hrdy, *Mother Nature: A History of Mothers, Infants, and Natural Selection* (New York: Random, 1999), 126.

Father's Day

1 Adrienne Burgess, *Fatherhood Reclaimed: The Making of the*

Modern Father (London: Vermilion, 1997), 22.

2 J. Adler, "Building a better dad," *Newsweek* (June 17, 1996), 58–64.

3 Charles Lewis, *Becoming a Father* (Open University Press, 1986), 33.

4 Philip A. Cowan, "Becoming a Father: A Time of Change, An Opportunity for Development," in *Fatherhood Today: Men's Changing Role in the Family.* (pp 13–35). P. Bronstein and Carolyn Pape Cowan, eds. New York: Wiley, 1988.

5 Carolyn Cowan and Philip Cowan, *When Partners Become Parents: The Big Life Change for Couples* (New York: Basic, 1992), 102.

6 Jenny Kadz et al, *Working Long Hours: A Review of the Evidence*, Vol. 1 – Employment Relations Research Series No. 16 (London: Department of Trade and Industry, 2003), 16.

Summer Solstice/John the Baptist Day

1 Maureen Murdock, *The Heroine's Journey* (Boston: Shambhala, 1990), 108.

2 James George Frazer, *The Golden Bough: A Study in Magic and Religion* (Abridged ed. New York: Collier, 1950), 622–632.

Friday the 13th

1 Winnifred B. Cutler, Wolfgang M. Schleidt, Erika Freidmann, George Preti, and Robert Stine, "Lunar Influences on the Reproductive Cycle in Women," *Human Biology*, December 1987, Vol. 59, No. 6, 959–972.

Halloween

1 Jack Santino, ed., *Halloween and Other Festivals of Death and Life* (Knoxville: University of Tennessee Press, 1993), 88–90.

2 Joel Best and Gerald Horiuchi, "The Razor Blade in the Apple," *Social Problems*, June 1985 (Vol. 32, No. 5), 488–499.

Guy Fawkes' Night

1 See, http://www.channel4.com/history/microsites/H/history/treason/story.html

262 — *Gabriella Kalapos*

Remembrance Day

1 The United States also commemorates November 11th but they call it Veterans Day. It was formally known as Armistice Day but was given its new name after World War II. The Unites States has two days to honour war veterans, Memorial Day (May 30th or sometimes the last Monday in May) and Veterans Day (November 11th). Memorial Day is dedicated to remembering and honouring military personnel who died in service to their country. While the dead are also remembered on Veterans Day, this day is mainly dedicated to honouring all who served in the military, be it during war or peace time. The poppy is traditionaly worn on Memorial Day in the United States.

2 As an interesting side note in 1940, after Hitler marched into France and occupied it, Hitler required that the French sign their capitulation in the same railroad car where the terms of the Armistice were signed at the end of World War I. This signing resulted in the now famous image of Hitler walking away from the railroad car with the papers stating that Germany now occupied France and dancing the jig. In reality, he was not dancing the jig—it was the result of a BBC news editor who looped Hitler's gait creating an edited version that made Hitler look like he was dancing the jig.

Thanksgiving

1 Proclamation issued by Canadian parliament on January 31, 1957.

2 Penelope Revelle and Charles Revelle, *The Global Environment: Securing a Sustainable Future* (Jones & Bartlett, 1992), 143, Table 6-3.

Christmas

1 Robert Briffault, *The Mothers*, Vol. 3 (New York: MacMillan, 1927), 169–170.

2 See, http://members.aol.com/wdwylie6/1650-1699.htm

BIBLIOGRAPHY

Armstrong, Karen. *The Gospel According to Woman: Christianity's Creation of a Sex War in the West*. London: Pan, 1987.

Armstrong, Karen. *A History of God: The 4000 Year Quest of Judaism, Christianity, and Islam*. New York: Alfred A. Knopf, 1993.

Banfield, A. W. F. *The Mammals of Canada*. Toronto: University of Toronto Press, 1974.

Baring, Anne, and Jules Cashford. *The Myth of the Goddess: The Evolution of an Image*. London: Penguin, 1991.

Barnstone, Willis. *The Other Bible*. New York: Harper & Row, 1984.

Batten, Mary. *Sexual Strategies: How Females Choose Their Mates*. New York: G. P. Putnam's Sons, 1992.

Begg, Ean. *The Cult of the Black Virgin*. New York: Arkana Penguin Books, 1985.

Bently, Peter, ed. *Dictionary of World Myth:* London: Duncan Baird, 1995.

Bevilacqua, Michelle, and Brandon Toropov, eds. *The Everything Christmas Book: Stories, Songs, Food, Traditions, Revelry and More*. Holbrook, MA: Adams Media, 1994.

Bierlein, J. F. *Parallel Myths*. New York: Ballantine, 1994

Blum, Deborah. *Sex on the Brain: The Biological Differences Between Men and Women*. New York: Penguin, 1997.

Briffault, Robert. *The Mothers: A Study of the Origins of Sentiments and Institutions*. 3 Vols. New York: MacMillan, 1927.

Burgess, Adrienne. *Fatherhood Reclaimed: The Making of the Modern Father*. London: Vermilion, 1997.

Burne, Charlotte Sophia. *The Handbook of Folklore: Traditional Beliefs, Practices, Customs, Stories, and Sayings*. London: Senate, 1995.

Cabot, Laurie. *Celebrate the Earth: A Year of Holidays in the Pagan Tradition*. New York: Doubleday, 1994.

Cade, Sharon. *Special Days: History, Folklore and What Not*. S C Enterprises, 1984.

Cahill, Thomas. *How the Irish Saved Civilization: The Untold Story of Ireland's Heroic Role from the Fall of Rome to the Rise of Medieval Europe*. New York: Doubleday, 1995.

Campbell, Joseph. *The Flight of the Wild Gander: Explorations in the Mythological Dimensions of Fairy Tales, Legends and Symbols*. New York: HarperCollins, 1990.

Campbell, Joseph. *The Hero's Journey: Joseph Campbell on His Life and Work*. New York: Harper & Row, 1990.

Campbell, Joseph. *Oriental Mythology: The Masks of God*. New York: Penguin Group, 1962.

Campbell, Joseph. *Primitive Mythology Vol. 1, The Masks of God*. New York: Penguin, 1968.

Chapman, J. A. and G. A. Feldhamer. *Wild Mammals of North America*. Baltimore: John Hopkins University Press, 1982.

Chernin, Kim. *Reinventing Eve: Modern Woman in Search of Herself*. New York: Harper Perennial, 1987.

Clarke, David, and Andy Roberts. *Twilight of the Celtic Gods. An Exploration of Britain's Hidden Pagan Traditions*. London: Cassell PLC, 1996.

Cohen, Hennig, and Tristram Potter Coffin, eds. *Folklore of American Holidays*. Detroit: Thomson Gale, 1987.

Coontz, Stephanie. *The Way We Never Were: American Families and the Nostalgia Trap*. New York: Basic Books, 1992.

Cooper, J. C. *The Dictionary of Festivals*. San Francisco: Aquarian Press, 1990.

Cosman, Madeleine Pelner. *Medieval Holidays and Festivals: A Calendar of Celebrations*. London: Piatkus, 1981.

Cowan, Carolyn Pape and Philip A. Cowan. *When Partners Become Parents: The Big Life Change for Couples*. New York: Basic Books, 1992.

Cowan, Philip A. "Becoming a Father: A Time of Change, An Opportunity for Development," in *Fatherhood Today: Men's Changing Role in the Family*. (pp 13–35). P. Bronstein and Carolyn Pape Cowan, eds. New York: Wiley, 1988.

Cox, Harvey. *The Feast of Fools: A Theological Essay on Festivity and Fantasy*. Cambridge, MA: Harvard University Press, 1969.

Davis-Kimball, Jeannine. *Warrior Women: An Archaeologist's Search for History's Hidden Heroines*. New York: Warner, 2002.

Delaney, Janice, Mary Jane Lupton, and Emily Toth. *The Curse: A Cultural History of Menstruation*. Chicago: University of Illinois Press, 1988.

de Paor, Máire, and Liam de Paor. *Early Christian Ireland*. London: Thames and Hudson, 1958.

Donzelot, Jacques. *The Policing of Families*. Trans. by Robert Hurley. New York: Pantheon, 1979.

Dossey, Donald E. *Holiday Folklore, Phobias and Fun: Mythical Origins, Scientific Treatments and Superstitious Cures*. Los Angeles: Outcomes Unlimited Press, 1992.

Dunwich, Gerina. *The Pagan Book of Halloween: A Complete Guide to the Magick, Incantations, Recipes, Spells and Lore*. New York: Penguin, 2000.

Eisler, Riane. *The Chalice and the Blade: Our History, Our Future*. San Francisco: Harper, 1987.

Eisler, Riane. *Sacred Pleasure: Sex, Myth, and the Politics of the Body–New Paths to Power and Love*. New York: Doubleday, 1996.

Eliade, Mircea. *The Myth of the Eternal Return: Cosmos and History*. Trans. by Willard R. Trusk. Princeton: Princeton University Press, 1954.

Eliade, Mircea. *Shamanism: Archaic Techniques of Ecstasy*. Trans. by Willard R. Trusk. Princeton: Princeton University Press, 1964.

Eliot, Alexander. *The Timeless Myths: How Ancient Legends Influence the Modern World*. New York: Truman Talley/Meridian, 1996.

Fausto-Sterling, Anne. *Myths of Gender: Biological Theories About Women and Men*. New York: Basic Books, 1985.

Fraser, Antonia. *The Gunpowder Plot: Terror and Faith in 1605*. London: Orion, 1996.

Frazer, James George. *The Golden Bough: A Study in Magic and Religion*. Abridged ed. New York: Collier, 1950.

Freke, Timothy, and Peter Gandy. *The Jesus Mysteries: Was the "Original Jesus" a Pagan God?* London: HarperCollins, 1999.

Freke, Timothy, and Peter Gandy. *Jesus and the Lost Goddess:*

The Secret Teachings of the Original Christians. New York: Three Rivers Press, 2001.

French, Claire. *The Celtic Goddess: Great Queen or Demon Witch?* Edinburgh: Floris, 2001.

French, Marilyn. *From Eve to Dawn: A History of Women*. Vol. 1: *Origins*. Toronto: McArthur & Company, 2002.

Frymer-Kensky, Tikva. *In the Wake of the Goddess: Women, Culture and the Biblical Transformation of Pagan Myth*. New York: Ballantine, 1992.

Gaer, Joseph. *Holidays Around the World*. Boston: Little, Brown & Company, 1953.

Gould Davis, Elizabeth. *The First Sex*. New York: Viking Penguin, 1972.

Graves, Robert. *The White Goddess*. New York: Farrar, Straus and Giroux, 1948.

Gregory, Ruth W. *Anniversaries and Holidays*. American Library Association, 1983.

Griffen, Robert, and Ann H. Shurgin, eds. *The Folklore of World Holidays*. Michigan: Thomson Gale, 1999.

Griswold, Robert L. *Fatherhood in America: A History*. New York: Basic Books, 1993.

Gulevich, Tanya, ed. *World Holiday, Festival, and Calendar Books: An Annotated Bibliography of More Than 1,000 Books on Contemporary and Historic Religious, Folk, Ethnic, and National Holidays, Festivals, and Celebrations*. Omnigraphics–Frederick G. Ruffner Jr. Publishers, 1998.

Hallam, Elizabeth, ed. *Gods and Goddesses: A Treasury of Deities and Tales from World Mythology*. New York: MacMillan, 1996.

Harrowven, Jean. *Origins of Festivals and Feasts*. London: Kay & Ward, 1980.

Heinberg, Richard. *Celebrate the Solstice: Honoring the Earth's Seasonal Rythms through Festival and Ceremony*. Wheaton, IL: Quest, 1993.

Helfman, Elizabeth S. *Celebrating Nature: Rites and Ceremonies Around the World*. New York: Seabury Press, 1969.

Henderson, Helene, and Sue Ellen Thompson, eds. *Holidays, Festivals, and Celebrations of the World Dictionary*. 2nd ed. Omnigraphics, 1997.

Henes, Donna. *Celestially Auspicious Occasions: Seasons, Cycles and Celebrations*. New York: Berkeley, 1996.

Highwater, Jamake. *Myth and Sexuality*. New York: New American Library, 1990 .

Hooke, S. H. *Middle Eastern Mythology*. Harmondsworth, U.K.: Penguin, 1963.

Hopkins, Keith. *A World Full of Gods: The Strange Triumph of Christianity*. New York: Penguin, 2001.

Hrdy, Sarah Blaffer. *Mother Nature: A History of Mothers, Infants, and Natural Selection*. New York: Random, 1999.

Husain, Shahrukh. *The Goddess: Power, Sexuality, and the Feminine Divine*. London: Duncan Baird, 1997.

Ickis, Marguerite. *The Book of Festivals and Holidays the World Over*. New York: Dodd-Mead, 1970.

James, E. O. *The Cult of the Mother Goddess*. London: Thames and Hudson, 1959.

James, E. O. *Prehistoric Religion: A Study in Prehistoric Archaeology*. London: Thames and Hudson, 1957.

James, E. O. *Seasonal Feasts and Festivals*. London: Thames and Hudson, 1961.

Jobes, Gertrude. *Dictionary of Mythology, Folklore and Symbols*. Vol. 3. New York: Scarecrow Press, 1962.

Kirsch, Jonathan. *The Harlot by the Side of the Road: Forbidden Tales of the Bible*. New York: Ballantine, 1997.

Larrington, Carolyne, ed. *Woman's Companion to Mythology*. London: Pandora Press, 1992.

Layton, Bentley. *The Gnostic Scriptures: Ancient Wisdom for the New Age*. New York: Doubleday, 1987.

Leakey, Richard. *Origins Reconsidered: In Search of What Makes Us Human*. New York: Random, 1992.

Lewis-Stempel, Jackson, ed. *Fatherhood*. London: Allen & Unwin, 1984.

Lindahl, Carl, John McNamara, and John Lindow, eds. *Medieval Folklore: A Guide to Myths, Legends, Tales, Beliefs and Customs*. Oxford: Oxford University Press, 2000.

McVickar Edwards, Carloyn. *The Storyteller's Goddess: Tales of the Goddess and Her Wisdom from Around the World*. 2nd ed. New York: Marlowe & Company, 2000.

Miles, Clement A. *Christmas Customs and Traditions: Their History and Significance.* Reprint, New York: Dover, 1976.

Moore, Thomas. *The Soul of Sex: Cultivating Life as an Act of Love.* New York: HarperCollins, 1998.

Morris, Joan. *The Lady Was a Bishop: The Hidden History of Women with Clerical Ordinations and the Jurisdiction of Bishops.* New York: MacMillan, 1973.

Murdock, Maureen. *The Heroine's Journey.* Boston: Shambhala, 1990.

Moussareff-Masson, Jeffrey. *The Emperor's Embrace: Reflections on Animal Families and Fatherhood.* New York: Simon & Schuster, 1999.

Neumann, Erich. *The Great Mother.* Trans. by Ralph Manheim. New York: Bollingen, 1963.

Nowak, Mariette. *Eve's Rib: A Revolutionary New View of Female Sex Roles.* New York: St. Martin's Press, 1980.

Pagels, Elaine. *The Gnostic Gospels.* London: Weidenfeld and Nicholson, 1979.

Pagels, Elaine. *The Origin of Satan.* New York: Random, 1995.

Pagels, Elaine. *Adam, Eve, and the Serpent.* New York: Vintage, 1988.

Parrinder, Geoffrey, ed. *World Religions: From Ancient History to the Present.* New York: Hamlyn, 1971.

Pennick, Nigel. *The Pagan Book of Days: A Guide to the Festivals, Traditions, and Sacred Days of the Year.* Rochester, VT: Destiny, 1992.

Phillips, Graham. *The Marian Conspiracy: The Hidden Truth About the Holy Grail, the Real Father of Christ and the Tomb of the Virgin Mary.* London: Pan, 2000.

Picnett, Lynn. *Mary Magdalene: Christianity's Hidden Goddess.* New York: Carroll & Graf, 2003.

Pieper, Joseph. *In Tune with the World: A Theory of Festivity.* Trans. by Richard and Clara Winston. New York: Harcourt, Brace & World, 1965.

Pomeroy, Sarah B. *Goddesses, Whores, Wives and Slaves: Women in Classical Antiquity.* London: Robert Hale and Company, 1975.

Popenoe, David. *Life Without Father: Compelling New Evidence that Fatherhood and Marriage are Indispensable for the Good of Children and Society.* New York: Free Press, 1996.

Ranke-Heinemann, Uta. "Female Blood: The Ancient Taboo and Its Christian Consequences," in *Eunuchs for Heaven*. London: Andre Deutsch, 1990.

Robbins, Tom. *Jitterbug Perfume*. New York: Bantam, 1984.

Robins, Gay. *Women in Ancient Egypt*. London: British Museum Press, 1993.

Rutherford, Ward. *Celtic Mythology*. London: HarperCollins, 1987

Rybczynski, Witold. *Waiting for the Weekend*. New York: Penguin, 1992.

Santino, Jack. *All Around the Year: Holidays and Celebrations in American Life*. Chicago: University of Illinois Press, 1994.

Schauffler, Robert, ed. *Mother's Day: It's History, Origin, Celebration, Spirit and Significance as Related in Prose and Verse*. Reprint, Omnigraphics, 1990.

Sharman-Burke, Juliet, and Liz Greene. *The Mythic Tarot Book*. Sydney: Simon & Schuster Australia, 1992.

Shlain, Leonard. *The Alphabet Versus the Goddess: The Conflict Between Word and Image*. New York: Penguin, 1998.

Sorell, Walter. *The Dance Has Many Faces*. Chicago: A Capella, 1966.

Steiner, Rudolf. *Festivals and Their Meaning* Trans. by M. Barton. London: Rudolf Steiner Press, 1996.

Stone, Merlin. *Ancient Mirrors of Womanhood: A Treasury of Goddess and Heroine Lore from Around the World*. Boston: Beacon Press, 1990.

Stone, Merlin. *When God Was a Woman*. London: Virago (Quartet), 1976.

Straffon, Cheryl. *The Earth Goddess: Celtic and Pagan Legacy of the Landscape*. London: A Blandford Book, 1997.

Taylor, Timothy. *The Prehistory of Sex: Four Million Years of Human Sexual Culture*. New York: Bantam, 1996.

Telesco, Patricia. *The Wiccan Book of Ceremonies and Rituals*. Sacramento, CA: Citadel Press, 1999.

Thompson, Lana. *The Wandering Womb: A Cultural History of Outrageous Beliefs About Women*. Amherst, NY: Prometheus, 1999.

Thompson, Sue Ellen, ed. *Holiday Symbols: A Guide to the Legend and the Lore Behind the People, Places, Foods, Animals, and*

Other Symbols Associated with Holidays and Holy Days. Omnigraphics, 1998.

Thomson, William Irwin. *The Time Falling Bodies Take to Light: Mythology, Sexuality, and the Origin of Culture.* New York: St. Martin's Griffin, 1996.

Tresidder, Jack. *Dictionary of Symbols: An Illustrated Guide to Traditional Images, Icons and Enblems.* San Francisco: Chronicle, 1998.

Tyldesley, Joyce. *Daughters of Isis: Women of Ancient Egypt.* London: Viking, 1994.

Urdang, Laurence, and Christine Donahue. *Holidays and Anniversaries of the World: A Comprehensive Catalogue Containing Detailed Information on Every Month and Day of the Year.* Detroit: Gale Research, 1985.

Walker, Barbara G. *The Woman's Encyclopedia of Myths and Secrets.* New York: Castle, 1983.

Walker, Barbara G. *Restoring the Goddess: Equal Rites for Modern Woman.* Amherst, New York: Prometheus, 2000.

Waring, Philippa. *The Dictionary of Omens and Superstitions.* London: Souvenir Press, 1978.

Weidegger, P. *Menstruation and Menopause: The Physiology and Psychology, The Myth and the Reality.* New York: Alfred A. Knopf, 1976.

Wosien, Maria-Gabriele. *Sacred Dance: Encounter with the Gods.* London: Thames and Hudson, 1974.

INDEX